BETTER MUST COME

Exiting Homelessness in Two
Global Cities

Matthew D. Marr

ILR PRESS

AN IMPRINT OF

CORNELL UNIVERSITY PRESS   ITHACA AND LONDON

First published 2015 by Cornell University Press
First printing, Cornell Paperbacks, 2015

Printed in the United States of America

Library of Congress Cataloging-in-Publication Data

Marr, Matthew D., 1971– author.
    Better must come : exiting homelessness in two global cities / Matthew D. Marr.
        pages cm
    Includes bibliographical references and index.
    ISBN 978-0-8014-5338-0 (cloth : alk. paper) —
    ISBN 978-0-8014-7970-0 (pbk. : alk. paper)
    1. Homelessness—California—Los Angeles. 2. Homelessness—Japan—Tokyo.
3. Homeless persons—Services for—California—Los Angeles. 4. Homeless
persons—Services for—Japan—Tokyo. 5. Shelters for the homeless—California—
Los Angeles. 6. Shelters for the homeless—Japan—Tokyo. I. Title.
    HV4506.L67M37 2015
    362.5'920952135—dc23   2014029973

Cornell University Press strives to use environmentally responsible suppliers and materials to the fullest extent possible in the publishing of its books. Such materials include vegetable-based, low-VOC inks and acid-free papers that are recycled, totally chlorine-free, or partly composed of nonwood fibers. For further informa- tion, visit our website at www.cornellpress.cornell.edu.

Cloth printing   10 9 8 7 6 5 4 3 2 1
Paperback printing   10 9 8 7 6 5 4 3 2 1

I've been trying a long, long time;
Still, I can't make it.
Everyt'ing I try to do seems to go wrong.
It seems I have done something wrong.
Why they trying to keep me down?
Who God bless, no one curse.
Thank God I'm not the worst!
Better must come one day. Better must come.
They can't conquer me!

—Delroy Wilson, "Better Must Come," 1971

Contents

Prologue

Growing up in culturally and socioeconomically diverse Long Beach, California, I spent a good deal of time skateboarding in parking lots, alleys, parks, and schoolyards. It was the 1980s, and I saw more and more people living in these public spaces. They seemed to be victims of all the inequalities and contradictions of contemporary urban society I heard about in the constant stream of punk rock, hip-hop, and reggae music that filled my ears. Also, they seemed worthy of all the compassion stressed at St. Barnabas Catholic Church, where on any given Sunday my brother and I were likely to be serving as altar boys. Homelessness had also become a national concern and had received ample coverage in mainstream news and even presidential politics.

My more direct confrontation with homelessness came as a college student. As part of a service and scholarship program of the Center for Social Concerns at the University of Notre Dame, I was assigned to work and live for a summer at the Midnight Mission in Los Angeles's Skid Row district in 1992. The student volunteer from the previous year tried to persuade program administrators and me to halt work there because the Mission and Skid Row were too dangerous. This only piqued my interest, and a few weeks later I got off a Blue Line train at the 7th and Metro station in downtown Los Angeles and walked east across Broadway, Spring, and Main streets to the old Midnight Mission at 4th and Los Angeles streets. After spending daytime hours in the Mission's dayroom distributing bed tickets and clothing and helping serve meals to hundreds of people, I would try to refresh myself in a dimly lit locker-room style shower. A few feet away, men coming in directly from the streets would be body-checked for lice and contagious diseases. I would sleep on an iron cot with a thin mattress in the second floor dorm with about one hundred men in various stages of homelessness. We were summarily woken at six every morning by the loud banging of a metal flashlight on the foot of the cot frame.

These arrangements took a while to get used to, but those whom I lived and worked alongside at the Mission befriended, protected, and impressed me. Al, a massive middle-aged man with a gentle character, once saved me from a flying metal trashcan thrown amid a nasty fight in the dayroom. But what left a deeper impact were our conversations in the early evenings as he ironed his dress shirt while getting ready to head to a large weekly twelve-step meeting across town in upscale Brentwood. He would talk about his focus on keeping his heroin addiction in check in order to find a job so he could reunite with his son, his ultimate goal. Tony, a street-smart man in his early thirties who ran the dayroom, amused me with constant jokes as we worked but moved me with his keen eye for those with immediate, pressing needs and a willingness to bend the rules if he felt it was truly beneficial. Jermaine was younger and wilder. After only a few weeks of being on staff, he relapsed on crack cocaine and made the move back to client. But others ostracized him, and he was ashamed, so he went over to the nearby Union Rescue Mission. It was these experiences at the Midnight that made me want to develop some professional capacity to help create better solutions to address homelessness as a social problem. I knew that passing out food, providing beds, and employing people who were formerly on the streets to deliver these services did help a few like Al and Tony attain some financial and housing stability in preparation to move on with their lives. But I also knew there were many others like Jermaine who fell through the cracks.

My time in Skid Row in the early 1990s also served as an unexpected boon to another interest that I thought at the time to be quite distant and unrelated to homelessness. A few years before, I began studying Japanese through the Center for International Commerce Program at Long Beach Polytechnic High School. Then in college I double majored in government and Japanese and spent a year as an exchange student at Nanzan University in Nagoya, Japan. After graduating amid a dismal job market in 1993, I preferred the Midnight Mission to my parents' new home in the distant suburbs of Los Angeles's sprawl. Back in Skid Row, I was able to continue my study of Japanese by skateboarding a few blocks to Little Tokyo to participate in a free conversation exchange supported by the Los Angeles Unified School District. A few months later, I learned that my application for a Japanese Ministry of Education fellowship had been accepted and that I would spend the following year at Nagoya University, furthering my study of Japanese language and culture. While spending late nights skateboarding in parks under the highway near Ōsukannon temple and around the downtown shopping districts of Sakae, I came to know some of the middle-aged men who were seeking refuge in these public spaces as the Japanese economy sputtered and unemployment increased. Seeing encampments and soup lines reminded me of Skid Row, albeit without the open illicit drug use and with much less violence. When given the assignment of conducting a graduate-level research project entirely in Japanese, I elected to focus on the causes of rising homelessness in Nagoya as well as the public- and private-sector response. I got involved with an informal volunteer group led by a Christian minister and activist named Matsumoto-san, and I participated in weekly patrols. A few years later, while a master of arts student in sociology at historically black Howard University, I was able to go back to Japan to conduct brief ethnographic fieldwork on homelessness in Kobe after the Great Hanshin Earthquake of 1995. As in Skid Row L.A., I was moved, impressed, and motivated by those I encountered in the public spaces of Nagoya and Kobe. Their stories defied the images of laziness in the media and claims of lack of morality from Japanese I met outside the volunteer group.

Upon my return to the United States, I was fortunate to land a job at Shelter Partnership, Inc., a Los Angeles nonprofit organization (NPO) that addresses policy issues related to homelessness. In addition to researching how emerging welfare reform policies affected homelessness, I became increasingly aware of the limitations of shelters and short-term, time-limited housing in reducing homelessness, even amid the extended economic growth of the late 1990s. Also, as I read about homelessness becoming apparently entrenched in major cities across the world, I became more eager to return to Japan to see firsthand how the problem was changing there.

Perhaps naïvely, I also thought I might have something to share from my experiences in Los Angeles's NPO sector. I participated in an exchange program between American and Japanese organizations sponsored by the Japan-U.S. Community Education and Exchange (which is now defunct). They placed me at Sanyūkai, a free medical clinic in San'ya, Tokyo's historical day labor ghetto that was rapidly becoming a district of street homelessness and welfare. It was refreshing to observe the director's ability to banter with and befriend clients while pouring tea daily in the clinic's consultation room; the familial atmosphere of the clinic starkly contrasted with the professionalized climate of the NPO I worked at in Los Angeles. At the cusp of the new millennium, the Japanese government had just passed legislation to promote the development of nonprofit organizations and was preparing new legislation to address swelling homelessness as the economy lagged. I saw a similar reliance in both countries on time-limited group living situations (transitional housing) that required people to first address personal issues such as flawed work ethics before securing conventional housing on their own. This approach ran counter to everything I had learned in my studies of sociology about the structural roots of urban poverty that pointed to shifting and bifurcating labor markets, housing markets, and social services. Therefore, upon acceptance to the PhD program in sociology at UCLA, I was inspired by my experiences to begin the research on which this book is based. For my dissertation project, I decided to look at how transitional housing in Los Angeles and Tokyo differentially affects individual and societal efforts to escape homelessness, and how these efforts relate to processes of globalization.

Along this long journey, I was blessed to have the support of an expanding network of friends and family. My friends from Long Beach, including Richard, Jason, Jerami, Kevin, and Nicole, and my college roommate Jason, have always supported my unconventional path as they pursue their own. The clinic Sanyūkai has become my surrogate family in Tokyo. I am always invigorated when I haul my bags on trains from Narita Airport to San'ya to be serendipitously greeted at the "Bridge of Tears" (Namidabashi) intersection by staff, volunteers, or clients calling out "Welcome home!" (*Okaerinasai!*). But more recently I have been fortunate to join a new family in Japan with the love of my life, best friend, and beautiful wife, Naoko, who as of this writing is carrying our daughter, Sara Frances. Of course, the longest and most steady support has come from my parents, Warren and Bivian, my brother Tim, and my grandparents, as well as uncles, aunts, and cousins far too numerous to list by name. I am especially indebted to my older brother who put me up throughout graduate school and always encouraged me in the toughest of times. I thank you all and love you very, very much.

As I will show in this book, major endeavors in life, sizable research projects and exiting homelessness included, often require not only help from family members but the support of communities embedded in organizations. I would like to thank the intellectual communities I have been part of at Florida International University's Department of Global and Sociocultural Studies and Asian Studies Program, the Maureen and Mike Mansfield Foundation's U.S.-Japan Network for the Future, Harvard University's Reischauer Institute of Japanese Studies, UCLA's Department of Sociology and Center for the Study of Urban Poverty, and Howard University's Department of Sociology and Anthropology. For feedback and encouragement on this project at various stages, in particular I would like to thank Rebecca Jean Emigh (and all fellow "Emight" advisees), David Snow, Abel Valenzuela Jr., Geoff DeVerteuil, Kate Cooney, Steve Heine, Sarah Mahler, Laura Ogden, Bin Xu, Mary Brinton, Akiko Hashimoto, Silvia Domínguez, Benedict Giamo, Jooyoung Kim, Rene Almeling, Gavin Whitelaw, Christopher Bondy, and Teresa Gowan. Colleagues who have provided invaluable input and assistance in Tokyo include Yasue Suzuko, Aoki Hideo, Tamaki Matsuo, Kitagawa Yukihiko, Yamaguchi Keiko, Koike Takao, and Gotō Hiroshi. I thank the other organizations and programs from which I have received support for this project. These include the U.S. Department of Housing and Urban Development's Doctoral Dissertation Fellowship, the National Science Foundation's Doctoral Dissertation Research Improvement Grant, the Japan Foundation's Doctoral Dissertation Fellowship, the Social Science Research Council's Japan Studies Dissertation Workshop, and the Aurora Foundation's Challenge Grant. Also, I would like to express gratitude to the organizations and staff persons who facilitated my data collection, especially the dedicated frontline workers who responded in interviews. Last, but certainly not least, I would like to thank Fran Benson, my editor, for taking immediate interest in this manuscript and seeing it into print.

I dedicate this book to the people who amid very difficult circumstances let me into their lives and shared their stories. I hope this book does their efforts some justice and, as they hoped, helps improve public understanding of homelessness and how it can be overcome personally and socially.

Abbreviations

APB	all-points bulletin
DPSS	Department of Public Social Services (Los Angeles County)
GDP	Gross Domestic Product
GED	General Educational Development (high school equivalency exam)
GR	General Relief (Los Angeles County)
HEARTH	Homeless Emergency Assistance and Rapid Transition to Housing (United States)
HPRP	Homelessness Prevention and Rapid Re-Housing Program (United States)
HUD	Department of Housing and Urban Development (United States)
LAHSA	Los Angeles Homeless Services Authority
MHLW	Ministry of Health, Labor, and Welfare (Japan)
MTA	Metropolitan Transit Authority (Los Angeles)
SCAG	Southern California Association of Governments
SDF	Self Defense Forces (Japan)
SAMHSA	Substance Abuse and Mental Health Services Administration (United States)
SHP	Supportive Housing Program (United States)
SOAR	SSI/SSDI Outreach, Access, and Recovery (United States)
SRO	single room occupancy (hotel)
SSA	Social Security Administration (United States)
SSDI	Social Security Disability Insurance (United States)
SSI	Supplemental Security Income (United States)
TMG	Tokyo Metropolitan Government
VA	Department of Veterans Affairs (United States)

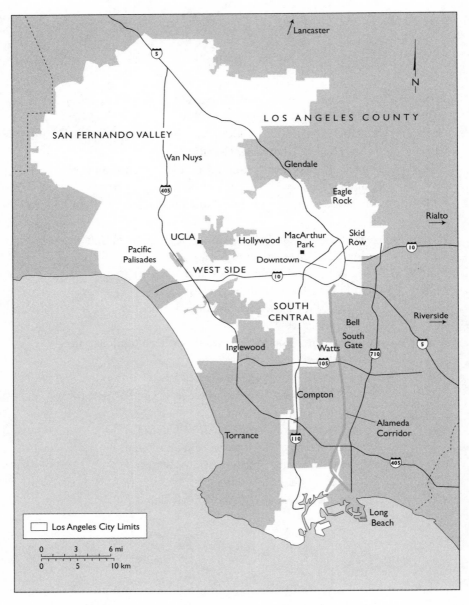

Los Angeles County with key municipalities and neighborhoods

Tokyo's twenty-three wards with key municipalities and neighborhoods

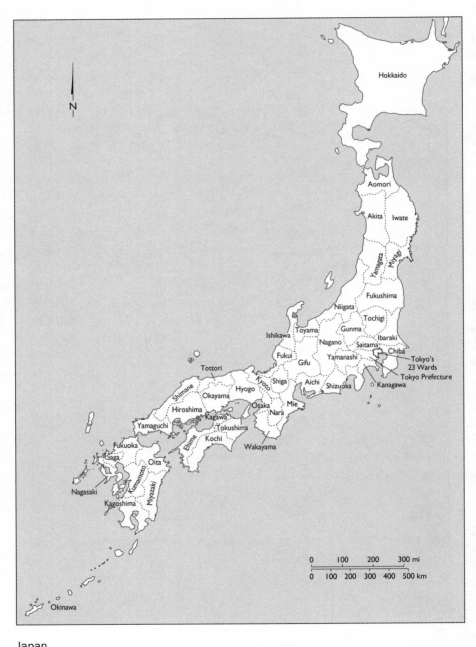

Japan

The United States

Part I

HOMELESSNESS AND GLOBAL CITIES

Exit Stories: Carlos and Takagi-san

Carlos

On a sunny fall day in 2003, I sat with Carlos, a short and stocky fifty-one-year-old Mexican American, on folding chairs in a church parking lot in Los Angeles's Skid Row district to hear about his experiences living in a transitional housing program nearby.[1] Born in El Paso, Texas, he moved with his family to Bakersfield, California, when he was an adolescent. His father died a few years later, and Carlos dropped out of school after the tenth grade to help his mother, a farmworker, raise his eleven siblings. Although he continued to contribute to his family, he also had a case of wanderlust. "See, I'm the kind of person that, I used to see the mountains, and that's where I wanted to be, whether it was cold or not. But I enjoyed it because I wanted to see the world. I was young, I was like a big old bull, strong, and nothing would stop me from working."[2] So he began traveling between California and Nebraska, working most often on farms slaughtering cows or in restaurants as a cook. He became active as an organizer in the farmworker movement led by Cesar Chavez, where he met his wife with whom he eventually had seven children. His family stayed in Bakersfield, but he continued to migrate for work. The hard physical labor wore on him, and when the men he played pool with suggested an easier way to make money, he began couriering packages of cocaine and heroin.

Carlos was captivated by the easy money and started trafficking drugs up the West Coast, through the Midwest, and to Northeastern cities, sometimes getting caught by police and serving time along the way. His wife initially waited for him, but as time passed she found a new man who could provide her with a more stable and fulfilling relationship. While at first he did not use hard drugs, he eventually tried heroin with a woman he met on the road, got hooked, and was addicted and homeless between the ages of roughly twenty-seven and forty. One lengthy stint in jail was the impetus to kick his habit, but for about a decade afterward he continued to traffic drugs, staying on the streets, in missions, and in motels when he could avoid jail. Eventually he made his way to Los Angeles and stayed in Skid Row missions. Trying to make a new start in life, he resisted the temptation to get back into the drug business, but he had to begin taking insulin for diabetes, had chronic pain in his feet, and even had thoughts of suicide.

One day he stopped by a Skid Row drop-in center in search of better housing and was referred to a transitional housing program. Carlos said, "That's where I met my case manager, Marisol. And we had some real good conversations. She's a very, very, nice person. And she helped me as much as she could, talked to me, counseled me, and tried to help me to go to this other counselor, things like that. And I saw her interest was not about money, it was about really helping the person. So I started talking to her—even going into my problems of (possibly) relapsing back into drugs and all that." Carlos saw Marisol, a Latina and a trained social worker in her late twenties, as being a person who offered sincere help when he was at a particularly vulnerable point in his life. At first, he was intimidated by the numerous program requirements, such as attending employment readiness courses, feeling that he could not keep up given his poor health. But once he felt he could trust Marisol, he was motivated to meet her high expectations for him to pursue his General Education Development certificate (GED), find a job, and secure housing.

He also pointed out other staff who aided him, describing the entire environment of the program as helpful and healing. "They treated me just like family. And I really love them, every one of them, how they work. I told Marisol one time, 'I don't hold back or I don't need to get mad at what you're trying to do for me. I know you're trying to help, but it's me that's gotta want help.' And that I was already determined that I was going to do something about my life. That little help they give me, something nobody ever done." Marisol and other staff provided Carlos an array of instrumental assistance in additional to emotional support. They arranged meals appropriate for his diabetes at the program cafeteria, enrolled him in GED courses, introduced him to an employment program for felons, referred him to health care services, and helped him put together an application for Social Security Insurance (SSI) benefits.

Despite medical documentation of his various disabilities, his application to SSI was rejected. The reasons largely escaped him, but he said he was told by a welfare office caseworker that he had to be at least sixty-five years old. He tried a job selling hotdogs at Dodger Stadium introduced by the program for felons, but had to quit after enduring a day of throbbing pain in his feet. With his lack of education and applicable job skills, limited contact with family and friends, and income of $221 per month from General Relief (GR),[3] Carlos's prospects for exiting homeless from the program appeared to be dismal. He reached a crisis point amid the stress of group living and felt that he might do something that would derail his progress. So he went to see Marisol. "I was about to bust. I was so mad. And I wanted to cry but I wasn't gonna cry in front of a lady, but I told her, 'You know what, Marisol? I need to move on. I'm living among nine other roommates. I'm in there with men. These are just the same feelings that I had when I was in prison. No respect, no privacy, no nothing.' Somebody stole my TV. I didn't do nothing about it. Nobody said nothing about it. I said, 'I need to move out. You know what? If I lose my control, I'll kill someone. And I don't wanna go back to jail.'" Fortunately for Carlos, Marisol was able to provide a solution to his predicament. "She told me to go see this lady at the Hayward Manor [a single room occupancy hotel]. And so she helped me to get into the housing. From there, they sent me to Section 8, the Housing Authority, and I paid $25 to see in the computer about my credit and felonies and stuff. Well, they approved me, and in two weeks, I was in. I said, 'Thank God!' I praise God for helping me get in there, but I also put a little blessing on the people at the [program] for helping me."

The last time we spoke, almost a year had passed since Carlos had left the transitional housing program, and he was still living in a subsidized room in the hotel. A long-term case manager from the transitional program was helping him apply for MediCal benefits from California's medical aid program for the very poor so he could get into a rehabilitation program for his leg pain. Since his only income was from GR, with about 30 percent going toward his subsidized room and another 10 percent tithed to his church, he relied on free meals at local missions or his church, but occasionally he had to skip meals for a lack of funds. His only contact with his large family was with his brother Mario, a truck driver with whom he talked by phone about once per month and who would take him out to eat whenever his route brought him through Los Angeles. However, he was thoroughly engaged with his church, studying to be a minister and substance abuse counselor, using a church van to bring Skid Row residents to services in nearby Eagle Rock. Sometimes he would even connect unemployed parishioners with jobs through contractors who worked on the church building. Although he was clearly still living in poverty, physically unable to do manual labor, and hoping to move somewhere with a private bathroom and kitchen, he did feel that he was in a much better material, emotional, and spiritual state than before he entered the program:

> I am learning through the help of programs like [the transitional housing program]. Because I came here with no goals, no direction, no hope,

The entranceway of the single room occupancy (SRO) hotel where Carlos lived in a subsidized room after leaving transitional housing

no nothing. By them opening the door and trusting and believing in me when I found, look this is my goal, this is what I want to do, and I am willing to do whatever I can. So they stretched out their hand for me and believed in me. Something that, in the world, nobody ever did. I was always afraid. Every little problem that came up, I solved my problems by getting stoned, doing drugs, drinking, and doing the craziest things. But they showed me how to set goals and to be able to achieve them. And I learned this because they had the faith to teach me and show me even though when I did wrong, they were patient to help me understand. If it wouldn't have been for the program, I don't know where I would have been. I probably would have been out there still.

Takagi-san

About one year after my first conversation with Carlos, and approximately fifty-four hundred miles across the Pacific Ocean in Tokyo, I sat down with Takagi-san,[4] a thirty-eight-year-old man from nearby Ibaraki Prefecture. Takagi-san was staying in a temporary emergency shelter funded by the Tokyo Metropolitan

Government that, due to widespread opposition from local residents, was placed in a parking lot adjacent to the large bayside Rinkai Park. With nothing better to do that day, unable to look for work until he was transferred from the shelter to transitional housing (called *jiritsu shien sentā*, or self-reliance support center), he sat with me on a bench in the park and described how he ended up in the shelter.

Takagi-san grew up in a working-class family, his mother a homemaker and his father employed first by a subcontractor of Tokyo Gas and then moving on to work as a taxi driver. When his parents divorced, he stayed with his mother and lost contact with his father. After completing junior high school, the highest compulsory level in Japan, he worked full time for eight years in a sushi restaurant. Since the job did not provide benefits, such as payment into a pension for retirement, or offer opportunity for upward mobility, he moved on to see new places and have new experiences, working as a sushi chef along the way. Aside from one stint at a restaurant in Yokohama where he rented an apartment, he usually stayed in the dorm of his employer, very rarely having a room of his own. He eventually began working at a "family restaurant" in Ibaraki and moved in with a girlfriend. But Takagi-san quit because his pay was lower than he was used to, and after a bit of unsuccessful searching he broke up with his girlfriend and went to Tokyo to find work. He used his 60,000 yen (about $538)[5] in savings to stay in small but cheap "capsule hotels" and all-night "comic book (*manga*) cafés" just outside of Tokyo in Matsudo City, Chiba Prefecture. He would bike to "Hello Work," the local public employment agency, to look for jobs. But his money ran thin, so he moved into scenic Mizumoto Park in nearby Katsushika Ward. He stayed there for about a month, sleeping on a bench under an awning to protect himself from the seasonal tropical rains of the early summer (*tsuyu*), enduring the humidity but feeling lucky that it was not during the winter cold. He fended for himself, keeping his distance from numerous other men who lived in the park, and used what money he had left to buy lunch boxes (*bentō*) and cup-sized ramen noodles from a convenience store.

Takagi-san had heard about programs for people in situations like his on TV, and after a few weeks in the park he went to the Katsushika Ward welfare office to seek help. "I was a little unsure. I thought I could find work, I really did. But then you need a guarantor if you get an interview [for a security job], right? That's no good. But I didn't have any money, so after talking to them [the welfare office staff] a bit, I decided to go for it." By chance, there was an opening in the emergency shelter and he was able to get in two days later. He was still in contact with his mother, but when I asked why he did not return to live with her he said, "Even if I try to go back, I have no place there. My mom remarried and I don't get along with her husband." He did not give her any details about his homelessness and initially refrained from asking her to be a guarantor, but instead had her send him some clothing once he was in the shelter. Takagi-san had about 900,000 yen ($8,007) in debt from predatory lenders (*sarakin*) and credit cards from a period of unemployment in the early 1990s when he tried to make ends meet by gambling on horse races. He hoped to get some assistance in dealing with his debt from the program or outside nonprofit organizations that sometimes visited the shelter, but at the time he was more focused on finding employment. He thought about getting a driver's license or training as a "home helper" for the elderly in case he was unable to find restaurant work, but he did not have time before being transferred to transitional housing.

After moving into transitional housing in Tokyo's working-class Sumida Ward, Takagi-san soon found work in a pub (*izakaya*) through the local Hello Work. However, he thought his boss was too picky and quit after one week. About one month later, he found another job through referral by a friend in the program. He began working as a register and stock clerk at a twenty-four-hour chain supermarket in Hatchōbori, central Tokyo, about a thirty-minute train ride away. Two other men from the center worked there alongside young students from China. His first three months was a training period where he worked forty hours per week with part-time status, and after that they would decide whether or not he was to become a full-time employee with benefits and security. His starting wage was 880 yen (about $7.18) per hour, and 1,110 yen (about $9.87) per hour for the night shift.[6] He preferred to work nights, from 11 p.m. to 8 a.m., not only for the higher wage but because he was used to working late in sushi restaurants and pubs. His assignment was to work twenty days a month for a take-home salary of about 130,000 yen (about $1,166) after paying social insurance (*shakai hoken*), pension (*nenkin*), and taxes. Despite rigid rules, he said he had no problems with the staff at the center. Still, he rarely sought them out for help. Most of his complaints were reserved for other residents. Since he shared a room with men who had not found work, he had trouble sleeping during the day in preparation for his night shift and even got into shouting matches with them. Feeling that the nonworkers were simply scamming the center and not trustworthy, he became friends with others who had found work and tried to get out with them on days off to bowl or play pinball-like gambling games (*pachinko*) for stress relief.

When I met him again two months after he left the transitional program, Takagi-san described himself as "living a normal life." He sometimes had difficulty making ends meet the week before his monthly paycheck but said, "Isn't that how it is for everyone? Even for people working normally as a salaryman?" He had moved into an apartment in Takenotsuka, on the fringes of Tokyo near Saitama Prefecture, renting for 42,000 yen (about $377), with a private "unit bath" so he did not have to use a public bath. He looked without help from the program staff and settled on the first place he was shown since he thought the rent was reasonable and it was close to a station, about a thirty-five-minute commute from his job. His move-in costs were approximately 170,000 yen (about $1,524), of which the center covered 60,000 yen (about $538). Also, Takagi-san got over his pride and called his mother, who agreed to serve as his guarantor. His training period ended and his hourly wage rose slightly to 900 yen (about $8.07) but his night shift wage stayed the same, barely increasing his monthly income. He felt his current work to be much easier than the long hours he would put in as a sushi chef. But he was concerned that he had not been made a full-time employee, which would have increased his wage more and provided seasonal bonuses, as well as more stability, respectability, and potential for upward mobility.

Life was not as stable for Takagi-san when I caught up with him again five months later. He quit his job abruptly because he was not promoted to full-time status. In hindsight, he acknowledged that he had reacted rashly, but he also just did not see any sense in being stuck in a low-paying part-time job and was confident in his ability to find a better opportunity. He had been out of work for about three months, paying rent with the last of his savings, leaving him without money to buy food. He did not have money for the following month's rent and arranged for his landlord to wait for a month as he looked for work. He had been going to Hello Work every other day and went on interviews but had no offers. "I didn't think it would come to this. I've been on a lot of interviews, about 10. I've been turned down by them all. I've gotten caught up because of my age. They were almost all jobs at restaurants. I haven't interviewed at chain restaurants because they are even stricter about age. They hire full-time employees, but only up to thirty or thirty-five. Thirty-eight and thirty don't sound too far apart, but I guess it makes a difference." Also, most restaurant jobs he saw in "sports newspapers" popular among working-class men were in Hachiōji in western Tokyo or Yokohama and other parts of Kanagawa Prefecture, too far to commute from his apartment. He also looked for work at *pachinko* parlors, but he found they also preferred younger workers in their twenties. He considered dispatch work in factories or event set-up that would pay about 6,000 yen (about $53) per day, but that would not ensure any long-term stability. As we talked in a fast-food restaurant in Kita-Senjū Station near his apartment he lamented, "There is no work. It's driving me crazy. I'm going to end up on the streets again."

He saw no use in contacting the transitional housing program staff about his problems, feeling that they would not be sympathetic because he had quit his job. Instead, he pondered going to the Adachi Ward welfare office, the closest to his apartment, to apply for welfare benefits called livelihood protection (*seikatsu hogo*). However, he had been there once already and was told that he needed to demonstrate he was sick. Otherwise, the only option was to apply for a 50,000 yen (about $449) loan from a social welfare organization (*shakai fukushi kyōgikai*) but the application process was complicated and required a guarantor. He was clearly demoralized by his situation, staring off into space, sighing, and saying he was simply tired ("*Mō tsukarechatta yo!*") and did not want to go back into a shelter or program. After sternly refusing my offer to buy him lunch several

The building in which Takagi-san rented an apartment after leaving transitional housing

times, he eventually relented. When we parted, he said he would try finding help again at the welfare office and I wished him luck and encouraged him to stay in touch by mail because I soon had to return to Los Angeles. A letter to Takagi-san I sent from the United States a few months after this meeting was returned with a stamp indicating he no longer lived in the apartment. Although I do not know his destination or whether or not he returned to a state of homelessness, it is clear that Takagi-san was struggling, largely on his own, in a labor market that offered few opportunities for stability and security.

Although there are glaring contrasts, the similarities in Carlos's and Takagi-san's experiences challenge popular images of homelessness as complete destitution, demoralization, defeat, and entrenchment. Their moves in and out of homelessness also contrast with scholarly research documenting and interpreting the worldviews, survival strategies, and experiences of "homeless people" lodged in a "homeless culture," "homeless identity," or "homeless community." Indeed, in my conversations with Carlos, Takagi-san, and other transitional housing program users in Los Angeles and Tokyo, they distanced themselves from these images and the people around them who they felt embodied the degradation of homelessness. In both cities, all persons I followed formed plans to improve their economic and housing stability, although these plans varied in detail, practicality, and alignment with program requirements. Neither their attitudes toward work nor their social networks could be best described as oriented toward acculturation into a homeless lifestyle, subculture, or identity. They fought hard to change their circumstances and improve their lives, with some overcoming tremendous challenges such as addiction, depression, social isolation, denial of state welfare benefits, tedious paperwork requirements to access aid, paternalistic programs, group living arrangements, a lack of myriad resources, and constrained opportunities in labor and housing markets.

In this book, I address two sets of research questions by analyzing the experiences of people who used transitional housing programs in Los Angeles and Tokyo. The first set of questions emerges from the shared goal of escaping homelessness exhibited by my interviewees. It includes the following: How do people get out of homelessness? How do they navigate the social and economic contexts that contribute to their homelessness to obtain income and housing? How is the process of exiting homelessness experienced and interpreted? Why do some people fail in their attempts to get out of homelessness? How are some people able to translate these exits into longer-term stability? Social science research has primarily focused on processes of becoming homeless and surviving materially, socially, and psychologically in that condition, without following people out of homelessness. Although this literature humanizes homelessness by highlighting the structural forces that push people into that condition and their individual and collective resilience in enduring it materially, socially, and emotionally, it does not say much about the aspect of homelessness that I found those experiencing it obsess about—how to get out of it. Thus, I push for a more balanced portrayal of homelessness by using a longitudinal, ethnographic approach that follows people experiencing homelessness as they seek to secure, and sometimes succeed in securing, more stable income, housing, and lives.

The similarities I found among interviewees in Los Angeles and Tokyo also drive my argument that homelessness, at individual and societal levels, should be viewed primarily as a predicament that is extremely traumatic and stigmatizing but surmountable, rather than as a stable condition, identity, or culture. This draws on anthropologist Kim Hopper's (2003) approach to homelessness as liminality, or a disorienting in-between space void of clear roles, but builds upon it by de-emphasizing how people adjust to this state and emphasizing the social processes that shape transitional process out of this ambiguity. By focusing directly on the process of exiting, I not only examine an understudied aspect of homelessness but also advance a shift in the understanding of homelessness, emphasizing the potential for its transcendence. I show how persons experiencing homelessness orient cognitively and behaviorally toward transcending the condition of homelessness itself. Instead of engaging in a debate for or against the influence of a culture or a social psychology of homelessness, a debate that can reinforce social boundaries of a housed "us" versus a homeless "them," I shift focus toward revealing how economic, material, social, emotional, and other resources such as information and trust are secured to exit homelessness. Moreover, I examine how access to such resources is affected by contexts at multiple social levels. Practically, this is important because truly ending homelessness at a societal level requires not just addressing individual vulnerabilities but also increasing access to living-wage employment, affordable housing, and social ties.[1] My focus on exits thus promotes a more holistic understanding of homelessness and how the social problem is created, sustained, and alleviated by the interaction of social contexts at multiple levels.

But the processes by which Carlos, Takagi-san, and others were able to exit homelessness differed in many ways between the two cities. My interviewees in Los Angeles generally relied on social ties with family, friends, and program staff to secure subsidized housing, having had little success in penetrating mainstream labor and housing markets. Their counterparts in Tokyo, however, succeeded in obtaining employment, albeit low wage and unstable, and moved into simple rental housing with very little help from family, friends, and program staff. The focus of this book is to explain how these similarities and differences in the process of exiting homelessness are produced by the interaction of social contexts at multiple levels, from the global to the individual. Where the experiences of my respondents in Los Angeles and Tokyo diverge, questions linking homelessness and broader social transformations occurring in global urban society emerge. How are processes of exiting homelessness affected by both global and local conditions? What are the conditions at different social levels that can promote exits from homelessness?

Critical urban scholars see homelessness as a result of neoliberal globalization—a process in which rising inequality and instability of employment and housing in global cities, the "command centers of the global economy," accompanies economic growth predicated on low-wage service-sector employment, financial and real estate speculation, and a state retreating from welfare and social service provision (Sassen 2001). While in this book I use the term "global city," my study provides insights beyond the limited set of cities that commonly receive that label, including what could be described as "globalizing cities" (Marcuse and Van Kempen 1999)—urban areas seeing broad trends associated with globalization.

In the current age of globalization, which began roughly in the early 1970s, goods, financial investment, workers, culture, and ideas move across borders at heightened levels and speeds. One ideology that has become increasingly powerful is that of neoliberalism, which posits that the logic of free markets aimed at macroeconomic growth should take precedence over state intervention and social redistribution (Harvey 2005). In the age of neoliberal globalization, economic inequality *between* nations has decreased, but socioeconomic inequality *within* nations, especially in cities that connect to the global economy, has widened (Förster and d'Ercole 2005). So while some people are becoming wealthy, and a select few fabulously wealthy, many more are finding opportunities for upward mobility or even basic stability eroding, with the most unfortunate falling into homelessness. The neoliberal response has not been social redistribution or bolstering safety nets, but an increased emphasis on "personal responsibility" for improving labor market competitiveness with limited help from programs like transitional housing. But amid these global tendencies, local variation in experiences of marginality, as evident in the stories of Carlos and Takagi-san, persists. Thus, with a longitudinal qualitative approach, my purpose is to explain how and why processes of exiting homelessness are different in two global cities, not whether the rate of exiting homelessness is higher in one city or why that might be.

Using analytical leverage provided by my comparison, I advance a second argument, that processes of exiting homelessness are not determined by any singular context, such as the constraining forces of neoliberal globalization, punitive state policies toward the poor, or individual-level resilience or lack thereof. Popular depictions of homelessness often favor either poor victims of a global trend toward heightened inequality and exclusion or defiant individual survivors fighting valiantly for a sense of worth amid demeaning conditions. However, neither the production nor amelioration of homelessness at individual and societal levels is determined by a singular context. Instead, my comparison demonstrates that processes of exiting homelessness are shaped by the interaction of multiple embedded contexts that operate at different social levels. Thus, even though economic, demographic, and (neoliberal) ideological globalization are driving forces behind "new inequality," "advanced marginality," and homelessness across global cities (Sassen 2001; Wacquant 2008), more local contexts, including labor and housing market structures, welfare state protections, social service settings, and predominant cultural views and practices, greatly shape the extent and content of experiences of marginality in any particular global city. Also, while surmounting the complex problems that drive people into homelessness requires substantial individual resilience, exits from homelessness also depend on *forgiving contexts* at multiple social levels—whether favorable conditions in local labor and housing markets, flexible and holistic social service settings, or cultural milieux that promote mutual aid among friends, family, and community. These are social contexts that work against the global and local trends driving inequality and that can promote exits from homelessness.

Comparing Los Angeles and Tokyo

I have selected Los Angeles and Tokyo for comparison because they are global cities that are seeing wide social polarization accompany both economic growth and stagnation, but they also contain different labor markets, housing markets, welfare policies, social service delivery settings, and cultural milieux. I draw on Esping-Anderson's (1999) classification of postindustrial *welfare regimes* to examine how state action interacts with labor markets, households, and community organizations in various ways to buffer the effects of market risks on individuals. The United States has a liberal welfare regime type, characterized by highly deregulated labor markets, individualized risk, and lean welfare state outlay restricted to needs- rather than rights-based assistance. Also, the American welfare regime is criticized for institutional discrimination against African Americans and Latinos and for taking a punitive approach to rising social insecurity via welfare retraction and mass imprisonment of the "war on drugs" (Wacquant 2009). Japan has a hybrid welfare regime, combining elements of the liberal type with the corporatist type of continental Europe. Japan's regime is more interventionist in labor markets than its American counterpart, placing primary responsibility on employer protections for a male breadwinner/female homemaker family model, and augmenting it with a lean welfare state (Estévez-Abe 2008; Miura 2012; Schoppa 2006).

At the city-region level, national welfare regimes intersect with local contexts, including *urban regimes*, or local political coalitions of government officials, business representatives, and community leaders (Dreier, Mollenkopf, and Swanstrom 2004). I use the concept *urban welfare regime* to represent the interaction of national welfare regimes with more local conditions that shape processes of neoliberal globalization. Global influences are not making national or local agency and variation irrelevant, but various scales interact in complex processes of neoliberal "glocalization" (Brenner and Theodore 2002; Harvey 2006). Los Angeles is deeply penetrated by global capital and by labor migration, and it has a tax-averse public and a fragmented governmental structure with a weakened capacity to provide social services that caters to powerful financial interests, all of which have radically transformed the local labor market (Dear 2002; Keil 1998; Wolch 1996). These forces have produced highly spatialized racial inequality partially countered by a diverse civil society that is vibrant but overwhelmed by its inability to meet growing social needs (Davis 1990; Milkman 2006). Tokyo is less penetrated by global capital and labor and led by a strong developmental state, which is highly coordinated nationally and locally and has kept unemployment and inequality comparatively low and spatially even (Fujita 2003; Hill and Fujita 2000; Machimura 1998). But the developmental state has been increasingly ineffective amid global economic vicissitudes and has used a conservative approach to social welfare insufficient to meet rising needs, countered by a growing but still small and limited civil sector (Fujita 2011; Hasegawa 2006; Saito and Thornley 2003; Waley 2007).

I compare how Tokyo's more forgiving labor and housing market conditions, centrality of male breadwinners, and lean and paternalistic state social services affect efforts to exit homelessness differently from Los Angeles' more liberalized (and racialized) labor and housing markets, more gender-egalitarian households, and lean but privatized model of social service delivery. These institutional differences produce a larger and more diverse homeless population in Los Angeles but also pathways out of homelessness supported by family and friends, community organization staff, and subsidized housing amid meager chances for living-wage employment and affordable housing; in Tokyo, they produce a comparatively small and less diverse homeless population and pathways out of homelessness largely devoid of social ties but with opportunities for unstable low-wage employment and austere but affordable housing. My comparison contributes to the critical urban literature focusing on rising marginality amid globalization by showing how these varying structural and institutional contexts interact to affect experiences and interpretations of urban marginality in these two global cities. Although I do explore differences within each city by race, ethnicity, gender, and age where appropriate, in this book I give precedence to the comparison across the two cities.

Comparing exits from homelessness in two global cities sheds light on how processes of globalization interact with local variability, demonstrating how neoliberal globalization is a contingent rather than a monolithic force (Peck and Tickell 2002). Urban studies has long been criticized for an American and western European bias in the development of urban theory; more recently, scholars are making advances in transforming it into a truly global social science endeavor (Auyero 2011; Robinson 2010). Central to this advancement is inclusion of a diversity of cities in efforts to understand general urban processes amid globalization and how local contexts interact with them to result in on-the-ground similarities and differences, particularly in various forms of social exclusion and inclusion (Abu-Lughod 2007). In contrast to depictions of globalization as rendering national borders and institutions increasingly irrelevant, I use my comparison to highlight how different welfare and urban regimes affect a particular form of mobility at the margins of global urban society. As such, I use analogical theorizing (Vaughan 2004), comparing similar processes (exiting homelessness) across two different settings to refine theory in two sets of literatures, ethnographies of homelessness and critical urban studies. I generally follow the approaches of the extended case method and global ethnography (Burawoy 2009; Burawoy et al. 2000), demonstrating how broad social forces and institutions such as neoliberal globalization, national welfare regimes, and urban regimes shape lived experiences of urban marginality. I engage in a dialectical process in which theory is both explanatory of specific observed experiences and interpretations as well as reconstructed by these observations. Rather than attempt to use the standards of statistical inference to make generalizations about the representativeness of specific events, such as the rate of exit from homelessness among my interviewees in the two cities, my approach relies on logical inference, extrapolating (in this case developing and revising theories) based on the validity of in-depth qualitative analysis of a social process (Small 2009a).

Following Exits from Homelessness in Two Global Cities

I address my research questions and develop my arguments by following thirty-four people, seventeen each in Los Angeles and Tokyo, as they attempted to exit homelessness. Rather than taking a cross-sectional snapshot of these individuals amid homelessness in a single-time interview, I conducted longitudinal interviews with people participating in transitional housing programs in the two cities. These programs provided time-limited assistance to help their clients address perceived individual limitations so that they could secure stable income and housing. In Los Angeles, I had permission from the program to place flyers in the mailboxes of approximately two hundred program participants, inviting them to an onsite information session about the study. I recruited ten participants at the session and then an additional eleven more through snowball sampling and through requesting participation from others I met while observing at the program. I was able to maintain long-term contact after departure from the program with all but four of these people. In Tokyo, the semigovernmental body subcontracted by the Tokyo Metropolitan Government to operate transitional housing (*jiritsu shien sentā*, or self-reliance support centers) denied me access. So, I accompanied members of local nonprofit organizations when they visited the programs and emergency shelters where transitional housing users were required to stay before moving in. There, I distributed flyers about my study and requested participation. Twenty-six persons agreed to the first interview, with two providing introductions to two more participants. I lost contact with more people in Tokyo (nine), likely given my limited access to program sites there and primary residence in Los Angeles. In both cities, those who left the study did not demonstrate substantial differences in their experiences of homelessness, demographic characteristics, and the circumstances they needed to overcome in order to exit. Although my data are not statistically generalizable to all clients and staff in the programs I studied in the two cities, it is important to remember that attempting to replicate representative sampling techniques in qualitative case studies often does not meet standards of statistical inference because of low response rates for cold-called, in-depth interview requests and the limits of small sample sizes and populations (Small 2009a). Instead, I used theoretical sampling to capture a diversity of program experiences by ensuring that my interviewees had demographic characteristics (age, gender, race/ethnicity, and so forth) and lengths or forms of homelessness that reflected the client populations in the programs.

My longitudinal interviews began in the summer of 2003 in Los Angeles and in the summer of 2004 in Tokyo. I followed interviewees for at least one month after they left these programs, but in many instances I followed them for several months, and for some, for several years afterward. I conducted recorded interviews with them two to six times over a period ranging from three months to eleven years, with a median of one year. My interviews started off semistructured, using a rough guide of questions about how they fell into homelessness; their upbringing; their experiences amid homelessness on the streets, in shelters, and in programs; and their hopes and plans for the future. However, subsequent interviews were less structured and aimed to capture a diversity of experiences related to homelessness and exiting that my interviewees deemed important. I also spent time with some outside of these interviews, "going along" on daily routines (Kusenbach 2003), accompanying them on job interviews and as they searched for employment, and for those who were able to exit homelessness, visiting them in their homes. In a few instances, more so in Los Angeles, I was able to witness interviewees reconnect with family and friends and even build new families. These longitudinal interviews and other meetings allowed me to understand the outcomes of their efforts in these programs, and, for some, the implications for longer-term trajectories.

I also collected data from the organizations and staff responsible for fostering exits from homelessness. In both cities, I interviewed several staff persons in the transitional housing programs who interacted with and attempted to aid my program participant interviewees. I was given full access to the program in Los Angeles and thus was able to observe in classes, dorm rooms, case manager offices, hallways, and dining halls. In Tokyo, I was denied access to observe by authorities administering the programs, but I was able to informally interact with a few staff outside of the program when they were "off the clock." Also, I observed the support activities of a few private nonprofit and volunteer groups in Tokyo that supplement the self-reliance support centers. In both cities, I also interviewed local government officials, NPO representatives, activists, and researchers and collected secondary materials to understand the broader political, economic, and institutional contexts in which my primary interviewees were attempting to exit homelessness.

These data sources are supplemented by my other research projects and applied work on homelessness in the United States and Japan spanning some twenty years. This work has taken myriad forms and led me through various "homeless geographies" (Murphy 2009), including working, living, and observing in homeless shelters and other programs in Los Angeles's Skid Row and San'ya, To-kyo's major *yoseba* or *doyagai*;[2] and volunteering in shelters, programs, and street outreach in multiple cities across the United States (Los Angeles, San Francisco, Washington, D.C., and Miami) and Japan (Tokyo, Nagoya, Osaka, and Kyoto). Also, I have been able to interact with volunteers and staff of support groups and NPOs as well as research experts in both countries. These experiences have exposed me to the trauma, harshness, and demoralization of homelessness. But at the same time I have witnessed the fortitude that people experiencing homelessness must draw on to survive and improve their condition, sometimes obscured by stigma, emotional drain, disability, and addiction. *Better Must Come*, the title of this book, depicts the defiant optimism and persistence that individuals and communities in global cities need to muster to overcome obstacles at multiple social levels that create and sustain homelessness and urban marginality. In parts of this book, I discuss why some people I followed for this study were unable to exit homelessness during our contact. However, I do place a special focus on processes of exiting homelessness. I do so not to present a sanitized version of homelessness. Indeed, there are many stories of frustration, failure, misery, and degradation in these pages. But my focus on exits allows me to highlight what I believe to be transgressive resistance to homelessness (getting out of the condition rather than merely adapting to it in situ) and how it is shaped by economic, social, and cultural contexts.

Homelessness, Ethnography, and Culture

I first met Barry, a forty-one-year-old white man from Rhode Island, one early morning outside the Skid Row transitional housing program while waiting for a job preparedness class to begin. George, a fifty-three-year-old white man from Maine whom I interviewed the day before, was contemplating taking a Grey-hound bus back to New Orleans where he had sold hot dogs as a street vendor. The two men had long worked as day laborers, mostly distributing flyers in residential neighborhoods and on commercial thoroughfares. But they both complained they were excluded from Latino immigrant networks that had come to dominate Los Angeles's informal sector. George introduced me to Barry, telling me that he would probably be easier to keep track of for my interviews. Before I could even ask, Barry voiced his dissatisfaction with the transitional program—there were too many requirements to attend classes and he could get little support for what he saw as his only way out of homelessness, building up his flyer distribution business and moving into subsidized housing. When we sat beneath the trees outside the Los Angeles Central Library a few days later, he told me that he had been living on the streets, in shelters, and in unsubsidized single room occupancy (SRO) hotels[3] around Skid Row for nearly twenty years. He originally moved to California for the warm weather after he was honorably discharged from the military. His savings were stolen while he was staying in a cheap hotel near the Los Angeles International Airport. With few marketable skills as a high school dropout, he learned that there were day labor jobs available on Skid Row, and he got work from agencies like Minuteman and informal hiring sites like the one outside Martha's Kitchen, a deli. However, he struggled to find enough work to pay for his room, and he ended up building a plywood shack in a parking lot on the fringes of downtown, recycling cardboard to make ends meet.

Barry signed up for the local county welfare program (General Relief, or GR), but the $221 per month was not enough to keep him housed. With lower back pain from construction work, he applied for federal disability benefits (Supplemental Security Income, or SSI) that would provide more income than GR. Despite the help he received from staff of the nonprofit organization Legal Aid, his application was rejected and appealed multiple times over fifteen years. He tried the transitional housing program but eventually dropped out when he was told that he had to attend more job search classes, which would conflict with his flyer distribution work. He took the savings he accumulated from his year in the program and moved into an unsubsidized SRO. However, when money ran thin, he began alternating between staying at the Midnight Mission and on the streets. For his bed at the Mission, he had to line up every morning at 4 a.m. to ensure that he received a temporary cardboard bed ticket distributed at 7 a.m. Given the Mission's rules, which were implemented to ensure those who demonstrated the most need for a bed received a ticket, he had to come back at 8 a.m. after breakfast to get a laminated "real ticket" for his bed. Although this was a tedious and precarious way to secure housing, other programs, including those for veterans, also had course requirements that would prevent him from working day labor. He used his contact at Legal Aid to get help in applying for a federally subsidized SRO room, but demonstrating what urban poverty ethnographer Javier Auyero (2012) describes as the modal experience of state poverty relief, Barry was made to "sit and wait," as he did with his SSI application and bed tickets. In frustration, Barry said, "If you're working, you're on your own. You're a drug addict or an alcoholic, there's millions of places you can stay. That's wrong. I mean it's like they're rewarding you for being a drug addict or alcoholic."

Barry's experiences highlight a number of issues of central concern for scholarly research on homelessness in general, and specifically research that has taken an ethnographic approach. Since the reemergence of sizable and visible homelessness in U.S. cities beginning in the late 1970s, and in Japanese cities in the early 1990s, extensive research literatures on contemporary homelessness have developed. The most common theme in reviews of the American literature is the debate about individual and structural causes of homelessness (Lee, Tyler, and Wright 2010; Shlay and Rossi 1992). Whereas much of the early Japanese literature on homelessness consistently took a structural approach (Aoki 2000; Aoki et al. 1999; Iwata 2000), more recently there has been a focus on individual-level vulnerabilities such as mental illnesses and developmental disabilities (Morikawa 2013; Suzuki 2012). I see this debate as potentially being resolved by the work of Paul Koegel, Audrey Burnam, and James Baumohl (1996) on the complex mix of forces driving people into homelessness. Structural conditions such as deindustrialization, the rise of bifurcated labor markets, the decline of affordable housing stocks, and retreating social protections, including the restructuring of mental health systems, have created a sizable precariously housed population. Individual-level vulnerabilities, such as mental illness and substance abuse, and a limited ability to tap social ties, make certain people among the precariously housed more likely than others to fall into literal homelessness. These vulnerabilities are not distributed evenly across society in either prevalence or consequence. For example, from a social stress perspective, substance abuse and addiction as well as resource-poor social networks among extremely poor and disadvantaged racial or ethnic groups are likely to be at the very least partially a result of their marginalized position. This mix of structural forces driving precariousness and individual factors making some more vulnerable to homelessness is often exacerbated via traumatic, "triggering" events such as domestic violence, tragic accidents, the sudden death of intimates and caregivers, loss of employment, robbery, divorce, sickness, and the like, ultimately pushing people into homelessness. Thus, the setting for Barry's fall into homelessness was the broad shifts in Los Angeles's local labor and housing markets and welfare systems in which competition for low-skill living-wage paying jobs and affordable housing increased, and opportunities for adequate welfare aid were sharply cut back (Wolch and Dear 1993). Barry's lack of human capital and social ties ultimately made him among the most vulnerable to these changes; the theft of his savings pushed him to Skid Row, precarious day labor, and eventually literal, on-the-streets homelessness.

This structural approach contrasts with that of more applied fields such as psychology, social work, and mental health, which have tended to emphasize the disproportionate and varied vulnerabilities of those experiencing homelessness. The influence of this latter type of research has contributed to a medicalization of the problem of homelessness, especially in the United States, resulting in the embedding of a discourse of "sick talk" in an expansive "homeless archipelago" of housing and services (Gowan 2010). Although approaches based on a medical model, including the provision of subsidized housing with supportive services to persons with disabilities instead of emergency shelter, have been key to reducing street homeless populations in many national contexts (Hombs 2011), the medicalization of homelessness has major limitations. Such a model directs policy and resources toward addressing individual vulnerabilities instead of tackling the broader social, economic, and policy contexts that drive and sustain the social problem (Lyon-Callo 2004). As Barry experienced directly, medicalization can also exclude those without sufficiently documented disabilities from subsidized housing and other forms of aid.[4] Also, it can justify aggressive outreach to those who, due to mental illness, allegedly do not know what is best for themselves, and police and private security sweeps of the "service resistant" who remain in public spaces (Murphy 2009).

Sociologist David Snow and colleagues challenged the "distorting tendencies" prevalent in the booming field of research on homelessness, seeing much of it as reliant on cross-sectional—primarily survey—data, thus overrepresenting individual vulnerabilities in support of the medicalization of the problem (Snow, Anderson, and Koegel 1994; Snow et al. 1986). Since persons with disabilities tend to experience homelessness for longer periods of time, they make up a larger proportion of the point-in-time population compared to the population experiencing homelessness over time. Cross-sectional studies thus tend to exaggerate the prevalence of mental illness and substance abuse and fail to capture the contexts that generate severe depression and alcohol and other drug use, which can be seen as responses to extreme poverty and homelessness. Instead, Snow and others advocate longitudinal studies that are sensitive to context and avoid the overapplication of reductionist perspectives that see homelessness as driven by individual-level causes and dynamics.

In addition to resisting medical reductionism, a longitudinal ethnographic approach that pays attention to multiple social contexts *and follows people out of homelessness* challenges the tendency to narrowly focus on how people acculturate to, identify with, and become entrenched in homelessness. My interactions with Matsuyama-san over time in Tokyo revealed a much more complex process. I first met him as part of a weekly street outreach conducted by staff and volunteers of Sanyūkai, a private, nonprofit medical clinic in Tokyo's San'ya district. In the summer of 2004, a staffing manager from a packaging factory in nearby Saitama Prefecture contacted the clinic. The manager said that local young people would not work in his old factory because it lacked air conditioning in the summer and heating in the winter. He thought that the unemployed people the clinic served in Tokyo would be willing to endure those conditions. He offered 250,000 yen ($2,243) per month and a modest furnished apartment renting for 50,000 yen ($449). But since the company itself was "restructuring" its workforce of those over fifty by encouraging early retirement, we were asked to try to find job candidates in their forties or younger. That afternoon, next to the "water bus" (ferry) stop on the Sumida River near Asakusa (a major entertainment district), a few other volunteers and I approached a group of men who were resting and drinking. They had spent the entire previous night scavenging through several nearby neighborhoods for aluminum cans. Most of the men appeared to be closer to their sixties than their forties, but I struck up a conversation with a much younger-looking man in grubby pants with a towel tied around his head to keep the sweat from his eyes. When Matsuyama-san told me that he was in need of work, I asked his age and he replied "forty-eight." I explained the opportunity in Saitama and although he thought it sounded good, he wondered if his somewhat older friends could get hired as well. Also, he said, "In fact, I've only been here [the riverside park] two days. I just got out of a live-in construction job (*hanba*) and my friend, or someone I thought was my friend, stole my savings. I'm really too tired so I'm not in any condition to go to an interview."

We exchanged information, and Matsuyama-san showed up at the clinic the next morning. I sat in on his interview, in which the staffing manager berated Matsuyama-san for being tricked out of his money and becoming literally homeless. Beads of sweat multiplied on Matsuyama-san's neck as he was questioned, and eventually he broke into tears when repeatedly asked by the manager if he was truly ashamed ("*Honto ni nasakenai desu ka?*"). The manager went on to explain the details of the job, and Matsuyama-san kept expressing interest, asserting that he would grow through the work experience. In contrast to the tense beginning of the interview, it ended with Matsuyama-san planning to move to Saitama the next day and the two smoking cigarettes and chatting casually. However, when I arrived at the clinic the following morning, I was told that Matsuyama-san had called from a pay phone to say that he would not be taking the job. The staff person that took the call relayed that Matsuyama-san said, "I have too much baggage" (*Ni ga omosugiru*), which he interpreted as obligations to the men in the park for their help. Also, the men apparently told Matsuyama-san that he probably would not be paid, a form of exploitation not uncommon among underground job recruiters (*tehaishi*) who prey on unemployed and vulnerable men in Tokyo's parks and stations. It appeared that Matsuyama-san simply did not trust the manager, the clinic as an organization, the staff and volunteers, or any of us.

A week later, Matsuyama-san was sitting outside the clinic in the morning with glazed eyes and a lazy smile reflecting that he had enjoyed a beer or two after his night of recycling. I had visited the factory and apartment in Saitama and told him that the job was legitimate. He told me that he was not bothered by the manager's brash approach and was extremely thankful for what he thought was a tremendous opportunity, but everything was just too "heavy" (*omoi*)—he would have to borrow money up front, interview again at the company with an application falsified by the manager to hide periods of unemployment, and he was beginning to wonder why we were so focused on him. The staff and I phoned the manager, who was willing to be flexible and provide a trial period where he would not incur debt and they could resolve his concerns about the second interview. However, when I relayed this, Matsuyama-san thanked me sincerely and refused the offer. As he turned to walk back toward his small hut (*koya*) along the Sumida River, he smiled and said, "I'm satisfied with my life" (*Jūjitsu shiteru yo*). The staff, the manager, and I were baffled by someone turning down a rare offer that would immediately remove them from the harshness of literal homelessness. At a staff meeting, the director of the clinic, often featured in the media for his insight into the hearts and minds of the dislocated men who come to San'ya, said, "If you've been on the streets long enough, you depend on your companions (*nakama*) and you can't leave them."

If my interactions with Matsuyama-san had ended with this weeklong exchange, I may have concluded that his case demonstrates a micro process of acculturation into a homeless culture and identity. This process seemed unaffected by what we thought was a fix to the structural problem of a lack of employment and housing. Although the stage was set for his homelessness given his marginal position as an informal live-in construction worker, once he was pushed into homelessness, he began a new process of learning to "do homelessness" (*hōmuresu wo yaru*) (Margolis 2008). However, I was able to keep in touch with Matsuyama-san long enough to see that this was not the best way to understand his experience of and orientation toward homelessness. Nearly a year after we first met, Matsuyama-san and many of his neighbors in the park were able to take advantage of a special Tokyo Metropolitan Government "housing first" program in which they moved directly into subsidized housing and were provided with public work while they looked for longer-term employment. Many residing in Sumida Park, like Matsuyama-san, were initially skeptical of the promises of work and housing, a hesitance viewed by some observers as indicating acculturation and entrenchment, and even a preference for homelessness. However, gradually outreach workers for the program built up trust through periodic, low-pressure interactions, and were able to assure program participants that they would be provided adequate housing and employment. Matsuyama-san moved into a simple apartment on the edges of San'ya and began working as a cook, his chosen trade, in a small soba noodle restaurant. Although he noted that those he cooperated with in eking out subsistence in the park were the first in his life to show him the true "goodness of people" (*hito no yosa*), he preferred that they all move on to a more humane (*ningen rashii*) living situation in which they would be free to visit each other as they liked. Thus, rather than illuminating a process of acculturation and entrenchment in homelessness, a longitudinal approach to experiences of homelessness that follows people out of homelessness can high-light how exits are shaped by access to a variety of resources, including economic, human, social, and emotional resources, as well as information and trust.

A chapter in sociologists David Snow and Leon Anderson's (1993) classic eth-nography *Down on Their Luck* analyzing the temporal dynamics of "homeless careers" provides an uncommon break from the focus on processes of becom-ing homeless and adapting to or resisting the condition in situ. They develop a framework for understanding various factors that contribute to exits from homelessness. They note that people "recently dislocated" or newly homeless often exit homelessness through employment and social ties. Those who do not exit enter a liminal phase as "straddlers," some of whom become more or less permanently "institutionally adapted" by working and living in shelters. Oppor-tunities for exit remain but diminish rapidly over time as people move toward long-term homelessness and an entrenched, acculturated status as "outsiders." They estimate that it takes about two years of street and shelter homelessness to reach outsider status, a state where one's identity and behavior is primarily ori-ented toward homelessness. Four factors affect the career any individual might follow—personal resource (human, economic, and social capital) deficits; insti-tutional factors (relief organizations); group-based ties (friends on the streets); and cognitive factors (specific plans to exit or lack thereof). Snow and Anderson place a particular focus on how a lack of resources, accommodative relief orga-nizations, street-based networks, and cognitive limitations interact over time to trap people in long-term homelessness. But this framework would have largely written off Matsuyama-san and many others in Los Angeles and Tokyo who ex-ited after much longer than two years of homelessness. Also, it does not antici-pate that personal resource deficits such as physical and mental disabilities could allow for better access to welfare benefits, programs, and housing as suggested by Barry's experiences.

I find many aspects of Snow and Anderson's framework to be accurate, but it is also in need of update and revision. In particular, I problematize the focus on a linear progression toward acculturation in which the potential for exit erodes over time. In a sense, this aspect of their theory is similar to the adage on the streets of Tokyo that "if you've done homelessness three days, you can't quit" (*Hōmuresu mikka yattara yamerarenai*). Their emphasis on this process in their theory is likely an artifact of a focus on "homeless street people" and the different organizational terrain of homelessness aid that has developed since their research in the 1980s. Their target population and research sites (streets and emergency shelters) most likely maximized contact with persons who were homeless over the long term, thus amplifying the focus on factors that lead to entrenchment rather than exits. Also, at the time relief was most likely to be "two hots [meals] and a cot" and accommodative, whereas programs designed to help people secure the resources to get out of homelessness expanded tremendously in the 1990s and 2000s (Burt et al. 2001; Hombs 2011). Through my focus on exits among transitional housing users, I centralize Snow and Anderson's emphasis on access to myriad resources, and decenter their focus on linear acculturation to homelessness. In particular, I show that social ties, especially those embedded in relief organizations, are more facilitative of exiting, and that cognitive factors play a much more minimal role. More broadly, my comparison of the process in two global cities advances their framework by showing how different contexts at various social levels shape the process of exiting in particular ways, and by identifying the more forgiving contexts that promote exits from homelessness.

Teresa Gowan's (2010) immersive ethnographic work on homelessness in San Francisco spanning several years does not focus on exits from homelessness but provides an alternative to the "culture wars" of demonstrating or disproving a pathological culture of homelessness. Instead, she looks at culture as three predominant discourses of homelessness (medicalized "sick talk," moralistic "sin talk," and structural "system talk") and how they deeply shape the experiences of people living primarily on the streets. I share her empirical focus on how culture operates in the speech and actions of people experiencing homelessness, but I move in a different direction away from the culture wars by examining the effects of cultural contexts on exits from homelessness in global cities embedded in two distinct national and urban contexts. Drawing on recent advances in ethnographic studies of urban poverty (Harding 2010; Small, Harding, and Lamont 2010), I take a cognitive view of culture, seeing it as a tool kit of symbols, stories, and worldviews that are used to understand, interpret, and act in the social world (Swidler 1986). This tool kit serves as the culturally available understandings and strategies that shape, but do not determine, one's behavioral choices. Empirically, I analyze these as "frames," or ways to understand the workings of the social world, embedded with information about the consequences of behaviors in context, and "scripts," or ways to address a problem, achieve goals, or act in any given situation (Benford and Snow 2000; DiMaggio 1997). Thus, I examine how culture interacts with the structural contexts of labor markets, housing markets, and welfare systems to affect key decisions related to securing the economic, social, emotional, and other resources necessary to exit homelessness. I do not use a deterministic understanding of culture but see repertoires of cultural frames as making certain behaviors more likely, rather than inevitable. These include decisions about work and housing, seeking out welfare benefits, securing aid through organizations, and getting help from family and friends. Although I do not take a rigid approach to national culture by seeing it as homogeneous within national borders, I do examine how broad differences in U.S.

and Japanese welfare regimes, as well as Los Angeles and Tokyo urban regimes, shape the cultural tool kits of people experiencing homelessness. This comparison allows me to not only shed light on the social contexts that are facilitative of exits from homelessness but also to contribute to critical urban studies' efforts to understand the relationship between global and local contexts in shaping experiences of urban marginality.

Nuancing Critical Urban Studies

Over the past three decades, sizeable populations experiencing homelessness have become a hallmark of wide inequality and deep marginality in global cities, the socially polarized command centers of an increasingly dispersed but connected global economy (Sassen 2001). The same can be said of globalizing cities, the broader set of cities that may not be major nodes but that still are seeing trends associated with globalization. As these cities have deindustrialized amid global economic restructuring, service-sector employment has expanded and inequality in incomes and potential for wealth accumulation have widened. High-skill workers, especially those in high-profit financial and business services, seem to have boundless opportunities, whereas low-skill workers in low-paying and precarious retail, cleaning, and other supportive occupations struggle to provide for themselves and their families. In addition to the decline of living-wage employment, affordable housing is scarce given the tendency of developers to target high-income households, fostering gentrification and real estate speculation. With state protections also eroding amid declining resources and widespread ideological opposition to tax increases and government spending, gaps in safety nets that have prevented homelessness and other forms of marginality have widened. Critical urban scholars see these global trends toward greater inequality as driven by a broad shift to postindustrial, neoliberal urban society, where private economic growth in the global marketplace is prioritized over social contracts, labor interests, and Keynesian intervention that characterized the Fordist and Toyotist (named after Toyota) periods (Aoki 2003; Wacquant 2008).

Despite its potential to alleviate inequality and marginality, state response to heightened insecurity amid economic globalization appears to have taken a punitive turn (Wacquant 2009). In post-Fordist cities, led by those in the United States, response tends toward punishment of poverty via mass imprisonment by the penal state and the replacement of entitlement benefits with disciplinary workfare that promotes participation in the precarious low-wage labor market. This expansion of the penal state directly contributes to homelessness. With felony records, eroded social ties, and little to no rehabilitation or transitional services, those paroled from prison are susceptible to unemployment, precarious housing, and homelessness. Also, stepped-up crackdowns on survival behavior like sleeping, panhandling, and relieving oneself in public render people experiencing homelessness susceptible to rearrest, entangling them in a "prison-homelessness nexus" (Gowan 2002). New York City's attacks on "quality of life" crimes, which were fully embraced by the Rudy Giuliani administration, are seen as emblematic of the rise of this new punitive paradigm of social control that has replaced the liberal goal of improving the lives of the poor (Mitchell 2003; Vitale 2009). Following a "broken windows" model of crime reduction, the New York Police Department, largely under the leadership of Commissioner William Bratton, increasingly targeted and penalized "antisocial" behavior and petty crimes like drinking in public and obstructing public spaces in a broader effort to establish order and reduce more substantial crimes like theft and violence. In the mid-1990s the Tokyo Metropolitan Government began looking to U.S. cities such as New York and Los Angeles for policy models to address homelessness; it seems at least to have been reassured if not inspired by the quality-of-life approach. In 1996 and 1998, police engaged in violent clashes to remove encampments of well over one hundred makeshift abodes in Shinjuku Station to make room for a moving walkway linking the station to the new Tokyo Metropolitan Government headquarters (Hasegawa 2006).

The expansion of this "no tolerance" approach to visible disorder gained momentum when Bratton was police chief of Los Angeles between 2002 and 2009. Beginning officially in 2006, the Los Angeles Police Department's Safer Cities Initiative aimed to have law enforcement remove a dense concentration of street encampments in the Skid Row area (Stuart 2011). Rooted in the broken windows theory, it was expected that eliminating the encampments would produce a broad reduction of various forms of crime in the area, such as drug sales and use, theft, and violence. A sophisticated evaluation, controlling for citywide trends in crime rates, shows that these efforts led to a modest but statistically significant decrease in violent, property, and nuisance crimes within the police district containing Skid Row (Berk and McDonald 2010). However, critics claim that during the first ten months of the Safer Cities Initiative, 2,218 persons were arrested for misdemeanors (mostly sleeping on sidewalks during the day and public urination/defecation), with only 17 percent referred to shelters (Blasi et al. 2007). Also, although street encampments did decline in the area and a modest reduction in crime was achieved, the intervention came with an expensive price tag, about $6 million per year for deployment of officers, and about $118 million for processing arrests made over the first few years of the program, resources that could have been better spent on permanent supportive housing (Culhane 2010a; Vitale 2010). The rise of the quality of life paradigm and antihomeless

laws restricting access to public space is thus seen to socially and politically exclude, creating a severely constricted public sphere barren of rights to housing,
livelihood, and health care (Mitchell 2003; Vitale 2009). This punitive approach
to extreme urban poverty portends to be globalized from its "living laboratory"
in American cities, with Bratton moving on to be an international consultant on
crime and risk to global cities spread across six continents[5] before returning to
the police chief position in New York in 2014.

However, much of critical urban studies focuses narrowly on punitive approaches to street homelessness, neglecting more ameliorative approaches being
implemented in major cities across the globe. Since the early 2000s, many cities
in North America, western Europe, and Australia have embraced assertive "housing first" approaches that provide subsidized housing and supportive services
and aim to reduce if not eliminate any time persons spend in shelters (Hombs
2011). This approach was applied in many American cities in the late 1990s and
eventually embraced by the U.S. Department of Housing and Urban Development (HUD) under the George W. Bush administration. These efforts have reduced "chronic" street homelessness among persons plagued with disabilities
and experiencing homelessness long-term (HUD 2011).[6] The approach is based
on research demonstrating that people with disabilities experiencing long-term
homelessness use up a tremendous amount of resources in shelters, emergency
rooms, jails, and other public facilities. Dennis P. Culhane, Stephen Metraux,
and Trevor Hadley (2002) showed that the cost of having "chronically homeless" persons cycle through New York City's institutional nexus of homelessness could be greatly reduced with subsidized housing and supportive services
("permanent supportive housing"). Also, despite being largely ignored by both
critical urbanists and advocates of Los Angeles's Safer Cities Initiative, targeted
programs using supported housing have been effective in reducing entrenched
street homeless encampments. These programs were pioneered during the quality of life crackdown era in the late 1990s, with federally subsidized housing and
supportive services being combined by private nonprofit organizations to reduce
street homelessness in Times Square and Penn Station in New York City.

After a visit to New York City in 1999, some of the Tokyo Metropolitan Government (TMG) homelessness policy leaders were so impressed by subsidized
housing projects around Times Square that it became the model for a housing first program that was unprecedented in Japan.[7] Between 2004 and 2009,
the "Moving to Community Life Support Program" (Chi'iki Seikatsu Ikō Shien
Jigyō) targeted large encampments near many of Tokyo's prime commercial and
residential spaces, such as in Sumida, Ueno, Shinjuku Central, Yoyogi, Toyama,
and Miyashita Parks. Residents of the parks, like Matsuyama-san above, were offered subsidized private apartments for which they would pay 3,000 yen (about
$27) per month for two years. Between 2004 and 2008, 1,945 people took up

the offer (or about 60 percent of those offered the deal), reducing the encampments in these parks by 66 percent with a fall from 2,695 to 925 tents (Chi'iki Seikatsu Ikō Shien Jigyō Kōka Kentō Iinkai 2011). By the end of the program in 2010, 84 percent of them remained in housing, with 57 percent on welfare and 26 percent "self-sufficient" through employment. Critics point out flaws in the program, such as poor-quality housing, spatial dispersal that has caused social isolation, and subsequent obstruction and forced removal of encampments (Yamada 2005). Nevertheless, a steady decline in street homelessness, high retention rates, and the clear decline in visibility across many of Tokyo's prime spaces suggest that the program has been successful in reducing encampments. Although a bit late, even Los Angeles has more fully embraced a targeted housing first approach. Well after Los Angeles's Safer City Initiative had criminalized street homelessness in Skid Row, public and private sector actors implemented a pilot Project 50 project, an intervention in which fifty of the most vulnerable (and costly to public services) persons on the streets of Skid Row have been provided with supported housing, with 80 percent remaining over the long term (Goffard 2010). Although the program is part of a broader public-private effort to increase supportive housing in Skid Row and other parts of Los Angeles, it is rather modest compared with New York City's ongoing objective of creating ten thousand supportive housing units in a five-year period (Culhane 2010b).

So rather than a singular punitive approach to homelessness in global cities, responses are multiple and varied, with some appearing to contradict one another. Through my comparative analysis of the longitudinal experiences of transitional housing program users, I aim to improve understanding of the differentiated nature of these state-led interventions to address homelessness, as well as to explain how they interact with the multilevel structural contexts of global cities embedded in different welfare regimes. This allows me to add nuance to critical urban studies by demonstrating how homelessness and exits are not simply driven by a singular context of monolithic neoliberal globalization.

Transitional Housing

In addition to viewing homelessness at an individual level as a state of limbo or liminality, Kim Hopper and Jim Baumohl (1994) theorize societal-level interventions such as emergency housing as warehousing institutions in an "abeyance process," absorbing surplus populations that do not fit into the established social order. Transitional housing has become a core element of major national interventions to address homelessness in both the United States and Japan, but it is unclear whether such programs simply warehouse, mainly serve to discipline amid a broader punitive framework, or are effective in helping people reconnect with conventional work and housing. In both places, transitional housing was developed to improve on emergency shelters that brought people in from the streets but did little more. However, transitional housing is criticized as being part of a larger neoliberal retreat away from state provision of guaranteed benefits toward time-limited support that promotes engagement with the low-wage labor market through disciplinary programs (Lyon-Callo 2004; Tamaki 2002). Transitional housing provides various forms of time-limited assistance to persons experiencing homelessness to enable them to secure income and housing, generally in the marketplace, and move out of shelters. It was a core element of Continuum of Care programs promoted by HUD under the Clinton administration in the mid-1990s. In Japan, transitional housing programs (*jiritsu shien sentā*) were the major component of the "Special Law on Temporary Measures to Support the Self-Reliance of Homeless People" (Hōmuresu no Jiritsu no Shien Nado ni Kan-suru Tokubetsu Sochi-hō), Japan's first homelessness-specific legislation, which was enacted in 2002. Although newer approaches, such as housing first and permanent supportive housing, have emerged in both countries, transitional housing remains a central policy measure for those not inhabiting prime urban spaces or without clearly documented disabling conditions that would render them eligible for welfare benefits and more supportive measures.

In addition to expanding supportive housing, there has also been movement toward emphasizing prevention of homelessness in both countries in response to rising unemployment rates amid the global economic crisis that began in 2008. The American Recovery and Reinvestment Act of 2009 created the Homelessness Prevention and Rapid Rehousing Program (HPRP). This program provides short- or medium-term rental assistance; housing search services and mediation with landlords; legal and credit assistance; help with security and utility payments; and assistance with moving costs. People who are homeless or at risk of homelessness are eligible, including those whose income is less than 30 percent of the area median and who frequently move due to economic need, live in a doubled-up arrangement or a motel, or are exiting an institution. This preventative approach has been expanded with the 2009 passage of the Homeless Emergency Assistance and Rapid Transition to Housing (HEARTH) Act that promotes supported housing and preventative assistance over criminalizing and costly warehousing models in addressing homelessness (HUD 2011). In Japan, the "Lehman Shock" of fall 2008 roused public concern about a nosedive of export-led manufacturing and subsequent widespread layoffs of dispatch and contract workers living in factory dorms. Savvy homelessness and labor activists joined forces to create a "dispatch village" (*haken mura*), a protest encampment providing aid to displaced workers, in front of the Ministry of Health, Labor, and Welfare (MHLW) in central Tokyo's Hibiya Park (Shinoda 2009). Intense media coverage encouraged a sympathetic response from the ministry, which opened the doors of some of its buildings to provide shelter, encouraged local welfare offices to expand access to people dislocated by the economic crisis, and bolstered loans and supportive programs to keep people in housing while they search for employment.

In both the United States and Japan, shifts in investment toward supportive housing and prevention seem to have helped keep surges in homelessness at bay amid the ongoing global economic recession. In both countries, long-term, entrenched, and visible street homelessness appears to be on the decline, even amid heightened unemployment and poverty. In the United States, point-in-time chronic street homelessness decreased 18 percent, from 82,108 people in 2007 to 67,247 people, in 2012 (HUD 2013a). Also, "unsheltered" persons inhabiting public spaces[8] decreased by 23 percent, from 278,658 persons in 2007 to 213,515 persons in 2013. Decreases in broader definitions of homelessness in the United States have been more modest. According to HUD (2013b), overall point-in-time homelessness (including persons on the streets, in shelters, and in transitional housing) declined 9 percent, from 671,888 people in 2007 to 610,042 people, in 2013. The declines in street homelessness have been attenuated by the general stability of the population in emergency and transitional housing programs, which has fluctuated between 390,000 and 400,000 people. Also, there have been recent small but alarming increases in familial homelessness concentrated in America's suburbs (HUD 2011; National Coalition to End Homelessness 2013), suggesting that new preventative and rapid rehousing programs are not fully meeting the need generated by the housing bubble collapse.

In Japan, homelessness, narrowly defined as persons living in public spaces, has declined 67 percent, from a peak of 25,296 persons in 2003 to 8,265 persons in 2013 (Ministry of Health, Labor, and Welfare 2003, 2014). This decline has occurred across major urban areas as well as in smaller regional cities and suburbs. Generally, the decline is attributed to expansion of access to welfare benefits, a trend that began in the early 2000s but gained steam with the dispatch village campaign of 2008–09. However, activists and researchers in Japan have highlighted the existence of a sizable precariously housed and "housing poor" population that does not meet the narrow definition of street homelessness (Inaba 2009; Yuasa 2008). In 2007, after media reports roused public concern about a "hidden homeless" population living in all-night Internet cafés, the MHLW attempted to estimate its size. They found that nationally about 5,800 (8 percent) of 60,900 overnight users of these cafés did not have any other place to stay (Ministry of Health, Labor, and Welfare 2007a). Also, a national study by academic and applied researchers found that one hundred organizations surveyed provided intermediary housing for 1,519 people in October 2010 (Kōgi no Hōmuresu no Kashika to Shiensaku ni kan suru Chōsa Kentō Iinkai 2011). In the same study, 878 public welfare offices throughout the country (67 percent of all welfare offices in Japan) reported providing welfare benefits in February 2011 to 1,889 individuals who were homeless when they applied. A portion of these persons may have ended up in "poverty businesses," which Okuta Tomoshi, director of the National Homeless Support Network, estimated in 2010 to be providing substandard housing and aid to between six thousand and seven thousand people and profiting off their welfare (*seikatsu hogo*, or livelihood protection) benefits (Terao and Okuta 2010). This suggests that while welfare benefits are being used to get people off the streets, only some could be seen as moving into a form of "supportive housing" (with aid from welfare offices and private NPOs), with some being warehoused and exploited. Together, these estimates demonstrate that there is a sizable precariously housed population across Japan that would fit a broader definition of homelessness. However, since there have not been follow-ups to these studies to date, it is not possible to discern whether or not these hidden homeless populations are growing.

Even though supportive housing and preventative measures are being expanded and contributing to declines in street homelessness in major cities of both countries, emergency and transitional housing is still widely used to address homelessness. In the United States in 2012, transitional housing made up about 28 percent of the 661,230 beds in national residential programs addressing homelessness, with emergency shelters making up about 33 percent, and permanent supportive housing about 39 percent (HUD 2013a). In Japan, nationally funded emergency and transitional housing grew substantially after the passage of the 2002 legislation. By 2011, there were approximately sixty-four emergency shelters in forty-three localities throughout the country with a point-in-time capacity of 2,192 persons. Transitional housing programs were operating in ten localities, with twenty-four programs in total and a point-in-time capacity of 2,224 persons.[9] Despite shifting policy and declines in street homelessness in both the United States and Japan, given the persistence of structural trends, such as widespread precarious employment, housing, and welfare aid, exacerbated by global economic crisis and stagnation, the flow of people pushed into homelessness has not stopped. Recently dislocated people, many without clearly diagnosed disabilities, are often missed by prevention programs and are generally not eligible for subsidized housing. They instead turn to time-limited transitional housing programs in their efforts to get out of homelessness. Indeed, just as the number of persons on the streets continues to fall, largely due to the investment in subsidized supportive housing, the number of people using these transitional programs in American and Japanese cities remains relatively stable.

Participants in these programs generally are relegated to the realm of neoliberal disciplinary workfare, provided with time-limited housing, and required to participate in programs that address their individual shortcomings and to secure income and housing in a precarious market. Thus, transitional housing programs are strategic sites to analyze how discourses and practices of neoliberalism interact with discourses and practices of care and aid (Cloke, May, and Johnsen 2010) to shape the lives of poor people in global cities. Also, because a general consensus has developed around a permanent supportive housing model as the most cost-effective measure to address chronic street homelessness, researching transitional housing provides an opportunity to examine a more contested area. Exit rates out of homelessness using transitional housing in both countries generally hover around 50 percent (HUD 2010a; Ministry of Health, Labor, and Welfare 2011). With a continued flow of persons into these programs, it is important to understand both the strengths of these programs, which help some of their users, as well as their weaknesses, which can be improved on. Through my focus on the experiences of transitional housing users, I aim to expand the dialogue about ending homelessness in both countries beyond long-term and disabled populations, to include the recently dislocated. It is only by addressing the needs of this population, as well as those of other forms of homelessness, that the predicament of homelessness can be ameliorated at a societal level.

Book Outline

This book consists of three parts, each preceded by "exit stories"—descriptions of exits from homelessness that demonstrate the themes of the chapters within each part. The first part introduces my study and the issue of homelessness in two global cities, Los Angeles and Tokyo. This introduction has presented my research questions, summarized my argument and contributions to the literature, described my methodology, and situated my study population. In Chapter 1, I weave secondary data with individual narratives to explain how trends associated with globalization have transformed and interacted with national- and local-level contexts to produce differences in the size and composition of populations experiencing homelessness in Los Angeles and Tokyo. Interviewees in both cities generally saw their fall into homelessness as being driven by individual failures, but their stories reveal how shifting global, national, and local contexts interacted in different ways in the two cities to pave pathways into homelessness of varying breadth and contour.

The second part turns to the main focus of the book, exiting homelessness, with an exploration of how transitional housing users experience state aid and markets differently in the two cities. Chapter 2 focuses on how my interviewees oriented themselves to state welfare and the systemic and informal barriers that resulted in their virtual exclusion from forms of state aid that would immediately end their homelessness. I also examine how a few interviewees were able to break through this exclusion, but generally only with the aid of a seasoned advocate. Chapter 3 shifts the focus to labor and housing markets, identifying barriers preventing access and strategies to overcome them. Interviewees in Tokyo were much more able to access income from the labor market and use it to purchase rental housing, although a greater ability to access subsidized housing in Los Angeles appeared to be a better long-term buffer from the precariousness of markets. This contributed to many of those who exited homelessness in Tokyo framing their exits as being precarious and possibly short term, whereas many interviewees in Los Angeles framed their exits as stable, but involving a hiatus from mainstream labor and housing markets.

The third part of the book focuses on the differentiated role of two types of social ties in processes of exiting homelessness. Chapter 4 looks at how ties with transitional housing program staff can facilitate exits from homelessness. It shows how different organizational cultures produce a greater level of trust in staff in the Los Angeles program, and thus greater use of ties with staff in exits there compared to Tokyo programs. Conditions from welfare and urban regimes enable or constrain frames and practices within organizations that promote these ties. Chapter 5 focuses on how broader cultural currents, embedded in welfare regimes and other social contexts in the two countries, affect efforts to rekindle ties with friends and family as a means to exit homelessness. Transitional housing users in Tokyo were nearly completely out of contact with family, whereas contact was common in Los Angeles, and for many there it was a key source of material and emotional aid in exiting homelessness. Tokyo interviewees more often framed their relations with family as completely severed, whereas Los Angeles interviewees sometimes hesitated to seek help due to concerns about independence, the financial ability of family members, and constraints placed by the penal state, but generally they at least sought out family for emotional aid.

The fourth section of the book bridges the individual experiences of my interviewees and the issue of ending homelessness at a societal level. It begins with an exit story, the description of an "actually existing counterfactual," a man from Tokyo who moved to Los Angeles and found himself homeless for nearly two decades, eventually exiting through the transitional housing program. His story highlights the persistent importance of multiple local contexts amid the globalization of homelessness. In the conclusion, I summarize the theoretical implications of my findings in terms of sociological research on homelessness as well as critical urban studies of globalization and marginalized populations. I also outline the policy implications of my analysis. Here, I describe the need to expand dialogue and efforts to end homelessness beyond those who experience it chronically to the sizable population without well-documented disabilities pushed into homelessness amid the vicissitudes of global urban society.

1

THE GLOBAL AND LOCAL ORIGINS OF HOMELESSNESS IN LOS ANGELES AND TOKYO

Surges in homelessness in recent decades in cities as varied as Berlin, London, Los Angeles, Moscow, New York, Osaka, Paris, Sao Paulo, Seoul, and Tokyo[1] call our attention beyond local levels. The emergence of homelessness in these cities has origins in labor market, housing market, and state social safety net transformation related to neoliberal globalization (Sassen 2001; Wacquant 2008). Since the early 1970s, increased international economic competition has generated a profit squeeze, and manufacturing firms in advanced capitalist countries have sought lower costs through offshore and flexible production. International finance and management of production, as well as the broader service sector, have risen in prominence, and all sectors have increasingly used nonstandard employment arrangements. This has caused increased precariousness through layoffs, unstable employment, and high levels of inequality and poverty. At the same time, transnational migration from developing countries has fed into economic restructuring in advanced economies by providing an ample labor force to work in low-wage, unstable employment. This influx, while fundamental to economic growth, has also increased competition for employment and housing. Welfare state supports, facing growing demand due to increases in poverty and inequality, have also been eroded by the ascendance of a neoliberal ideology that emphasizes individual responsibility and the strength of markets and communities to address social problems. Together, these trends increase economic insecurity and housing costs and weaken supports from the state to prevent extreme poverty and homelessness.

However, populations experiencing homelessness vary considerably in size and scope across global cities. As I show in the following section, the population experiencing homelessness in Los Angeles is larger than that in Tokyo and has larger shares of diverse subpopulations including families, people with serious mental health issues, and emancipated foster-care youth. Then, through description of structural changes driving homelessness in the two cities, I address the question, *why is the population that experiences homelessness in Los Angeles larger and more diverse than that found in Tokyo?*

Populations Experiencing Homelessness in Los Angeles and Tokyo

Sizeable surges in homelessness were reported in Los Angeles from the late 1970s through the 1990s (Wolch and Dear 1993). However, it is difficult to precisely measure increases due to the methodological complexities of counting a population that is hard to define and reach in a consistent manner. The first enumeration used data on the housing status of welfare applicants and estimated about 84,300 individuals experiencing homelessness on any given day and 236,400 individuals experiencing homelessness between July 1993 and June 1994 (Shelter Partnership, Inc. 1995). In addition to people in shelters and on the streets, this count included those doubled up in short-term temporary housing.

In 2005, the Los Angeles Homeless Services Authority (LAHSA 2006) used field counts within a sample of census tracts, counts in shelters, and telephone surveys to find persons doubled up or in structures not meant for habitation. LAHSA estimated the 2005 countywide point-in-time population to be 88,345 persons and the yearly population to be 221,363 persons. Although recent enumerations have refined procedures, HUD (2010b) has questioned their consistency and reliability. LAHSA reported an extraordinary 40 percent decline in the population between 2005 and 2009, with much of this decline among the street population in a single year (HUD 2011; LAHSA 2008, 2010). More recently, a 2013 enumeration found 57,737 people experiencing homelessness in the county on a single day, a 15 percent increase from 2011 (LAHSA 2012, 2013), with most of this increase among the "hidden" or "doubled up" population. Los Angeles has seen an expansion of its supported housing stock in the past fifteen years and federally funded preventative measures more recently. Thus, it is likely that the size of the population experiencing homelessness has followed the national urban trend of general decline between the mid- to late 2000s (albeit possibly not as dramatic as reported in LAHSA data) and increases from the early 2010s, as intertwined global and local economies rebound slowly while economic stimulation spending focusing on prevention expired.

By contrast, the Tokyo Metropolitan Government (TMG) has consistently conducted direct counts of persons living on the streets since the mid-1990s. TMG limits its definition to persons living in public spaces to the exclusion of those in shelters, housing programs, all-night commercial establishments such as Internet cafés and saunas, or doubled up (TMG 2007). Also, the TMG only uses direct counts of areas where encampments and more mobile populations are known. These figures are likely underestimates, but counts using consistent definitions and methods at similar times of night and year show steady growth of the street population in the late 1990s. The number peaked at fifty-eight hundred in 1999 and stabilized until 2005, when the effects of an improving economy and targeted supported housing programs became visible in a decrease to forty-three hundred persons. This trend toward decline has continued despite growth in unemployment during the global economic crisis, with the street population down to eleven hundred in 2013.[2]

Although there have been decreases in street homelessness in both cities, this trend has generally not carried over to shelters and other programs. In Los Angeles, between 2005 and 2011 the percentage of the total point-in-time population staying in emergency, transitional, or other kinds of shelters grew from 12 percent (9,874 persons) to 37 percent (16,882 persons).[3] In Tokyo, the number of persons in emergency and transitional housing grew considerably after the passage of 2002 national legislation to expand such programs. In 2009, there was a local stock of three hundred beds of emergency housing and 358 beds of transitional housing (Tokubetsu-ku Jinji Kōsei Jimu Kumiai Kōseibu 2010). The number of people using these facilities has been stable since, with 2,674 persons using emergency housing over the course of 2009, of which 1,389 moved on to use transitional housing. Also, with widening access to welfare benefits (*seikatsu hogo*), there is a sizable population in special facilities for recipients. Although there is little longitudinal data on this population in Tokyo, a point-in-time estimation for 2008 found approximately twenty-one hundred households living in these facilities (Kitagawa 2011).

Surveys from periodic enumerations also depict demographic patterns in the two cities. In 2005, approximately 24 percent of persons experiencing homelessness in Los Angeles were with family members, with 4 percent of them children under eighteen years of age. Single adult males made up 55 percent, single adult women 19 percent, and 1 percent identified as transgender. In Tokyo, nearly the entire street population is made up of single men, around 98 percent in 2007 (MHLW 2007b). Although gender is often only inferred in street counts, and the narrow use of street homelessness obscures the extent of homelessness among women in Japan (Maruyama 2013), men are overrepresented to a greater extent in Tokyo compared to Los Angeles. This is due to a mix of factors, including the disproportionate employment of men in construction and manufacturing, industries hit hard by economic stagnation and turbulence since the early 1990s; a tendency for welfare offices to be more likely to provide aid to an unaccompanied female than a male; and families being more likely to support an unemployed woman who provides household labor than an idle male (Maruyama 2004). Additionally, the age distribution of the street population in Tokyo is strongly biased toward older men, with a mean age of fifty-nine years in 2007, and with 88 percent being fifty and over. This skew toward middle aged and older men likely results from a combination of factors, including the aging of the postwar baby boom generation; the greater likelihood of older men to lose jobs in restructuring amid economic stagnation; the limited ability of men to compete in casual and day labor markets as they age; the tendency for men to completely sever ties with family after divorce; and an unwillingness among older unemployed men to utilize the welfare system. In Los Angeles, however, homelessness affects a broader set of age groups, with a mean age in 2005 of forty-three years, with 58 percent between thirty-one and fifty years old.

But it is important to note that while Tokyo's street population is homogenizing by remaining overwhelmingly male and becoming older in age (Abe 2010), the "hidden" population and those in welfare facilities is diversifying. These facilities house more women, 13 percent in one study (Tokyo Metropolitan Government 2003 as reported in Murayama 2004), and younger people, with the percentages in their twenties and thirties growing between 1998 and 2007 (Kitagawa 2011). Also, a 2007 survey of national all-night cafés found that, compared to the street population, those living in these establishments were more likely to be young, female, and working in part-time employment, reflecting how labor markets have become unstable for Japanese youth (Brinton 2010; MHLW 2007a).

Exemplifying national differences in overall demographics and structural racial inequality, racial and ethnic patterns of homelessness are much more evident in Los Angeles than in Tokyo. In the 2005 Los Angeles survey, 39 percent of respondents were black (versus 9 percent of the total county population), 29 percent white (29 percent), 25 percent Latino (47 percent), 3 percent Native American (0.3 percent), 1 percent Asian (13 percent), and 4 percent other or multiethnic (2 percent).[4] The dramatic overrepresentation of blacks demonstrates how structural changes driving increases in homelessness have disproportionately affected Los Angeles's black communities. However, the underrepresentation of Latinos, who are overrepresented among the local poor population (68 percent in 2000), reflects the "Latino paradox" in which family and immigrant networks often lead to employment and housing, preventing homelessness but not poverty (Gonzales-Baker 1996). A pervasive ideology that Japan consists of a single, pure race has been criticized as a "hegemony of homogeneity" that masks ethnic, regional, and class diversity (Befu 2001). Thus, official data on race and ethnicity are rarely collected or made available. But the TMG 2007 street survey found that about

30 percent of respondents once procured work in San'ya, Tokyo's day-labor ghetto (*yoseba*). Researchers of these neighborhoods have long speculated that ethnic and status groups such as resident Koreans, *burakumin* (descendants of premodern social outcasts), Okinawans, and Ainu are overrepresented among *yoseba* day laborers, but evidence is thin (Fowler 1996).

Although household, gender, and race/ethnicity characteristics in Los Angeles's population experiencing homelessness have been generally stable, there has been a decline in the proportion that is disabled and experiencing homelessness over the long term, thus falling under the label of "chronically homeless." Point-in-time surveys tend to exaggerate the prevalence of this population, but consistent longitudinal measures can provide insight into trends. About 49 percent of those surveyed in 2005 were determined to be chronically homeless, a figure that dropped steadily until it stayed even at 24 percent in 2009 and 2011 and increased slightly to 25 percent in 2013. This decline is likely due to supportive housing programs that have targeted this population, discussed in the introduction. Until very recently, there have been little data on the mental health of people experiencing homelessness in Tokyo or other parts of Japan (Morikawa 2013). As many other advanced capitalist countries were deinstitutionalizing the mentally ill in favor of community-based treatment beginning in the 1960s, Japan was expanding its mental hospitals. Although Japan has made a shift toward deinstitutionalization through measures like the Disabled Persons Self-Reliance Support Act of 2005, by the late 2000s Japan still had about three mental hospital beds per one thousand persons, compared to an average of less than one bed per one thousand persons in the United States, Germany, Great Britain, and France.[5] However, the negative effects of emerging deinstitutionalization may be unfolding. The percentage entering Tokyo's welfare (*seikatsu hogo*) shelters with a mental illness increased from 18 percent in 1998 to 35 percent in 2007 (Kitagawa 2011).

Given varying definitions and enumeration strategies, "unsheltered" (including people in structures not meant for human habitation on private property) and street homeless populations in the two cities provide perhaps the most valid, albeit imperfect, basis for direct comparison. In 2011, Los Angeles had a rate of approximately thirty-two unsheltered persons per ten thousand people (31,627 per 9,889,056 total population), compared to slightly over one person on the streets per ten thousand people in Tokyo (1,600 per 13,189,000 total population).[6]

Transforming Labor Markets in Los Angeles

Broad industrial change in Los Angeles played a prime causal role in the increase of homelessness in the region since the late 1970s (Wolch 1996; Wolch and Dear

1993; Wolch and DeVerteuil 2001). Los Angeles's Fordist economy, its heyday spanning from the bombing of Pearl Harbor to the 1965 Watts Riots, was centered on the manufacturing of durable goods such as automobiles, rubber, glass, steel, and aerospace equipment (Abu-Lughod 1999; Keil 1998; Soja 1996). But in the late 1960s and early 1970s the local economy began a shift to service and high- and low-tech manufacturing and employment in the public sector shrank. Politically, Los Angeles's urban regime wavered from liberal to conservative but consistently maintained an entrepreneurial stance focused on financial deregulation and labor market flexibility to remain competitive in global markets (Dreier, Mollenkopf, and Swanstrom 2004). The current industrial mix in Los Angeles is dominated by services such as finance, insurance, and real estate (FIRE); entertainment; international trade; tourism; retail sales; and communications equipment, electronics, clothing, and furniture manufacturing (Ong and Blumenberg 1996; Southern California Association of Governments 2000, 2005, 2007). While the FIRE, entertainment, trade, and tourism industries provide many high-salary jobs in management, they also generate many unstable low-wage jobs in administration and maintenance services. The new post-Fordist manufacturing industries encompass a smaller share of the labor force and use a more flexible organization of production, new technology, and larger numbers of low-wage workers who are generally not unionized (Soja 1996).

Together, deindustrialization, reindustrialization, public-sector contraction, and service-sector expansion have generated considerable economic dislocation, poverty, and income inequality in Los Angeles. Although unemployment in the county has fluctuated, it was at a generally lower level in the 1970s (around 6 percent at decennial censuses in 1970 and 1980) than later in 1990 (7.4 percent) and 2010 (12.4 percent), although unemployment dipped to 5 percent at the peak of late 1990s economic growth.[7] Household income inequality showed a more linear increase, with the Gini ratio increasing steadily from around 0.35 in 1970 to 0.49 by 2010.[8] Poverty measures, although likely underestimates given a lack of adjustment for increased housing and other costs, provide perhaps the clearest indication of growing deprivation. The official poverty rate for Los Angeles County has grown steadily in the post-Fordist period, increasing from 10.9 percent in 1970 to 15.1 percent in 1990, reaching 17.9 percent by 2000, and decreasing very slightly to 17.5 percent by 2010. With the overall county population growing, this naturally resulted in tremendous increases in the number of people in poverty.

As in other major metropolises in the United States, poverty in Los Angeles has taken on a particularly concentrated, racial, and destructive form. By the 1980s predominantly black and Latino neighborhoods of South Central and East Los Angeles, as well as those along the Alameda Corridor of manufacturing such as South Gate, Compton, and Long Beach, had become known for unemployment, poverty, drug trafficking, substance abuse, crime, and street gang warfare (Davis 1990). Beginning in the 1970s, most predominantly black neighborhoods became increasingly Latino with growing immigration but remained poor as those with lower educational levels in the two groups often competed for similar low-skill jobs in the service sector (Grant, Oliver, and James 1996; Ortiz 1996). At the same time, occupational and housing segregation eased and many higher educated blacks and Latinos climbed up the occupational scale and moved out to suburban areas. The devastation of concentrated and racialized poverty combined with heightened levels of illicit substance use and trafficking and increasingly punitive measures. Between 1985 and 1990, 14 percent of the black population (82 percent of them adult males) left the county for institutionalized group quarters, many of which were prisons (Grant, Oliver, and James 1996).

The impact of these economic and social shifts in inner-city Los Angeles on processes of becoming homeless can be seen in the experiences of Jill, an African American woman from Watts. In 1973, at the age of twenty, Jill began working for Xerox as an electronics assembler, soldering circuit boards, only to be laid off three years later when the company began downsizing. Then she had the same experience with Hughes Aircraft and General Motors. Jill's limited employment stability, driven by major shifts in the local manufacturing industry, intersected with her increased use of drugs. In the 1970s, cocaine had become a popular party drug among her childhood friends in Watts, and after her parents unexpectedly died in her early twenties, she overdosed on PCP. By the time she was working for GM, Jill said, "I'd get up in the morning and eat breakfast, and I'd take me about two snorts. I'd be good for the day." Jill was able to remain functional, going to work and paying her bills. But then the GM plant closed, right about when she and her friends got into a "new high"—smoking "freebase," cocaine diluted and solidified into "rock" form with baking soda. For Jill, the high was more powerful but also more addicting and debilitating. When I asked if she thought her layoff affected her substance abuse, Jill replied, "It had a lot to do with it! Because I had too much leisure time and then I worked so hard there. And you know then getting laid off like that after makin' that good money! That's a big disappointment. It discouraged me. I was upset with the world. Oh, I didn't think about no work. I was mad at GM for a long time." Unemployed again, frustrated with repeated layoffs, and developing a taste for crack cocaine, Jill dove into her addiction. When she used up all of her severance benefits, she began nearly two decades of hardcore drug abuse, unemployment, precarious housing, and homelessness.

Much of the growth of both the total and relative sizes of the poverty population in Los Angeles County has coincided with a tremendous influx of immigrants (which made up about 36 percent of the county population in 2000 and

2010), many of them without the human or social capital needed to compete for high-wage employment. This growth, largely from Mexico, Central America, and Asia, was fueled by a growing demand for low-skill labor brought on by the expanding service sector and the downgraded manufacturing sector. Thus, in addition to contributing to overall economic growth, the influx has been shown to contribute to declines in both the employment rates and income levels of poorly educated young black males in Los Angeles (Ong and Valenzuela 1996). Certainly not all immigrants to Los Angeles are able to use social networks, low-wage service-sector employment, and shared housing arrangements to avoid homelessness. I will show this later through the examples of Magdalene, a Caribbean immigrant who struggled to secure stable employment in Los Angeles that paid enough to house her family, and David, a thirty-five-year-old whose father was Italian American but who moved as an infant to Mexico City with his Italian and Mexican mother, and who felt alienated from other migrants and was unable to break into service-sector employment to avoid homelessness despite having American citizenship.

Whereas the accounts I have presented in this section highlight the negative impacts of the decline of manufacturing, concentrated poverty, and immigrant competition, in other vignettes in this and other chapters, especially in Chapter 3, I show how Los Angeles's precarious service sector also contributes to homelessness by not providing income sufficient to purchase housing in an increasingly expensive rental market.

Transforming Labor Markets in Tokyo

Tokyo was at the center of Japan's Toyotist economic and social base, which shared the Fordist focus on manufacturing, expanding domestic consumption, export-led growth, and social contracts, but contained distinct Japanese characteristics (Fujita and Hill 1995). In contrast to the liberal American state's focus on competitive markets, Japan's developmental state provided "administrative guidance" and financial supports to industry, minimizing competition in favor of steady growth, and promoting employment stability and compressed wage structures through "Japanese style management" practices such as lifetime employment, seniority promotion, and enterprise unions (Hill and Fujita 2000). Tokyo's Toyotist period spanned roughly from the end of the American occupation in 1952 to the bursting of the bubble economy in the early 1990s (Machimura 1998). Tokyo's labor market began to change in the 1970s with a substantial contraction of manufacturing and primary industries, coinciding with the expansion of services (Sassen 2001). But expanding services and financial sectors have not globalized extensively, and Tokyo has primarily been a strategic location for the global head-quarters of Japanese firms (Waley 2007). Even though the Tokyo Metropolitan Government conducted "world city" campaigns to promote its attractiveness to global capital, it retained a developmental approach through the early 2000s, promoting stable business growth by supporting firms in targeted industries rather than using a competitive entrepreneurial approach with tax relief incentives (Fujita 2003; Saito and Thornley 2003). This fostered investment in high-tech industries such as environmental technology, life science, information technology, and nanotechnology. But at the same time, national deregulation of labor markets and corporate restructuring eroded traditional management practices, and the ranks of those in nonstandard employment in Tokyo expanded (Hasegawa 2006). Also, a continued focus on exports, especially to the United States, without stimulating domestic consumption rendered Tokyo's economy vulnerable to the 2008 global economic crisis (Fujita 2011). Subsequently the developmental state has moved further toward a post-Toyotist service- and finance-based economy, yielding to more neoliberal approaches and making it unable to keep growing inequality at bay (Tsukamoto 2012).

As a result of these shifts and interventions, unemployment, inequality, and poverty have expanded in recent decades in Tokyo, albeit in a more muted fashion than in Los Angeles. Although unemployment doubled from the very low levels of the bubble economy, Tokyo's rate remained around 5 percent between 2000 and 2013, spiking but not exceeding 6 percent amid the post-2008 global economic recession. This has had a particularly negative effect on older workers, with the ratio of employment for persons forty-five years and older declining steadily since the onset of the recession in 1991, from 40.4 percent in 1990 to 34.1 percent in 2003.[9] Poverty rates, adjusted for household size and cost of living, grew steadily from 7.6 percent in 1992 to 13.8 percent in 2002, dipping to 12.6 percent in 2007 before the global economic crisis (Tomoro 2013). In terms of income inequality, Tokyo's Gini coefficient has generally hovered around 0.3 throughout between 1999 and 2009 (Ashida 2005).[10] Tokyo has seen a steady increase in immigration in recent years but it remains relatively low, with the share of registered foreign residents growing from 1 percent in 1970 to 3.2 percent by 2010.[11] Also, although income-based residential segregation grew in Tokyo in the late 1990s, it was at a level of about one half that of Los Angeles, muted by the developmental state's decreasing but still important promotion of mixed-use and mixed-income neighborhoods (Jacobs 2005; Fujita and Hill 2012), likely preventing threats to social networks and cohesion seen in more highly segregated American cities (Wissink and Hazelzet 2012).

Data from Tokyo's first large-scale street and shelter survey in 2000 showed that over 75 percent of respondents worked in unstable jobs in manufacturing or construction prior to becoming homeless (Hagiwara 2001). The experiences of Yamada-san, a fifty-five-year-old native of Chiba, Tokyo's neighboring prefecture, demonstrate how labor market changes in Tokyo rendered him vulnerable to homelessness. A longtime nonstandard worker in manufacturing, he quit a live-in job just prior to the end of a two-year contract because he could no longer endure sharing a one-room apartment with two other workers. He used his savings (about 1,400,000 yen or around $12,558) and unemployment insurance payments to rent a small apartment for 35,000 yen (about $314) in the mixed industrial and residential district of Ōta Ward and began searching for work. However, he found factories were either not hiring workers in their fifties or required computer skills that Yamada-san was unable to acquire as a seasonal worker. Here, he describes how he became discouraged after years of unsuccessful searching and ultimately fell into homelessness.

> I started feeling inferior. Every year you report your income, right? So, for me it was always zero. I wasn't paying any taxes—residency taxes. Basically, if you are not paying taxes you are not a respectable adult, right? When I got turned down by about fifty places, I began to see things a certain way. There are no jobs, no jobs, no jobs, and when I find a job that I am qualified for, I get turned down. Then I start thinking, "Okay, this is not good." Security jobs were no good. They asked for two guarantors. There was no cleaning work, none, nothing working eight-hour shifts. So I figured that I could make about 100,000 yen [about $897] a month gambling, more than I would make in a part-time cleaning job. But it didn't work out. Eventually I ran out of money, and the next day I left my apartment and ended up sleeping in Heiwajima Park.

Like others in both cities, Yamada-san often framed his fall into homelessness strictly in individual terms, attributing it to his gambling and a lack of skills. However, a broader look at his labor market experiences reveals how his vulnerable position rendered him susceptible to unemployment and homelessness.

Additionally, the graying of the day laborer population, a growing pool of native and foreign-born part-time workers, and the extended recession have driven changes in employment practices at the fringes of the construction industry. The construction industry in Japan has long utilized boarding houses (*hanba*) where workers live and are dispatched to local construction sites, but this practice may have increased as hiring out of day labor ghettos (*yoseba*) dwindled. Living conditions can be quite squalid, and management will charge high fees for housing, bathing, food, alcohol, and cigarettes. Operators are sometimes affiliated with violent organized crime syndicates (*bōryokudan*). Brokers (*tehaishi*) recruit in parks and stations that are known to have sizeable mobile populations such as

Shinjuku, Ueno, and around the Sumida River, as well as advertising in sports newspapers popular among older working-class men. Although some *hanba* provide workers with an ample amount of jobs that allow for some savings, some lure in desperate workers and provide scant work while continuously extracting fees. Thus, for many who attempt to utilize *hanba* to avoid homelessness, they generally serve as dismal temporary respites and oftentimes actually increase vulnerability to homelessness.

Within the expanding service sector in Tokyo, there has been growth in a number of occupations with relatively low wages and nonstandard employment arrangements, rendering a growing population vulnerable to economic instability. At the same time, predatory cash lenders (*sarakin*) have been active. These lenders provide easy access to cash, usually only with proof of employment, and sometimes with even lower requirements, to persons strapped for cash, usually due to some combination of low and stagnant earnings, high household expenses, and excessive drinking or gambling. In addition to charging high interest rates, these agencies sometimes use a practice called *toritate* in which collectors intimidate debtors by relentlessly calling and visiting them at their homes and places of employment and even threatening violence. Particularly problematic are those connected to violent crime syndicates, which charge illegally high interest rates well over 20 percent (*yamikin*).

Shimada-san, a tall, stocky twenty-four-year-old from the northern prefecture of Iwate, provides an example of how low-wage service-sector employment, gambling addiction, and debt to predatory lenders can intersect to push even younger workers into homelessness. Unable to pass an exam to enter the police force, and after five years working in a low-wage, high-stress security job, Shimada-san got a taxi driver's license and a job in Tokyo. At first, the job paid a decent salary, but new regulations opened the local market to competition and his earnings declined.

> When I first started working as a taxi driver, it was fun, but there were a bunch of taxis coming in from the Kansai [around Osaka, Kyoto, and Kobe] area. In bad times I would only make 120,000 or 110,000 [about $1,076 and $986] per month. So, no matter what I did, I couldn't make ends met. Since I was working I had no time to practice judo. So I had no other way to relieve my stress. With *pachinko* it's strange because sometimes you win. When I won, I didn't really think, "Oh, this is good enough." I've seen it on TV, where they talk about gambling as an addiction, a kind of sickness. I think that is what I have. So, after work, that is where I would go. But, then I would use all of my money—my pay was so low anyway. Then I turned to lenders (*sarakin*)—even though

I wasn't a regular company employee, I was a taxi driver and I had a driver's license, so I got the cash loans easily. In the end, I was three months' late on my rent plus I had to pay about 200,000 yen [about $1,794] to renew my lease. I had no electricity, no gas, no water, and I was showering in the bathroom at the soccer stadium nearby, but still

A pachinko parlor in central Tokyo

going to work. Plus, I had the collectors from the *sarakin* on my back so I left.

Subsequently Shimada-san tried to avoid literal homelessness through help from family, working short term in live-in construction (*hanba*), and gambling on horse races. But his luck and money ran out so he began sleeping in Ueno Park. Although his gambling problem may have triggered his fall into homelessness, his work as a low-paid taxi driver in a sector being liberalized and seeing heightened competition set the stage. Also, his long work hours and solitude in a big city far from home littered with *pachinko* parlors made gambling a plausible form of stress relief—one that may have remained benign absent his unstable income.

Withering Social Safety Nets in Los Angeles

The withering of social safety nets just as there were surges in unemployment, poverty, and inequality has also contributed to the growth of homelessness in Los Angeles. With the inability to increase property taxes due to Proposition 13, a state ballot measure passed in 1978 that capped real estate taxes, the County of Los Angeles resorted to three tactics to address the financial problem posed by heightened welfare demand: cutbacks, closures, and coercion (Wolch 1996). The monthly cash benefit allocation for the county's welfare program for extremely poor households without children, General Relief (GR), is one of the lowest in the state ($221) and has not been adjusted for inflation. In the late 1980s, the county violated state law by reducing the value of GR cash benefits and was eventually forced to pay out the reductions after a class action suit of recipients was successful. Since the late 1990s, recipients deemed able to work can only receive a maximum of nine out of twelve months of benefits conditional on meeting job search and workfare requirements (Reese 2002). Also, the county's Department of Public Social Services (DPSS) has reduced staff, closed offices, and used a low bar for termination of GR benefits, including appearing late for a meeting with a case manager.

The experiences of Sally, a thirty-six-year-old white woman from Long Beach, shed light on how the low benefit levels of GR can fail to prevent a slip into homelessness for persons struggling to secure a place in the low-skill service sector. Sally worked for ten years as a baggage clerk at a U.S. naval base commissary, but she lost the job when the base closed amid disinvestment in the region's defense industries. Subsequently she cycled through low-wage jobs at retail outlets, citing conflicts with management and casual, on-call arrangements as contributing to her employment instability. Sally quit a job as a product demonstrator at a supermarket when she had difficulty communicating with bosses who would often change, the last straw coming when she was unable to obtain a paycheck. Sally was able to avoid homelessness through about three years of unemployment from 1999 to 2002 due to the generosity of a high school friend with whom she lived since graduating. During this time, Sally would turn over her GR check and food stamps to her roommate to pay for some of the household expenses. However, her friend eventually tired of the arrangement and decided to move out. Long Beach's Multi Service Center told Sally about a shelter in Compton called Compassion in Action that charged her $200 per month for a bunk and her food stamps to cover meals. When she reached the nine-month time limit on benefits, she was unable to cover her second month's fee, so she was turned out of the shelter and began sleeping on the rooftop of a nearby Rite Aid.

Although the focus of this book is single individuals and their efforts to exit homelessness, it is important to remember that families, often headed by single parents, are an alarmingly substantial proportion of the population experiencing homelessness in the United States (Burt et al. 2001; HUD 2011). Although welfare reform, beginning with the ascendance of conservative Republican administrations at state and national levels in the 1980s and culminating in the Personal Responsibility and Work Reconciliation Act of 1996, has increased employment and lowered welfare rolls, it has not reduced poverty and vulnerability to homelessness (Danzinger 2010). There is widespread state and local variation in implementation, but California has used time limits on lifetime receipt of CalWORKs (as the program is called there) benefits and penalties for failure to comply with workfare requirements (Reese 2005). Even though a direct causal link is difficult to establish, the correlation of welfare reform and growing familial homelessness at national levels is alarming.

Additionally, various social services and penal systems in Los Angeles County have been strained financially in recent decades, limiting their ability to transition their wards to stable housing arrangements, causing them to dump people in areas with a high density of service provision, such as Skid Row. Many outpatient mental health clinics were closed, disproportionately in low-income black and Latino neighborhoods, damaging their ability to absorb rising demand given the closure of large state mental institutions and legal changes that prevented holding mentally ill persons against their will if they were not demonstrably dangerous to themselves or others (Wolch 1996; Wolch and Dear 1993). It is likely that the closure of these mental health facilities has contributed to the high prevalence of chronically mentally ill persons experiencing homelessness as well as Los Angeles County Central Jail's reputation as the largest de-facto mental hospital in the country, with the "Twin Towers" holding about fifteen hundred to two thousand people with mental illness (Rivera 2005). In addition to the numerous departments from cities in the area that have been accused of dumping persons picked up in their jurisdictions with nowhere to go into Skid Row, former Los Angeles County sheriff Lee Baca publicly stated that as many as fifty persons per day are released from the Central Jail in downtown directly to the streets without housing (Rivera 2005). Many of these people wander into Skid Row, rendering themselves vulnerable to substance abuse relapse, crime, violence, and street homelessness. Although city and state programs addressing substance abuse have increasingly implemented therapeutic models, the expansion of imprisonment during the war on drugs has entrapped a sizable population in Los Angeles's prison-homelessness nexus (Gowan 2002).

My chance meeting with Stephen, a white Angeleno in his midthirties, on Crocker Street in Skid Row provides an example of how inadequate assistance in transitioning out of incarceration encourages street homelessness. I was interviewing Premier, a black man in his thirties from the South Bronx, under a blue tarp propped up with a stick and tied to a shopping cart. Stephen happened to walk by fumbling with an empty aluminum can. Premier spotted Stephen as someone looking for a relatively inconspicuous place for a heroin fix and invited him in. As Premier lit up a crack rock from his visitor's stash, Stephen pricked at his arms in a frustrating search for a viable vein and described how his day had unfolded. Shortly after sunrise, he was released from Central Jail—he thought because of overcrowding—after serving only forty days on a year sentence for a "petty with a prior" drug-related shoplifting conviction. Premier asked Stephen if he was eager to get his first fix:

> Yeah, I started getting that psychological jump, that little nervousness a little bit but I was fine, I didn't need to do this. You know what's funny, *I did try to stay clean*. I got the fuck out of downtown! I got on the train [without paying] and I went to Hollywood and Vine because my stepsister lives over there and she is the most nonjudgmental and understanding, even though I jacked them for their digital camera while I was staying with them last time. I got it back out of a pawnshop but there is still a trust issue there. But what's funny I'm thinking alright, I'm done, done with drugs. I don't need to commit any crimes. I'm going to prison if I get another theft charge. I just need to get out of downtown away from dope. So I go there and didn't have change to call her. I can't call her collect. I can't show up at her door on the weekend because her mom would be there, my stepmom, who is cool, but not that cool. So, I gotta get money for the phone but I don't feel like panhandling. So I do

what I do best and I go into the store and I jack just enough [instant] coffees and razors to fuckin' fence on Broadway and buy three bags of dope [heroin], a fuckin' nickel [five dollars' worth] of cavy [crack cocaine], a pack of smokes, and here I am.

[MM: When you were getting out they didn't help you try to find somewhere to go?]

No, they don't give a fuck! In fact, all over the goddamned jail now they got little flyers saying, "Your wristband is no longer acceptable for the bus, for the train. The County is not responsible for giving you a ride home." But they sure were there for me when they brought me here to jail!

By the time we parted that late afternoon, Stephen was pondering where he was going to sleep that night, and whether he would ever have the courage to try to get back in touch with his father. So, the lack of transitional aid from the corrections system, even transportation out of the immediate drug-ridden neighborhood, interacted with Stephen's broader vulnerability, namely his lack of social ties, his fragile state given the loss of two brothers in tragic accidents within the previous five years, and his lingering addiction disorder, to push him into homelessness.

Additionally, other public social services such as hospitals and foster care have been affected by budget reductions during the county's periodic financial crises and cutbacks, impeding the ability of these institutions to help their wards get back into mainstream housed society and increasing the number of persons at risk of homelessness. With many working and nonworking poor lacking health insurance, physical injuries and health complications can precipitate an experience with homelessness. There have been reports of hospitals sending discharged patients, even some on gurneys, in wheelchairs, and in hospital gowns without anywhere to go, in hospital vans or taxis to shelters on Skid Row (DiMassa 2006). Judy, a forty-eight-year-old white woman from Riverside County, first experienced homelessness after being discharged from Harbor UCLA hospital where she had an operation related to her cervical cancer. She worked double shifts at a Texaco gas station up until about two years prior to the operation but was fired after missing a shift due to a doctor's appointment. Unable to cover her rent, Judy went to stay with a friend and her mother in a trailer in Torrance. Judy was released from the hospital on a Friday but they were unable to help her find a place to stay until the following Monday, leaving her in the emergency room for two days. Finally, a social worker at the hospital sent her in a taxi to the Henderson Community Center, an emergency shelter south of downtown Los Angeles, where she had been for a year when we met. She was still awaiting a verdict on her application for Supplemental Security Income (SSI) disability benefits and wondering if the shelter was going to extend her stay.

Withering Social Safety Nets in Tokyo

National and local developmental states have muted the impact of rising inequality in Tokyo through employment-centered development and broad social programs such as pensions and universal health insurance, supplemented by expanding but lean welfare entitlement outlays (Fujita 2003; Fujita 2011; Jacobs 2005). However, this system is weakening and has excluded marginally attached workers extremely vulnerable to homelessness. I will explore in more depth in Chapter 2 how the livelihood protection (*seikatsu hogo*) welfare system relates to exits from homelessness among transitional housing users, but these benefits are legally available to all who fall below a minimum standard of living and provide considerably more financial support (approximately 130,000 yen per month, or $1,166) than the Los Angeles GR program. Eligibility qualifications for livelihood protection benefits have been especially strictly enforced on persons who are homeless or who cycle through unconventional arrangements such as live-in construction, capsule hotels (where the "rooms" are capsules with just enough space to lie down), and all-night *manga* (comic book) or Internet cafés. Men determined to be physically able to work are often denied benefits for lack of sufficient effort to find work and because frontline staff are unable to investigate whether or not a person with no address has assets. When in need of medical attention, applicants may get medical assistance (*iryō fujo*) for out- or in-patient treatment, but they won't get regular benefits unless their physical problem is severe and a long-term condition. Persons in these situations are usually channeled into the homeless services and shelter system, and if they are part of the small minority (about 20 percent) determined eligible for livelihood protection benefits, they are often required to live in group quarters or institutional environments (Tokubetsu-ku Jinji Kōsei Jimu Kumiai 2010). As I will demonstrate further in Chapter 3, these strict qualifications for eligibility interact with a cultural stigma against able-bodied men's relying on welfare benefits. This stigma manifests in the resistance of many middle aged and older men to seek benefits as well as the strategies used by frontline staff to discourage applications. In a survey of about nine hundred persons lined up for free meals (*takidashi*) along Tokyo's Sumida River over two days, 45 percent preferred to fend for themselves amid homelessness rather than apply for livelihood protection benefits, 20 percent said that they dislike group living situations, and 18 percent said that they were treated poorly by welfare office staff (Gotō 2010).

However, as discussed in Chapter 1, access to welfare benefits across Japan expanded in the early 2000s with the advocacy of lawyers and later growing public concern about the vulnerability of dispatch workers and other neoliberal reforms (Shinoda 2009). At the same time, a sizeable number of recently incorporated private nonprofit organizations emerged to provide housing to welfare recipients. However, some of these organizations are believed to be "poverty businesses" primarily interested in milking welfare funds out of clients while providing minimal aid (Terao and Okuta 2011). Like labor brokers for live-in construction, these organizations recruit in parks and stations where there are high concentrations of homelessness. Brokers will take a person to a welfare office in the jurisdiction where the organization has a facility, sometimes in a neighboring prefecture, and apply for welfare benefits on the person's behalf. Since for the welfare office's purposes many of these organizations are legitimate nonprofit organizations that provide housing and the actual legal criteria for welfare benefits are low, oftentimes offices will award benefits. In some jurisdictions, welfare offices refer to these organizations when they need to house recipients, an example of informal and nonprofit organizations contributing to welfare restructuring (Fairbanks 2009). However, these organizations sometimes house people in group-living conditions in old buildings, make residents work, and provide meager meals, but extract the great majority of residents' monthly benefits in fees. These substandard facilities generally serve the purpose of warehousing vulnerable people, only temporarily concealing visible homelessness.

Pak-san, a resident Korean from Nagasaki on the southern island of Kyūshū in his late fifties, had been diagnosed with schizophrenia and hospitalized for much of his adult life. He had been kicked out of welfare facilities for the mentally ill after violating rules about drinking and sexual relationships between patients. In our interviews over a two-year period, he often slurred his speech, had difficulty staying on topic, and became manic, exhibiting some clear symptoms of mental health problems. Despite also walking with a limp due to frostbite from sleeping by the Sumida River for a winter, he was scheduled to move into a transitional housing program to look for work. But he fled an emergency shelter in the middle of the night after he was mocked by staff who he had sought help from during an episode of insomnia. He ended up back on the streets and contemplating suicide, but he was recruited by an organization that placed him in a welfare facility in nearby Chiba Prefecture. There, he lived in cramped and shared quarters, and he was illegally sent out to construction jobs. He fled that facility and was recruited by another organization and sent to a welfare facility in Kanagawa Prefecture. There he lived in a subdivided room and largely survived off instant noodles. However, he received regular mental health treatment at a nearby hospital and, as evidenced in our later meetings and letters, his mental health seemed to have improved.

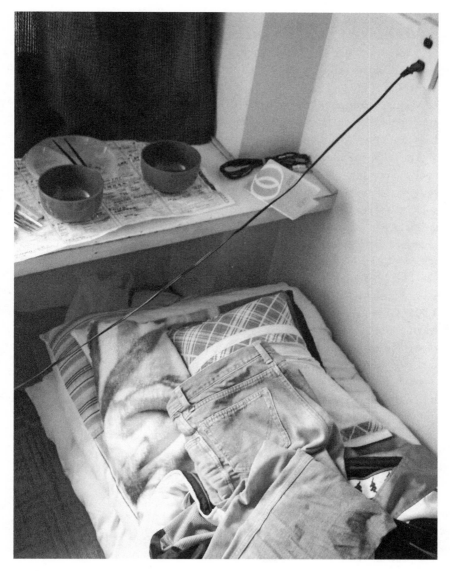

Pak-san's tiny room in a Kanagawa welfare facility

Social services, especially health care, are spread relatively thickly and evenly throughout Tokyo's urban landscape, bolstered by the national developmental state and active ward-level governments oriented toward social welfare (Fujita 2011; Waley 2007). State investment in urban infrastructure has prevented much of the degradation seen in racially segregated American low-income urban neighborhoods. This includes investment in neighborhoods often called *hisabetsu buraku* that were deemed appropriate for aid given historical neglect based on concentration of residents believed to be descendants of feudal-era stigmatized groups (Mizuuchi and Jeon 2010). Tokyo has also redeveloped crowded areas to protect against disasters as well as advanced a low-carbon policy to improve the environment (Fujita 2011). Much lower levels of income inequality and socioeconomic residential segregation combined with community based policing, including small police kiosks (*kōban*) and active neighborhood associations (*chōnaikai*), have also muted crime and disorder (Jacobs 2005; Waley 2000).

The buffering effect of Japan's universal health care system, as well as its incapacity to completely counteract the effects of labor market change, can be seen in the experiences of Higashi-san, a man in his late fifties from Miyazaki City on the southern island of Kyūshū. After separating from his wife, Higashi-san had been struggling to maintain his carpentry business amid the recession and his own deteriorating physical condition, all the while taking care of his preteen daughter. Eventually, his daughter found him passed out in a puddle of blood and he was hospitalized with a severe stomach ulcer. He stayed in the hospital for one month until his health stabilized, running up a bill that he estimated to be about 1,000,000 yen ($8,970), but he said the government picked up most of the bill, leaving him to pay only 170,000 ($1,525). But after leaving the hospital he was physically unable to do carpentry and took a job selling newspapers. This proved not to be a viable source of income, despite Higashi-san's bright, easygoing manner. When he could not make ends meet, he sent his daughter to stay with her mother for the summer as usual. Then, he emptied out his apartment and headed out to work a short-term live-in construction job he had found in a sports newspaper. He was able to string a few jobs together but never accumulated enough savings to last for more than a few days in a capsule hotel. So he began sleeping in a park in the commercial district of Ikebukuro.

Decreasing Affordability of Housing in Los Angeles

The growing ranks of Los Angeles's poor must compete for an insufficient stock of affordable housing given upward pressure on rents amid rising inequality. Los Angeles County's housing supply has not kept pace with the growth in the size of the total population and the change in its housing needs (Wolch 1996). Between 1970 and 2010, the county population increased by 39 percent from just over seven million to nearly ten million people. Since the 1970s there has been no construction of public housing in Los Angeles and very limited private-sector affordable housing produced in relation to the increase in demand. Local homeowner associations that favor slow growth have resisted the development of apartments, condominiums, affordable housing, and single-family homes in distant suburbs. Thousands of apartments, many of them multifamily units concentrated in low-income areas, and the vast majority of them low rent, were demolished or converted to commercial space each year during the 1980s. Instead, real estate has become a major focus of financial speculation, as reflected in the concentrated effects in Southern California of the real estate bubble that ruptured in 2008.

The mismatch between the supply and demand for housing has resulted in an extremely tight rental market: the vacancy rate for rental units in Los Angeles County was 3.3 percent in 2000 and 5.8 percent in 2010, compared to vacancy rates for all U.S. metropolitan areas of 6.8 percent and 9.2 percent, respectively. The HUD Fair Market Rent, a measurement of the dollar amount below which 40 percent of local standard-quality rental housing units rent, for an efficiency apartment in Los Angeles County increased 134 percent from $390 in 1983 to $911 in 2013.[12] In order to only pay one-third of one's income on rent, HUD's standard measure of housing affordability, for a Fair Market Rent efficiency apartment in Los Angeles in 2013 one would have to earn a wage of $17.52 per hour for a forty-hour workweek, or work about eighty-eight hours per week at a wage of $8 per hour.[13] Amid these conditions, many households double and triple up in dwellings meant for single households, giving Los Angeles County the highest rate of crowding in Southern California, a region with crowding at levels more than twice the national average (SCAG 2007).

The experiences of Magdalene, her five children, and two grandchildren demonstrate how tight local housing and labor market conditions, along with the failure of welfare benefit payments to keep up with housing and other costs, contribute to the precarious housing and vulnerability to homelessness of many poor families in Los Angeles. Magdalene, her husband, and their children legally migrated to Los Angeles in 1997 from Trinidad to escape bleak economic conditions, gaining citizenship through her husband's mother, who had naturalized. However, her husband left her for another woman who was living just below the family. This was disastrous for Magdalene since her arthritic hip was becoming increasingly debilitating, and her employer, the Los Angeles Unified School District, terminated her employment as it restructured amid budget constraints. After being delinquent on two months' rent, Magdalene was told by her landlord that he was going to have to evict her.

> We were trying to find another apartment but, with the size of my family, I have to get a three- or four-bedroom house. The cheapest rent for a three- or four- bedroom house is anywhere from $900 to $1,100. My check is only $1,000 so I couldn't do it. I'd be without electricity, gas, you know? Since November, I was homeless, because we came from

Trinidad so I don't have no relatives here, nobody, no aunts, uncles, daughters. I was on the street, sleeping in my car, sleeping in a motel whenever I had extra money and sometimes some people who I know, like, I worked with in the past, my neighbor, and they know the situation, they help me pay for a motel room, you know? It's difficult for me to find a shelter because my kids are too big. Shelters usually take kids from like ten and under. My kids are like teenagers so nobody's gonna want to take them.

Like some other immigrants I interviewed, Magdalene is largely unable to tap into networks with relatives to avoid homelessness—her connections to extended family were severed with her husband's betrayal. Since the combined amount of her unemployment insurance and CalWORKs benefits was only $1,000 monthly, she was unable to find an affordable rental that would accommodate her large family. Magdalene and her children were not even able to utilize family shelters that see teenage boys as potentially gang affiliated and prone to intimidate women, many of whom are fleeing domestic violence.

Downtown's Skid Row district and neighboring areas have undergone a long process of transformation and gentrification since the 1970s, resulting in a reduction of cheap, easily accessible housing for the extremely poor—single room occupancy (SRO) housing. More than half of the SRO hotels in Los Angeles's downtown had been destroyed by 1985 (Wolch 1996). This process intensified starting in the late 1990s as urban developers converted old office buildings into lofts for young professionals (Reese, DeVerteuil, and Thach 2010). Even some SROs have been converted into lofts, directly gentrifying the SRO housing supply. As a result, fees for these rooms have increased, and they more quickly exhaust the funds of persons precariously attempting to avoid homelessness.

Rita, an African American woman in her late forties with extensive secretarial experience, faced difficulty holding jobs over the long term, not due to her own work performance but because her employers merged with other companies, forcing sizeable layoffs. First, Union Bank of California laid her off when it merged with another company in the mid-1990s. Next, Rita got a job at the downtown headquarters of the accounting and consulting firm Ernst and Young through a temporary agency and was eventually hired as a full-time employee. She managed to survive two of Ernst and Young's mergers in the late 1990s, but her division fell victim to a third merger in mid-2001, and Rita was again out of a job. Rita benefited from the extension of unemployment benefits after 9/11 but was unable to find work amid the ongoing recession. She began temping, but she struggled to pay her rent; without time to look for full-time work, she moved out of her rent-controlled apartment and began staying with friends. This proved to be a costly decision because she began to feel like a burden on her friends and decided to move into the Cecil, an SRO hotel near downtown.

> I was paying a weekly rate of $174 or something, and I know it's $39 for the night, if it's paid by the night, so it's better to pay by the week. But it was kind of high for me, 'cause, you know, something like almost $700, I could get an apartment. I could've kept my apartment, it was something like $625. When I couldn't find a job, I just sort of like was in total denial, I just got up like I was going to work, got dressed, went to the gym [her membership paid by Ernst and Young was still valid] or went to the library or did something to fill my entire day. Came back at five, ate dinner, watched TV and went to bed, you know? When I ran out of money I left the hotel room and I didn't have any way to get to the welfare office so I had to walk and I could only take as much as I could carry.

At a downtown Department of Public Social Services office, Rita was given a referral to a Skid Row emergency shelter and began her efforts to escape homelessness.

Decreasing Affordability of Housing in Tokyo

Hasegawa (2005) points out that urban redevelopment has intersected with broader industrial change in producing Tokyo's surge in homelessness. Total floor space put under construction for office space in Tokyo more than doubled between 1985 and 1990 amid the bubble economy and local and national aspirations to ensure Tokyo's position as a leader of the global economy (Machimura 1994). Much of the development of office space has occurred at the expense of the housing supply in central city areas that catered to households of average and modest income (Cybriwsky 1998). Also, in the latter half of the 1980s, private rental housing in Tokyo targeting young urban professionals and small families grew rapidly. At the same time, the share of older wooden units, commonly used by low-income workers, dropped from 23 percent to 19 percent as a percentage of total housing units (Cybriwsky 1998). These trends were concentrated in areas of central Tokyo that contained "mixed districts" with low-income housing and small factories, including Shinagawa, Ota, Sumida, Arakawa, and Itabashi wards (Hasegawa 2005).

As a result of these changes, low-income workers have faced higher rents. Between 1978 and 1988, rent measured by *tatami* mat (about six by three feet) increased 54.8 percent for older apartments made of wood with private bathrooms and 44.1 percent for tenement housing with shared toilets (Cybriwsky 1998). Also, the Ministry of Construction estimated in a survey taken in 1988 that more than 13 percent of renters in Tokyo faced housing costs that were "too high to secure sufficient money to buy even the minimum necessities of life" (Tsukada 1991, 152, as cited in Hasegawa 2005). Monthly rent for housing owned by government or public corporations increased by 27 percent between 1990 and 2000 and remained largely level through 2004 while monthly rent for housing owned by private corporations increased by 18 percent between 1990 and 2000 but then continued to increase 7 percent more by 2004.[14]

Although there is substantial evidence for rising rents plaguing low-wage workers in Tokyo, conditions are less constraining than in American global cities, such as New York or Los Angeles (Hasegawa 2005). Population growth in Tokyo has been modest, increasing by only 14.3 percent between 1970 and 2010, less than half the rate in Los Angeles. Some of the housing in the aging working-class east side has been transformed by the development of large-scale apartment complexes (*danchi*), either by the Tokyo Metropolitan Government to alleviate the city's cramped housing conditions or private corporations to provide housing for their employees (Cybriwsky 1998). Additionally, there has been substantial development of housing in the suburban areas surrounding Tokyo. The developmental state became more entrepreneurial in fostering private development along the Tokyo Bay waterfront, contributing to an increase in spatial inequality in Tokyo during the late 1990s and early 2000s (Jacobs 2005; Saito 2003). However, in the wake of the real estate bubble collapse of the early 1990s, Governor Aoshima Yukio in the mid-1990s emphasized improvement of quality of life through affordable housing, limiting speculative development projects (Waley 2007). Thus, amid broader processes of development and gentrification, Tokyo retains an important stock of small, older apartment buildings with simple facilities.

Gentrification of Tokyo's inner wards has placed pressure on small firms that provide housing for low-wage employees, firms already challenged by the economic conditions described above (Hasegawa 2005). A number of these companies have been among the thousands that have gone bankrupt in Tokyo since the onset of the recession, pushing live-in employees and sometimes their owners onto the streets. Also, the number of SROs (*doya*) in San'ya, Tokyo's largest day labor ghetto, has declined steadily, from 199 in 1990 to 165 in 2013 (Jōhoku Welfare Center 1999, 2013). Many of the more affordable hotels were renovated in the late 1980s bubble economy to provide better facilities to skilled, and thus more stably employed, workers, enabling owners to boost fees. Beginning in the mid-1990s many of San'ya's *doya* have been transformed from simple lodgings with few amenities for day laborers into slightly more comfortable "business hotels" to serve budget travelers. Increasingly these include traveling businesspersons from other regions of Japan and East Asia, recent graduates looking for work in the capital, or tourists from throughout the world. This later group increased in 2002 when Tokyo hosted soccer games for the World Cup.

The experiences of Kawauchi-san, former San'ya day laborer in his midsixties, demonstrate how the confluence of declining day labor jobs in construction amid the recession and the rising cost of housing in San'ya's *doya* pushed many aging laborers to begin living in tents and huts along the Sumida River. Kawauchi-san first came to San'ya after chopping off his own finger in a ritual required to properly sever his ties to organized crime, since his involvement had become public and problematic for his sister, a local school teacher. Kawauchi-san originally worked as a carpenter, learning the trade from his father. So, in San'ya he was able to find ample day labor and short-term contracts, staying in *doya* even as their fees increased in the bubble years.

> Before, I could stay in a *doya* because I was working, even hiring people as a boss (*oyakata*). But then gradually I didn't have any work. It's a waste to spend that much money on a *doya*—1,500 yen or 2,000 yen [about $13.45 or $17.94] per night. So, even though I am sleeping here like this, I would never say that I am sleeping outside. I'm not just sugarcoating it. I don't care if this is the country's land or Tokyo's land or whatever. I am not asking anyone for anything. I am not bowing my head like a beggar and saying "Please help me." I have made a hut and am living on my own. I have all of the tools for life. I even have a fry pan here. Because I've gotten these things little by little when I have work. No one's gonna give me them, right? I know I could have gotten welfare two years ago, when I was sixty-three. But, as long as my body is fit and I can work, I have no desire to get on welfare. I am not going to be a burden on anyone.

Like many men whom I have met on my intermittent participation in outreach along the Sumida River for about 15 years, Kawauchi-san expresses a strong desire to survive on his own without receiving the support of government welfare programs. In Kawauchi-san's case, he even refused to endure the shame of lining up for a free meal just a short walk across Sakura Bridge from his hut.

The impact of three forms of globalization are evident in my structural account of homelessness in Los Angeles and Tokyo—economic globalization in the form of labor market restructuring, frequent economic downturns, income polarization, and growing employment instability and poverty; demographic globalization in the form of international and domestic migration, contributing to labor and housing market competition; and (neoliberal) ideological globalization in the form of weakening welfare protections, state investment in housing, and social services. However, differences in the extent and form of these structural changes show how processes of globalization are enacted in local contexts of national and urban regimes to produce pathways to homelessness of different breadth and contour. Thus, although both Los Angeles and Tokyo have seen substantial increases in homelessness in recent decades, the population in Los Angeles grew rapidly at an earlier point and is larger and more diverse than in Tokyo.

Overall, as summarized in table 1, structural pressures associated with neoliberal globalization have manifested themselves more prominently in Los Angeles than in Tokyo. This is because Los Angeles's urban welfare regime has taken a more neoliberal form, encouraging flexibility and instability in labor markets in response to heightened global competition. Demographically, Los Angeles's liberalized labor market has attracted a wave of internal migrant and international immigrant labor that dwarfs those in Tokyo. A highly tax-averse local public has enabled erosion of welfare supports and social services amid growing need in

TABLE 1 Local-level conditions driving contemporary homelessness*

	LOS ANGELES	TOKYO
Economic	Advanced shift from Fordism to post-Fordism: highly increased income inequality, unemployment, and poverty in a service-centered economy	Progressing shift from Toyotism to post-Toyotism: moderate increased income inequality, unemployment, and poverty
Demographic	Moderately aging native-born population	A rapidly aging population
	A sizeable wave of immigrant workers	A small influx of immigrant workers
	High population growth	Moderate population growth
Welfare	Retrenched liberal regime: advanced welfare reform, mass incarceration, deinstitutionalization, "dumping"	Retrenching developmental regime: emerging welfare reform, deinstitutionalization, "dumping"
Housing market	Extremely tight, less public investment in housing, high real estate speculation	Moderately tight, more public investment in housing, with a larger stock of low-rent, simple lodgings
Culture	Widespread racial discrimination toward blacks and Latinos in labor and housing markets	Limited discrimination against ethnic/ status groups, such as resident Koreans, burakumin, yoseba day laborers, Okinawans, and Ainu
	Presence of a drug culture, with high levels of use of a variety of highly addictive substances	Absence of a drug culture, although alcoholism and gambling addiction are prevalent

*Cells shaded in gray indicate more dire conditions in that particular locale in terms of increasing vulnerability to homelessness.

Los Angeles. Los Angeles has been exemplary of the American neoliberal state's assault on the black and Latino urban poor, incarcerating them through the war on drugs and disciplining them through welfare reform. Even though Tokyo's urban welfare regime is clearly influenced by neoliberal globalization, it retains a developmental tendency through bolstering labor markets and encouraging more even development. Older, working-class neighborhoods in Tokyo have seen gentrification, but there are not high concentrations of poverty comparable to those in racially and economically segregated Los Angeles. Although low levels of immigrant labor may impede Tokyo's macroeconomic growth, it may prevent more dramatic expansion of inequality and competition with its aging labor force. Therefore, the "glocalization" of neoliberalism has played out differently in the two cities, with urban welfare regimes producing varying structural vulnerabilities to homelessness and thus differences in the rate and composition of populations experiencing homelessness.

In the following two parts of this book, I explore how these and other differences in the structural contexts of homelessness shape pathways that persons experiencing homelessness follow as they attempt to escape their predicament.

Part II

EXITING HOMELESSNESS IN LOS ANGELES AND TOKYO

State Aid and Markets

Exit Stories: Michelle and Tsukada-san

Michelle

Michelle, a forty-one-year-old white woman from upstate New York, homeless for the first time in her life, walked the streets of Skid Row for a single night in the late spring of 2002. She had been living in an SRO hotel near MacArthur Park about three miles west of downtown Los Angeles but had depleted her savings and was searching for somewhere to stay. A friend from her church referred her to an organization in Hollywood, from which Michelle received information about shelters. A few that she contacted had arduous job search requirements and were located on Los Angeles's Westside, which would make it difficult for her to continue her pursuit of a certificate in human services at Los Angeles City College. Staff at the organization discouraged her from going to shelters on Skid Row, but Michelle had volunteered with her church there and was not intimidated. So she went to a Department of Public and Social Services office in downtown and received a two-week voucher for emergency housing on Skid Row. There, she learned that she could stay in a transitional housing program for up to two years while she finished school.

At her intake for transitional housing, she was asked if she had any debilitating conditions. When she responded that she was diagnosed with epilepsy at three years of age, she was given a single room and provided medication through the free clinic on the first floor of the building. Michelle initially came to Los Angeles in 1989 to look into new innovative epilepsy treatments. She graduated from college with a major in sociology several years before and worked for three years at a drugstore, but she had a seizure at the cash register and was reassigned as a stock clerk. Within a few months of moving to Los Angeles, she met her boyfriend who was living off a settlement from a motorcycle accident and disability benefits. His application for a subsidized Section 8 apartment in Hollywood was accepted after he spent a few years on the waiting list, and they moved in together. She worked part-time and took classes. Eventually her application for SSI was accepted, and she had surgery related to her epilepsy a year later. Her health improved, and at her third-year evaluation she was declared fit for work, and her benefits were abruptly terminated without any vocational rehabilitation. As their neighborhood faced gentrification accelerated by the development of a massive theater complex, their landlord opted out of government subsidies to pursue rapidly rising market rents. Her boyfriend received a Section 8 voucher, but it did not cover Michelle because they were not married. She returned to upstate New York to help take care of her ailing mother and worked as a register clerk in a clothing store for a few months, but she returned to Los Angeles after her mother died. She had broken up with her boyfriend, so she moved into a MacArthur Park SRO, got back into school, and managed to survive on her savings and part-time work at Los Angeles City College. But budget cuts at the college ate away at her work assignments, her savings eventually ran out, and she had to leave the hotel.

The college finally implemented a hiring freeze, and Michelle needed to find a new job. The job developers at the transitional program and her church did not provide any information that she could not get on her own at the local publically funded One Stop or WorkSource employment agency where she looked for various low-skill service sector jobs. Michelle said, "I try everything—magazines, the Internet, and everything. I try to sign up for temp agencies, and it's either seasonal or part-time, because I don't wanna be full-time while I'm in school, you know? That seemed to limit the agencies too much or something, I don't know. I don't have full transportation either. So every time I call them, 'Oh, yeah, we'll put you on the list,' and I never hear from them. So I started giving up on them." When I asked Michelle why she thought employers did not respond to her inquiries, she replied, "I never get any answer, you know. I always wonder if it's my credit. I started dumbing down my resume because maybe it's because I've got my bachelor's degree and I'm overqualified." Due to her reliance on epilepsy medication, she was also worried about testing positive in drug tests for employment or periodic random tests in the program.

Michelle became more and more stressed and eventually had what she described as a "minor breakdown" while meeting with a staff person at a job search program. She said, "I knew he [her former boyfriend] was cutting off my mail, and I said, 'Okay, where am I gonna get my mail. I need this amount of money for this. Is there gonna be enough on this check?' I still hadn't gotten a phone call back from the first job. I didn't really know what to do. So I just lost it." She participated in church activities a few times a week, and there was a parish nurse who she frequently helped out as well as talked with about her problems. Also, she got along well with Robert, a case manager who was encouraging. He referred her to stress management classes, where she learned breathing and meditation exercises. She also was in periodic contact with her former boyfriend and with her family in New York. She got along fairly well with the other women in the transitional program, considering some to be her friends, and they would share information about jobs and other resources.

About two months into her transitional housing program, Michelle replied to an advertisement for a job working as dispatched event staff. Most jobs were at the Los Angeles Convention Center, which she could walk to, or at Universal Studios and the Long Beach Convention Center, locations she could reach by the Metro rail system, albeit by traveling one hour each way. She would call in each Monday for her schedule and worked about 30–40 hours per month at minimum wage ($6.75 per hour), bringing home about $225. This was about the same she would receive on GR ($221), but Michelle detested all of the paperwork and preferred to work. She earned her general certificate in human services, and then she began a specialized certificate program in drug and alcohol abuse counseling. As she progressed in that program, she began thinking about applying for full-time counseling jobs. She interned at several of the major organizations addressing homelessness in Skid Row, so she had a broad practical understanding of the local social welfare system. However, Michelle was anxious about interviewing, especially about how to explain her lack of experience despite earning her bachelor's degree nearly twenty years earlier. She could explain her health problems, but she worried about disclosing too much. Her two-year time limit in the program was rapidly approaching and she had been unsuccessful in trying to get into subsidized housing. Although she had been able to save money, Michelle worried that her low monthly income would not allow her to survive over the long term in Los Angeles's tight rental market.

During her two years in transitional housing she saved about $5,000. So when she left she stayed in unsubsidized Skid Row hotels, paying $600 per month while looking for an apartment.

> At that point, I had twenty-eight days in the Cecil [an unsubsidized SRO] and I kept on waiting for this [subsidized] place west of downtown. The other staff lady that was doing the housing at the [transitional housing program] had gone back to grad school. I realized that all the new staff person was doing was collecting apps [applications].

So I couldn't keep waiting for her. My twenty-eight days[1] had expired so I moved on down the road to another SRO, and I realized that that was a *real* slum of a hotel. They don't even take care of the toilets. It's like those are outhouses every other day. And I was living with a little four-legged critter, a mouse. That's what got me out of there. *Anybody* who answers me [laughs]! I only took one week of that and got out of there. And initially that place looked like heaven compared [to the second SRO].

The studio apartment she found on craigslist.org was just across the 110 freeway from downtown, rented for $525 per month, and required three months' rent up front. Friends from church helped her furnish the room, but her building was old and the "slumlord" was slow to make repairs. She shared a bathroom and shower, which was under repair and inaccessible for a few weeks. After only a few months, the refrigerator her slumlord sold her broke down and her food began to spoil.

About four years later, in 2008, Michelle had received her specialist's certificate but said that state regulations for the license in drug and alcohol counseling changed, leaving her a few credits short. She was working two staffing jobs and her wage had risen to $8.50 an hour, but her hours fluctuated and she struggled to pay her rent. The slumlord's neglect was a blessing in disguise as other tenants pursued legal action, resulting in an award of $8,000 and her rent being halved for ten months. Michelle used that money to make up the difference between her income and monthly costs, and picked up her job search. She got some exposure to the medical field in an AmeriCorps assignment and took medical billing courses. She applied for jobs at two hospitals but worried about her ability to sell herself in interviews. Rent control on the building allowed her rent to increase only to $533, and the AmeriCorps program helped her pay down her school loans for her bachelor's degree. However, she still had to pay a little over $100 per month, and when she paid off the remainder of that $2,000 balance, she still had her other school loans and credit card debt. Although the slumlord conformed to minimum court requirements, his neglect of the building continued to bring cloaked blessings like poor phone service that obstructed loan collectors. She sometimes relied on food donations from church, but Michelle said she felt more stable in her apartment than in the transitional program, where staff could terminate her for issues beyond her control. She had received free professional health treatment through a church referral, but she was turned off by their recommendation for antidepressants. She summed up her feelings about her situation by saying, "Sometimes I've been kinda frustrated here and there but little by little I feel like I'm getting better without medication. I was surprised when I was talking to these girls in Bible study, 'I must be letting Him run my life because I just had enough to pay my rent last month and couldn't pay the student loan and another bill for about the same amount. I'm not sitting there going crazy.' I'm amazed because, I used to do that. Maybe it is a little faith thing, or hope."

A hallway neglected by Michelle's "slumlord"

Tsukada-san

Tsukada-san, a fifty-five-year-old man from nearby Saitama Prefecture, made his way into a Tokyo transitional housing program (*jiritsu shien sentā*, or self-reliance support center) via an emergency shelter in the summer of 2004. Immediately prior to emergency housing, he was sleeping rough near the statue of famed samurai Saigō Takamori in Ueno Park with about six other men. However, he heard that if he applied to the transitional housing program at the Taitō Ward welfare office nearby, he would be put in the center that was in a parking lot in the park. Word had spread that the men who went to that center faced added difficulty finding work because potential employers would be suspicious of an address that said "Ueno Park." So he first tried at the Chūō Ward welfare office but was turned away and told to try somewhere else. He served as a live-in volunteer (*hōshi*) at a Christian church for a week or so helping them prepare food for their free meals (*takidashi*), but then he was able to get into emergency shelter through the Adachi Ward welfare office after a few days on the streets in that jurisdiction.

Tsukada-san had been a public servant (*kōmuin*) for a city government in Saitama for fourteen years, beginning when he was eighteen years old. He worked in the planning department assessing and negotiating property transactions and in the water department implementing and developing computer systems, enjoying the stability and benefits of being a public employee. However, he had a conflict with his boss over the installation of a new computer system and quit. He had trouble finding a stable job at that time, so he worked for over a decade in live-in construction, usually short-term contract jobs that he found through people he knew or through labor brokers in train stations. He began borrowing money and accumulating credit card debt little by little when he was having difficulty finding work and his mother became ill. He took a job running a lathe (*senban*) in an auto parts factory in Saitama and moved into public housing with his mother until she died in 1999. He renewed his contract at the factory annually for eight years, but he had to quit when pain in his lower back and leg became unbearable. He survived off money borrowed from predatory lenders (*sarakin*), bringing his total debt to about 3,500,000 yen ($31,395). Eventually he could not keep up with his bills, so Tsukada-san moved out of public housing and worked live-in construction again for a few months.

When he was looking for more stable work at the Ōmiya public employment agency in Tokyo, his duffle bag holding his savings and licenses was stolen. He went to look for labor brokers in Yokohama Station and was approached by a man who told him he could help him get welfare benefits, housing, and medical attention for his lower back pain. Tsukada-san was awarded benefits to get treatment for his lower back, but he left the facility after a month because of the verbal conflicts and fights among the men staying in the cramped dorm. He moved between the streets and live-in construction until he entered another welfare facility to have a stomach ulcer and anemia treated. Given his previous experience as a bureaucrat, the organization put him to work processing applications and paperwork for welfare benefits and moved him into an apartment. However, after a few months he grew uncomfortable with the morally questionable actions of some staff and started having more health problems, so he quit the job and began sleeping in Ueno Park.

When we first met at the emergency shelter, Tsukada-san said that he wanted to get a job doing administrative work, but he thought it unlikely because employers preferred younger people and women for such jobs. He was thankful that applications to the transitional program were backed up, since it extended his stay in the shelter and allowed him to get medical treatment, including a new set of false teeth. He still had lower back and leg pain and was diagnosed with a heart valve disorder, so he was concerned about his ability to do anything beyond light manual labor. Nevertheless, Tsukada-san and his welfare office caseworker agreed that he should pursue "self-reliance" (*jiritsu*) through work rather than enter a welfare facility. When I later interviewed him in transitional housing, Tsukada-san had applied to four jobs and was not optimistic about his prospects:

> On the advertisement it said there was no age restrictions, but they wanted younger people. That was the job pressing aluminum. There were fourteen people applying for one job. Plus there were two or three guys who looked like they were in their thirties—one of them will get the job, right? Even they [the employers] said, "We prefer young people. So, sorry, but we are not checking anyone's character (*hitogara*) or anything like that." That is what they said at the interview! If that's the case, they should have never brought me there. I could have been out looking for another job. There is an Equal Opportunity Employment Law (Kōyō Kikai Kintō Hō), right? Because of that, even if they are not looking for men, if they are just looking for women, since there is an ad out, men are going to apply. Then we are told, "This job is for women." These are jobs cleaning toilets. You would think that men should clean men's toilets but in Japan, since men can't clean women's bathrooms, women do both. That is not gender equality.

Even though he did a training program in cleaning at the transitional program and looked for work through the public employment agency, Tsukada-san was not free from employers' age- and gender-biased practices. In an effort to avoid other barriers, and at the instruction of staff, he tried to mask his residence in the program by writing "Sumida Heights" for his address on applications to make it look like a private apartment building. When not sure about how to respond to questions about his housing at one interview, he said that he was on welfare (*seikatsu hogo*) and was looked at strangely. With only three weeks left before his two months to find work were up, Tsukada-san contemplated how to apply for welfare benefits. He was unable to talk to center staff about that since the program was designed specifically to help participants find work rather than rely on welfare. Also, he was told he might need surgery on his heart valve and cataracts in the future. Amid this uncertainty, he contemplated moving back into Ueno Park and contacting a local nonprofit organization to help him with the application process.

But he persisted in his job search and began focusing solely on cleaning and building maintenance jobs. He got along fairly well with the other men in the transitional program, but he knew that many had problems with drinking and gambling, so he would not serve as a guarantor, which was sometimes required for construction site security work. Occasionally they would go together to the Hello Work public employment agency and consult each other about writing resumes and about jobs. Tsukada-san found some of the job counselors to be too negative, focusing on what jobs program participants could not take (part-time jobs that paid less than 130,000 yen, around $1,155, per month, as formally required by the program, were far away, or were generally for women) when the options were not abundant. However, there was one counselor who he found helpful, so he made sure to seek help when that person was working. He applied for a janitorial job at a large office/retail building in the Nihonbashi business district, and he impressed the employer with his computer skills so he got the job. Although most of his work involved separating, bagging, and moving trash around, he liked that the job involved producing simple data reports on types and volume of trash. He even tried to create new programs on the computer when he had downtime. The job was full-time and with pension (*kōsei nenkin*) and health benefits (*kenkō hoken*), something Tsukada-san appreciated given his need for treatment for his various ailments. He was only responsible for one-third of nationally regulated medical costs, so he paid about 5,000 yen ($45) per month. He worked from 9 a.m. to 7 p.m., with a one-hour break for lunch, six days per week, earning 950 yen ($8.52) per hour, and 2.5 times that for his eight hours of overtime per week. So, he ended up taking home about 185,000 yen ($1,659) per month. He also found that one of the benefits of his job was that there was food thrown out that was still packaged and edible, so he often only had to spend money on rice.

When his four months in the program were up, staff allowed him to stay three extra days so he could manage his move, register his address, and complete out-take paperwork at the center. His rent for a small apartment in Adachi Ward was

46,000 yen ($413) and he had to pay 280,000 yen ($2,512) for his initial move-in costs, with the program covering 110,000 yen ($987). He was able to cover his portion with the approximately 300,000 yen ($2,691) he had saved in the program. The apartment came with a refrigerator and air conditioning, and staff put him in touch with a secondhand store where he bought a washing machine,

Tsukada-san's small and cluttered apartment

microwave, bed, rice cooker, and dresser. He also used some wooden wine boxes he found at work as a bookcase. With the help from an organization that provided low-cost legal aid, he declared bankruptcy and had his debt and record cleared, leaving him with a monthly payment of about 14,000 yen ($126) for a year or so, and a one-time payment to the lawyers of 52,500 yen ($471), which he planned to pay with his tax refund for the few months he had worked the previous year. However, he felt that until he paid off his debts he could not say that he had achieved "real self-reliance" (*hontō no jiritsu*).

As he established more stability, Tsukada-san reconnected with his family and reached out to help people who were experiencing homelessness. He had grown up in public housing in Saitama with his mother (a clothing factory worker), his grandmother, and an aunt, but he never knew his father. Tsukada-san had been out of touch with his aunt since his mother's death, but he eventually called her to let her know he was okay. When I met up with Tsukada-san a year and a half after he had moved into his apartment, he was in regular contact with his aunt. He had visited her a few months before in Saitama and brought his cousin a used laptop that he had bought in the Akihabara electronics district and rebuilt himself, saying, "It would be a pity if I didn't do what I could for a relative." Also, he had become a one-man outreach team, frequently bringing food from work to Ueno Park and sharing information about how to secure shelter, work, and welfare, as well as legal advice about debt. He was cautious about not upsetting his neighbors but sometimes brought people from the park home to use his shower and washing machine and cook them dinner. But he felt that he was not helping them achieve "self-reliance (*jiritsu*)" so he was making plans to create a website with information on available aid for people experiencing homelessness instead. He said, "I don't see the old guys anymore, it's a different group now. But it is like me just giving them a handout. So I went to a different group this time than last month. Next time, I'll go to another place. If I don't do that, I won't be helping them be self-reliant. So, I was bringing bread to them all the time. Stuff that has gone past 'Best if Sold By . . .' date or if it's on that day, right? I myself was getting welfare so I should at least give something back (*ongaeshi*). I need to do something in return for the welfare because I received citizens' taxes. In the past I was a bureaucrat so I have to think about these things."

SEARCHING FOR STATE AID

In the exit stories that opened the second part of this book, both Michelle and Tsukada-san had difficulty securing regular access to income support from the welfare state in times of need, which negatively impacted their housing stability. Although both had serious ailments, the welfare benefits they received from the state were partial and of limited reliability. Michelle was abruptly terminated from Supplemental Security Income (SSI) without any transitional employment assistance and was not allowed to move with her boyfriend when his Section 8 subsidy changed to a voucher. Obtaining General Relief (GR) was a tedious process. The $221 per month and about $200 in food stamps was insufficient to keep her out of homelessness, and whenever she found part-time work, her cash benefits were terminated. Tsukada-san was able to secure livelihood protection (*seikatsu hogo*) benefits only with the help of an advocate and because he had clearly diagnosable medical problems. However, he was unable to endure cramped and dismal conditions in welfare facilities run by organizations suspected of warehousing benefit recipients for profit. When Michelle and Tsukada-san sought out aid in public welfare offices on their own in a state of literal homelessness, they were not awarded welfare benefits that would allow them to secure access to stable housing of their own. Instead, they were filtered into transitional housing where they were expected to secure income through the labor market, save, and move into rental housing.

In both the United States and Japan, transitional housing programs are criticized as examples of neoliberal policy measures that allow governments to shirk their responsibility to provide adequate welfare benefits and push the poor into unstable labor and housing markets through substandard aid (Burt et al. 2001; Lyon-Callo 2004; Tamaki 2002). But limiting welfare rolls has been a primary function of welfare offices as a form of poverty management even prior to the rise of neoliberal globalization (Piven and Cloward 1993). For example, in the Fordist period states generally expanded welfare aid only to absorb surplus populations in times of economic stagnation, thus limiting social unrest. However, in the post-Fordist era the ascendance of neoliberal ideology has produced countercyclical contractions of state welfare functions even as the need for aid swells, buffered by the extension of the penal state (Wacquant 2009; Western 2006). In the United States, this has been manifested in welfare reform through which benefit amounts have stagnated or been cut, time limits have been placed on receipt of benefits, and workfare programs have expanded. In the latter, participants are disciplined through mandatory menial labor and job preparedness courses in exchange for aid, only to be pushed back into precarious low-wage labor as soon as possible. In Japan, there has not been a similar imprisonment binge, and welfare access has expanded in recent years in response to aging, rising poverty, and spikes in unemployment amid the post-2008 global economic crisis. But, amid this expansion, welfare programs in Japan recently have been facing American-style reform given rising costs for welfare. For example, one of the first initiatives of the conservative Liberal Democratic Party that regained control of the national legislature and executive branch in late 2012 was to pass legislation that reduced standard *seikatsu hogo* benefits by 6.5 percent to save an estimated 75 billion yen (about $800 million at the 2013 exchange rate) over three years.[1] In this sense, transitional housing is seen as one measure supporting the retraction of more substantial welfare benefits, keeping the poor off welfare rolls, disciplining them to aspire to compete in the low-wage labor market, and containing social spending in global cities.

In interaction with these system-level legal changes, which have been bolstered by the global spread of neoliberalism in recent decades, frontline welfare office staff have long used informal exclusionary practices of "street-level bureaucracy" to deal with the problems of insufficient resources and overwhelming demand (Lipsky 1980). Need for public services like welfare aid tends to exceed the supply, promoting an organizational tendency toward exclusion. So in a political climate in which governments face pressure to contain or even reduce social spending, inevitably welfare office workers have to differentiate between those who are deemed truly worthy and those deemed unworthy given a scarce supply of aid. Although formal criteria for state aid eligibility are rooted in welfare law, in practice eligibility for benefits in specific cases is determined in interactions between caseworkers and applicants in welfare offices. Whereas poor persons seeking aid from the state may see themselves as individuals struggling amid complex circumstances, caseworkers must treat them bureaucratically, placing them in categories that receive treatment routinized over time. This bias in treatment, a fundamental component of street-level bureaucracy, is justified by workers as being the best method to aid as many people as possible under existing conditions of scarce resources and massive demand.

However, acceptance of this bias by applicants must be secured through practices that attempt to control clients and dampen their claims on the state. These practices involve constraining client behavior in welfare offices and transmitting the message that welfare receipt is to be avoided in favor of labor market participation, even if poorly paid. Among their tactics to secure client control, welfare office workers use their more powerful position in the interaction and control over benefits, including their capacity to deny or make benefits harder to secure. Welfare office caseworkers also control the structure of interactions (when, where, and how they take place), the socialization into a client role (defining what constitutes transgressive behavior), and the allocation of psychological rewards and punishments. So, in addition to systemic forms of exclusion from state welfare aid such as benefit reductions and time limits, the organizational phenomenon of street-level bureaucracy allows for another level of exclusionary practices. These practices not only prevent some persons from receiving benefits but can have a psychological impact on applicants through the transmission of messages regarding worthiness and socialization into downgraded expectations for state aid. This exemplifies how, as urban ethnographer Javier Auyero (2012) argues, contemporary welfare states often stifle claims for aid by the poor and instill subordination through making them demonstrate deservedness by waiting quietly, making them "patients of the state."

In this chapter, I analyze the experiences of my transitional housing interviewees in Los Angeles and Tokyo to show how the formal, system-level structures of welfare programs (including welfare reform) have interacted with informal, street-level bureaucratic practices to generate general exclusion from state welfare aid that would be sufficient to allow them to expeditiously exit homelessness. In particular, I look at how different urban welfare regimes in two global cities can shape these processes of exclusion.

Exclusion from Welfare Aid through Systemic and Street-Level Practices in Los Angeles

In Los Angeles, many of my interviewees did not believe they were eligible for welfare benefits beyond General Relief and assumed that they would have to seek income in the labor market. However, seven of seventeen transitional housing program interviewees applied for SSI or Social Security Disability Insurance (SSDI)[2] while in the program. All these applications were rejected, and my interviewees either gave up or became entangled in an extensive appeals process. This was despite feeling they had clearly identifiable disabilities, often well documented in medical records. Their experiences exemplify a national trend of SSI applicants who are homeless and do not receive the help of an advocate, being awarded benefits only 10–15 percent of the time, compared to 32 percent for all adult applicants aged eighteen to sixty-five (Dennis et al. 2011). These denials are generally attributed to an office's inability to contact the applicant, missed appointments, and lack of adequate documentation for the application.

In addition to denials, there are often delays in rulings on applications and processing appeals. Since 2005, the U.S. Substance Abuse and Mental Health Services Administration (SAMHSA) has operated a program called SOAR (SSI/SSDI Outreach, Access, and Recovery) to help communities like Skid Row address barriers and increase SSI/SSDI access among people with disabilities who are experiencing homelessness. However, overall my interviewees in Los Angeles described being disadvantaged in an application process that lingered on and most of the time ended in rejection. Thus, applying for and obtaining SSI on their own was generally not a viable route out of homelessness even for those who felt that they had disabilities. Instead, those who were denied SSI and appealed rejections were largely trapped in a state of limbo until they secured help from a skilled, professional advocate, which still did not guarantee award of benefits.

The U.S. Social Security Administration describes the baseline for eligibility decisions on its website in three bullet points:

- You cannot do work that you did before;
- We decide that you cannot adjust to other work because of your medical condition(s); and
- Your disability has lasted or is expected to last for at least one year or to result in death.[3]

Many of my interviewees who were deemed ineligible for benefits felt that they had long-term physical limitations that prevented them from doing the physically demanding labor they had done in the past, and they needed education or training to break into new fields. Thus, many were confused, shocked, and offended when denied benefits.

Sinee, a documented immigrant from Thailand in her early fifties, entered a psychiatric ward at UCLA when she became emotionally and mentally unstable amid a separation from her child's father. Upon release, she moved between board-and-care facilities, shelters, and live-in cleaning jobs. She was diagnosed with bipolar and anxiety disorders by doctors at a nonprofit medical clinic where she received counseling and medication. Prior to entering the transitional program, a caseworker at a board-and-care facility helped her apply for SSI benefits so that she could live there over the long term. While her SSI application was being processed, she moved into the transitional housing program. There she completed job preparedness courses and did some cleaning work under the table for relatives and others in the local Thai community, but she refrained from looking for work in the mainstream labor market as she tried to stabilize her mental health. To meet the transitional program's income requirement, she applied to and began receiving GR. Since Sinee had a mental health condition, a county worker from the Department of Public Social Services helped her apply for SSI benefits independently of the board-and-care application. Her first application was accepted, but the county worker advised her to turn it down because once the second application was approved, she would be able to move into housing of her choice. Sinee preferred not to live in a board-and-care facility, so she followed the advice. Two weeks later, her second application was rejected because she was determined to be able to work. Luckily her child's grandparents took her in from the transitional housing program, but Sinee remained confused about the contradictory rulings and continued to pursue her appeal with the help of the county worker and caseworkers at a free medical clinic.

Like Sinee, many of the other interviewees had difficulty identifying and articulating the specific reasons why they were denied, because doctors diagnosed their maladies, but eligibility workers rejected their SSI applications. The lead case manager at the program in Los Angeles saw the application process for SSI as being set up to disadvantage vulnerable applicants. Here is her response when I asked her what she saw as the major difference between her clients who were awarded benefits and those who were rejected:

> The consistency of attending the appointments. What they [DPSS] want you to do is miss an appointment and not follow through and not fill out—they're going to ask you to fill out paperwork in triplicate. And if you don't fill it out correctly, you leave a lot of things blank, you miss a medical appointment without consulting them or letting them know "I can't make it, I don't have transportation." Because they'll help you get all that. They don't want you to have an excuse to not get the benefits. "Oh, we are going to send you to the psychiatrist and to a physician for specialty testing. Can you get there?" [If the client says], "Oh yeah, yeah, yeah, no problem," well, now you don't have tokens to get there, and we [the program staff] don't have tokens to give you, now you miss your appointment. It's easy to forget because the appointments

are like three months away and they only send you one reminder. No one's ever held them accountable before, so, you know, here you are, you have schizophrenia and paranoid tendencies, and someone is telling you, "You must go see this doctor." And now you've seen five different doctors and told them the same thing, you're going to start really having an issue with going back and being straightforward or not.

In terms of street-level bureaucracy, the case manager is pointing to the controlling and differentiating practices of welfare workers and systems through elaborate paperwork and setting requirements. In the face of insatiable demand given limited resources, those who are able to meet these requirements are more likely to be deemed as cooperative and deserving and are awarded benefits, and those who are not able are seen as uncooperative and undeserving. The latter applicants tend to get excluded. As the case manager points out, it is especially difficult for persons with mental health issues such as Sinee to navigate a system set up to exclude them, but even those without mental health problems face extreme difficulty in navigating the application process for disability benefits.

In addition to people whose SSI benefits were denied despite documented ailments, those in Los Angeles who did not feel eligible for SSI but had legal status in the United States turned to the local, secondary safety net of GR benefits. Since transitional program users were required to save 75 percent of their income, GR served as a crucial resource, helping many move into housing, although it was not sufficient for unsubsidized rental housing on its own. The eligibility requirements were much lower than for SSI, with any applicant household being eligible if they have less than $50 in cash or a bank account as well as a lack of other assets, and GR eligibility automatically makes one eligible for approximately $200 in food stamps.[4] In Los Angeles, GR provided $221 in monthly cash benefits for seven months of the year, with an additional two months of benefits if the recipient meets job search requirements. These included participating in the two-week GROW job preparedness program where they received instruction on how to write resumes, search for jobs, and interview for jobs. Many were also required to participate in workfare activities, which included assignments in public offices filing papers and other basic administrative and cleaning work.

Some interviewees with documented disabilities who had been denied SSI were placed on "GR Medical," which allowed them to forgo many of the job search and workfare requirements but receive monthly benefits year-round. Some of these interviewees, like Sinee, were provided with assistance from the local welfare office in applying for SSI, since from the county's standpoint, GR was substandard aid at their cost that obscured the federal government's exclusive approach. Also, many were trimmed from the GR rolls because they failed to keep up with the reporting requirements related to their job searches or missed appointments, and a few simply removed themselves from GR given tedious requirements for limited rewards. Thus, GR helped some transitional housing users accumulate savings to cover move-in costs for an apartment, but given the low amount and unreliability of the benefit, GR did not allow a recipient to exit homelessness without the aid of further benefits such as SSI, subsidized housing, or help from a relative or friend.

Additionally, the instability of GR benefits, fueled by exclusionary practices at systemic and street levels, in many instances actually impaired transitional housing users' efforts to secure employment and exit homelessness through mainstream labor and housing markets. For Rita, an African American former administrative assistant in her late forties introduced in Chapter 1, efforts to meet the requirements of GR often disturbed her school work and job search while in the program. While in emergency housing she applied to the transitional housing program; she moved in, began the required job preparedness courses, and searched for work on her own. A few months later, Rita was facing termination of her GR benefits and was wondering whether missing class and taking time away from her job search to meet administrative requirements for an extension was worth the meager and temporary benefits.

> I have to take paperwork back and forth, and I took one form, and then I get a new caseworker. Every time I get a new caseworker, then it's a whole new cycle that I fill all these forms out. I don't know what they're doing with 'em, but they keep losing my forms, so I've been up there at least a dozen times in the last couple of weeks. And I think that's what stressed me out, too. I'm doing all these things, and I've caught this cold, and I'm just like I can't wait to get out of here. You have to keep yourself focused. Because if you don't, then you blow up, and if I blow up at someone here, then I risk losing my housing. So, I keep my temper here. If I blow up at someone at the GR office, then I lose my benefits.

Here Rita describes a direct connection between the exclusionary practices of the DPSS office in downtown Los Angeles and her own precarious housing situation. She understands that waiting patiently is a way to demonstrate "deserving" aid. In this way, the need to stay cool about the frustrating interactions with the DPSS office is similar to her daily life in the shelter, where there are numerous opportunities for conflict and thus for termination from the program. In essence, Rita was being disciplined through street-level bureaucracy, and she incurred psychological costs. Rita became depressed given her lack of success in finding work, the frustrations she had in meeting GR requirements, and her inability to maintain her appearance on the low and unreliable nature of the benefit.

Exclusion from Welfare Aid through Systemic and Street-Level Practices in Tokyo

When they sought out aid at local welfare offices amid homelessness, the transitional housing users who I followed in Tokyo nearly uniformly saw themselves as ineligible for livelihood protection welfare benefits (*seikatsu hogo*) due to a lack of clear disability and being under sixty-five years of age. Instead, they expressed a desire to exit homelessness through employment. The fact that none of my interviewees assertively sought out *seikatsu hogo* is certainly biased by my sampling of transitional housing users, a group made up of people filtered in a formal assessment process that screens for disability status and desire to work. For the few who at least had *seikatsu hogo* in mind as a possibility when they sought help at local welfare offices, it was made clear to them in varying degrees of directness that they were not eligible. Shimada-san, the tall and broad shouldered twenty-four-year-old from the northern prefecture of Iwate introduced in Chapter 1, was firmly scolded when he first sought aid from the welfare office. He had developed a rash around his ear from sleeping rough, and other men living in the park urged him to get help at the nearby Taitō Ward welfare office. Here is how he described being received:

> I went to the ward office (*yakusho*) for the first time. I went to the welfare section, and the staff got really mad at me. They said, "Why are you living like this?!" and stuff like that. They really poured it on. So I started regretting that I went there. But, my ear was hurting, so I asked, "Please let me go to the hospital." They sent me to a special hospital, a big hospital in Sumida Ward. Then, when I went back to the welfare office, I saw a poster for emergency housing. I knew that they were going to be strict and that I was in no position to get *seikatsu hogo*. Just mentioning *seikatsu hogo* will get you yelled at. They'll say, "No, you're being lazy!" So, I said, "Excuse me, can you please let me use the emergency short-term housing?" And of course they got mad at me. They said, "What are you doing [on the streets]? Get yourself together!" I told them everything and they just got mad. The worker wouldn't understand, so I really had to lower my head to them.

Shimada-san lowered his expectations for aid, preventing him from seeking out *seikatsu hogo* benefits and pressuring him to concede to a second tier of aid, emergency and transitional housing. This street-level bureaucratic practice of outright exclusion from welfare benefits through shaming, along with alienation from his parents and later pressure from transitional housing staff, were likely sources of stress for Shimada-san. He was able to find work at the center, but he quit two jobs, fled the program, and began sleeping rough in Ueno Park again.

Street-level bureaucratic practices of exclusion from *seikatsu hogo* run counter to the spirit of Japanese welfare law (Hasegawa 2006). The Seikatsu Hogo-Hō (Livelihood Protection Act) of 1950, derived from Article 25 of Japan's constitution, states the purpose of the act as being "for the State to guarantee a minimum standard of living as well as to promote self-support for all citizens who are in living in poverty by providing the necessary public assistance according to the level of poverty."[5] So poverty or need appears to be the main criteria for assistance, rather than age or disability status. However, Article 4 of the act states that "a person who is living in poverty shall utilize his/her assets, abilities, and every other thing available to him/her for maintaining a minimum standard of living" prior to receiving benefits from the state. Also, any assistance available from a "person responsible for support prescribed by the Civil Code" must be exhausted before benefits are issued. The website of the Ministry of Health, Labor, and Welfare, the national body responsible for implementing *seikatsu hogo*, is a bit more specific in terms of eligibility criteria and lists five conditions for receiving *seikatsu hogo* benefits:[6]

> Conditions for aid: *Seikatsu hogo* is aid provided by the Public Assistance Act and implemented at the household level only after applying members' assets, abilities, and every other thing available, including aid from persons responsible for support (*fuyō gyōmusha*).
>
> Application of assets means: Please use savings and sell unused land or housing for your livelihood.
>
> Application of abilities means: For those able to work, please apply that ability.
>
> Every other thing available means: Please use pensions (*nenkin*) or allowances (*teate*), when eligible to get benefits from those systems.
>
> Persons responsible for support (*fuyō gyōmusha*) means: When you can obtain aid from relatives or others, please do so.
>
> When these conditions have been met, the household's income and a minimum cost of living determined by the Ministry of Health, Labor, and Welfare will be compared, and when the applicant's income is below the minimum standard, aid will be given.

These minimum standards are adjusted for geographic variation in cost of living (with the twenty-three wards of Tokyo included in the highest category), as well as age, disability status, receipt of other forms of aid, and number of household members. In 2012, the official minimum for a single man between forty-one and fifty-nine years old was 81,610 yen (about $873 at the 2013 conversion rate).

By many interpretations, all of my Tokyo interviewees should have qualified for *seikatsu hogo* benefits. They had all used up their assets, with most completely exhausting their savings and others with only a few thousand yen (less than $50) left when they went to the welfare office. All had looked for work, albeit with varying degrees of tenacity and certainly limited by their lack of housing, but none had been successful in finding anything stable that would keep them out of homelessness. A few had paid into pensions but all were too young to collect on them, and a few had received unemployment insurance but had exhausted it by the time they went to the welfare office. Practices vary by office, but "persons responsible for aid" is usually interpreted as being parents, siblings, and children of elderly people. As will be demonstrated and explored in Chapter 5, my Tokyo interviewees were almost completely out of contact with all family, and the few who were in contact, like Tsukada-san in the exiting vignette that preceded this chapter, felt that they were not in a position to ask for help given family members' limited resources. Although recent negative public sentiment toward growth of the *seikatsu hogo* rolls has called for more investigation of persons responsible for support (*fuyō gyōmusha*), none of my interviewees, even the few who later submitted applications for benefits, reported having family members contacted by the welfare office. However, this possibility could have prevented some from even asking about *seikatsu hogo*.

Although I have heard stories of overt exclusionary tactics in my broader fieldwork in Tokyo, the transitional housing users whom I followed generally did not even pursue *seikatsu hogo* when they reached the welfare office. Some were unaware of what aid was available, others had heard that caseworkers would respond negatively to requests for welfare benefits, and still others felt that they were able bodied and just wanted help finding work. Murata-san, a fifty-three-year-old former skilled factory worker from Hokkaidō who walked with a limp from a stroke, expressed this last view.

> According to the law, I should be able to get *seikatsu hogo* if I don't find work while I am in transitional housing. But I am about 90 percent sure they would not give it to me. I paid into a pension for twenty-nine years. I could get that once I'm sixty but my amount would be reduced for taking it five years early. If I had a major illness, or something, I could probably get welfare benefits temporarily. But in my case I even have a driver's license. At the least, I am able bodied. At best, I would be told by the welfare office, "*Seikatsu hogo* is for people that have nothing. You are able to do all kinds of work." Even in this economy, there are people who are earning money and eating by their own power, trying their hardest, even if they are crippled [sic]. So, I won't apply. Even if I die on the street at some point, at least I have tried my hardest.

Murata-san demonstrates a clear distaste for receiving welfare benefits and a preference to work as long as he is healthy. A victim of corporate restructuring,

Murata-san was often sharply critical of the growing inability of the Japanese government and Japanese firms to protect workers from the vicissitudes of capitalism. But in resonance with the broader neoliberal ideology of self-responsibility and the Japanese welfare regime's emphasis on the work responsibilities of men, he believed that it was ultimately his responsibility to find work and be self-reliant.

Murata-san's quote highlights the complexity of views toward *seikatsu hogo* and the role of masculinity in preventing many men from pursuing these benefits in times of need. Anthropologist Tom Gill (2012) has examined "failed manhood" among men living along riverbeds and in parks in urban Japan. As discussed in Chapter 1, there are many men who refuse to turn to state aid as a way to preserve their notions of masculinity as being self-reliant and certainly not dependent on the state. Also, there are those who are pragmatic and do not apply until the statute of limitations (generally five years) has passed on their debts in order to avoid having an officially registered address available to debt collectors. However, there are also men like Murata-san who are not willing to become fully dependent on the state but willing to receive more limited aid in the form of help finding work through transitional housing.

Once in emergency housing in Tokyo's self-reliance support system, men are evaluated for physical ability and desire for employment, and those deemed able to work are filtered into transitional housing. In 2003, about 60 percent of the men in Tokyo's largest emergency shelter (Ōta Ryō) moved into transitional housing (Tokubetsu-ku Jinji Kōsei Jimu Kumiai 2010). The next largest group (about 20 percent) went to hospitals, *seikatsu hogo*-funded welfare facilities, and other shelters, with a similarly sized group whose destination was not accounted for (about 20 percent). But despite being formally vetted for physical ability and their desire to work via assessment, my Tokyo interviewees who moved into transitional housing were not free of health limitations, as evident in Murata-san's case above. Also, Tsukada-san from the exit story preceding this chapter was found in his assessment at the program to have a heart valve disorder and cataracts, both of which may have required surgery. While in emergency housing, he received health care for his maladies, including dental care, but he still had to struggle with chest pain, vision problems, and leg numbness while searching for work and even after landing a job and moving into his apartment. So even my Tokyo interviewees who had some health issues while in emergency housing still felt that they were still physically able to work and expressed a desire to go to transitional housing during the assessment process.

Once in transitional housing, all of my interviewees were expected to search for employment and understood that the program would not help them secure *seikatsu hogo*. For the few Tokyo interviewees who did not find work, when their transitional housing was terminated, responsibility returned to their caseworkers at welfare offices to determine their eligibility for further aid. However, since transitional housing users had completed an assessment for the welfare office that determined them able to work, most who did not find work assumed they were ineligible and generally refrained from pursuing welfare benefits or even contacting their caseworker. When I asked Andō-san, a fifty-three-year-old from Niigata Prefecture, if staff at the center had explained his options should he not find work within two months of entering the program, he said, "No, not really. Just if the two months are up and you don't have work, that's it, you're out (*mō ojan ni naru*)." So I asked if there was any possibility of getting on welfare. He replied, "Only if your body is really messed up. So, everyone is there for two months and they can't find work. There were a lot of people there just to eat for two months [laughs]." Andō-san opted to sign up for a publicly funded training program he found on a flyer in San'ya, Tokyo's day labor ghetto. The program provided two weeks of housing and a small daily stipend, but no job. After that, he moved back into his tent on the Sumida River. When he became skeptical about his prospects for work while still in the program, he had a companion (*nakama*) hold his spot. Several months later, after returning to the Sumida River encampment, he felt that undiagnosed depression had been keeping him from finding stable work for years. He also complained that the transitional housing program and the welfare office were unable to help him, and he had no idea where to get treatment. He felt that the assessment process was simply recording his life history, and that there was a great need to screen for depression, a problem he thought he shared with many others in transitional housing.

Obtaining State Aid through the Help of an Advocate in Los Angeles

Venetia Cheatham,[7] whose exit story begins part 3 of this book, was one of the few transitional housing interviewees in Los Angeles who was able to obtain SSI benefits, but this was after she had left transitional housing. She was rejected numerous times, but a lawyer who had once judged appeals was able to navigate the process for her, in return for a portion of Venetia's back-paid benefits once awarded. Although there was general exclusion from SSI benefits absent a skilled advocate, my interviewees in Los Angeles were much more successful in tapping into another important source of state aid, federally subsidized housing in single room occupancy (SRO) hotels. But this also generally required crucial assistance in navigating the street-level bureaucracy. Oneita, a twenty-four-year-old African American woman from South Central Los Angeles, was able to exit homelessness to subsidized housing. As I will show in Chapter 3, Oneita looked hard for work but had difficulty finding viable employment while in the transitional housing program. She had completed all of the required courses in the program and had developed a tight bond with her case manager, Margaret, who consoled her when she first came to the program after fleeing an abusive boyfriend. But, like many of my other female Los Angeles interviewees, Oneita was bothered by the unwanted attention she received in a facility inhabited by many aggressive men, some straight out of prison. Also, she thought women in the program were jealous of her, perhaps because of her youth, her looks, or her lack of a substance abuse problem. She would dress down, trying to prevent men from talking to her, but then her case manager would get upset at her for not maintaining a better appearance for school, her job search, and her self-esteem.

Oneita was fortunate to be placed in one of the few single rooms in the program, but her neighbor complained that Oneita was too loud, and the two argued. Oneita felt that some of the anger management courses she participated in at the program helped her avoid conflicts by not engaging others who bothered her. She took a job at a nearby small mental health clinic, but the administration was in disarray, and the doctor failed to pay her on a regular basis. As she looked for more stable employment, she also pursued other housing options since she knew her time in the program was limited and she was unsure how long she could endure the institutional living situation. Here is how she responded when I asked if she was looking for new housing about six months into her stay in transitional housing.

> Oh, I've looked. I've applied for the projects. It's like in the Watts area. And they told me it would be a six-month wait and then after I wait my six months and now they talking about people that get SSI and disability get preference and it might be up to a year that I'm waiting. And I'm like, "Alrighty, then." And I tried to get into one of the SROs. And they said I couldn't get in because at that point in time I was working. They said that they're not taking nobody that's working. Or whatever. So it's like, "Alright then." And then like now a lot of them aren't accepting applications because they got so many applications. So I don't know. Wait another month.

Oneita's trouble finding subsidized housing that she qualified for was shared by many transitional housing program participants in Los Angeles, especially those without clearly diagnosable disabilities or meeting criteria that qualified them as "chronically homeless."

But within a month of her previous statements, after conflicts with her neighbor in the program escalated, Oneita was able to quickly move out of the program into a subsidized SRO room on the eastern edge of Skid Row. In contrast to her earlier struggle to navigate bureaucracies to access subsidized housing, she described a quick and seamless application process involving a single interview.

> Yeah, because I had Margaret [case manager] as one of my references. I had my boss and the dude that live here [who told her about the room], named Tikki—he used to live in the [transitional housing program], too. I had to fill out an application and bring it back. They gave me another one to take to the Section 8 [Housing Authority] building. Then like two days later, I did my little interview. They gave me my keys. Because they usually say it takes about a month, or two months to get in here. It took me about three days. The lady asked me what was my reason for wanting to move into the [hotel] or whatever, and was sort of like "I need a new surrounding." I'm living at the [transitional housing program], and I did my program, and now I felt like it was time for me to get on my own.

Oneita was proud of her ability to "stay on top of her business" and saw it as the key to getting in so quickly to her subsidized room. But she had been on top of paperwork before and had been unsuccessful. It was likely a combination of her tenacity, her having an "associate" from the program serve as a reference along with her case manager and former boss, and her positive attitude in the interview that helped her get the room. Perhaps the most crucial of these factors is her "associate" alerting her to an opening. Without that, her promptness, references, and good performance in the interview would never have been relevant. Also, she had quit her job at the clinic, and in Los Angeles's tight rental market her unemployment ironically helped her secure housing since some of the rooms in the building had been set aside for GR recipients.

Obtaining State Aid through the Help of an Advocate in Tokyo

As in Los Angeles, for my Tokyo interviewees the few who were able to secure welfare benefits required the assistance of an advocate, usually a staff person or volunteer at a private, nonprofit organization not associated with the transitional housing programs. These people provided help navigating the application process, including visiting the welfare office together, pressuring welfare office caseworkers to process applications for *seikatsu hogo*, and providing some assistance in securing housing. In some cases, these advocates even provided crucial information and emotional support to transitional housing users. However, in contrast to the experiences of my interviewees in Los Angeles who pursued SSI, those in Tokyo who were able to enlist the help of an advocate saw applications quickly processed, and began receiving benefits without long delays and disruptions from a confusing and apparently contradictory system. Takahashi-san, a fifty-five-year-old day laborer from Tokyo with a bad back, had to leave the transitional housing program after two months because the day labor construction job he took after failing to find full-time employment did not met the program's employment criteria. He moved into an unsubsidized SRO (*doya*) in San'ya and worked while hoping to be able to move into a public housing project to which he had applied before entering transitional housing. However, his job ended and his funds ran out, so he left his *doya* and began sleeping on cardboard in Asakusa and around Sumida River Park. There he was approached by Sugiyama-san, a seasoned volunteer in his seventies who was involved in a number of San'ya-based groups, during a street patrol of the area. Sugiyama-san accompanied Takahashi-san to the Sumida Ward welfare office. There a caseworker said that Takahashi-san would be allowed to try the program again, a rare exception usually reserved for those who lost jobs because their employer had experienced economic hardship. Here is how Sugiyama-san described the way he was able to draw on his experience to resist the caseworker's attempt to steer Takahashi-san away from welfare benefits.

> I told them, "You are not going to send him on the self-reliance center (*jiritsu shien sentā*) course!" Once the caseworker has decided to send them to the center, that is hard to reverse. I can do it when necessary. But, that time, I had him go to emergency housing and then go to SSS [a large nonprofit organization sometimes suspected of being a "poverty business"]. Because when he goes to SSS, that's welfare benefits [*seikatsu hogo*]. So I had them promise that. And, I have been going like this to the Sumida welfare office for three years. Now, the caseworkers all listen to me. There is the section chief, Katō-san. But now when I have gotten them to follow my advice, then the person I took and got them to help, that person screws up and then the worker complains, "That guy is not doing well" [laughs] So, it is a burden for me, too.

Sugimoto-san's pride in being a "pro" advocating for people at the welfare offices highlights that a good deal of expertise gained through trial and error is essential in resisting the street-level bureaucratic tactic of steering applicants away from benefits.

After two weeks in emergency housing, Takahashi-san spent a few months in the SSS facility. He said his job search was less frantic because there were no time limits on his welfare benefits. He eventually found a part-time job maintaining a small apartment building and then moved into a small apartment. He earned 900 yen (about $8) per hour, working four hours per day four days a week, bringing in about 70,000 yen (about $628) per month and receiving an additional 26,000 yen (about $233) per month from the welfare office in addition to having his rent paid. This half-work/half-welfare (*han-shūrō/han-fukushi*) approach was generally not an option for transitional housing users without an advocate. Although Sugiyama-san lamented that the welfare office did not get it right the first time when they sent Takahashi-san to transitional housing, Takahashi-san was extremely happy with his new life and job and appreciated the help from the welfare office and Sugiyama-san: "I think of the building I work at as my own house. Even the trash cans are all clean and shiny. When the residents smile and greet me, saying 'Good morning!' there is nothing better. It makes me happy. I try hard. I need to repay Sugiyama-san for his kindness." Takahashi-san described the help provided by Sugiyama-san as making possible a dramatic change in his life, both physically and mentally. Without his guidance and advocacy, the welfare office would have channeled Takahashi-san into transitional housing where he was disadvantaged in finding full-time work because of his bad back and age. Through Sugiyama-san's advocacy he was able to get into a privately run welfare facility that allowed him more time to find work, tolerated income from employment to be supplemented by welfare, and helped him transition into rental housing.

I have demonstrated how, through the interaction between systemic elements of state welfare systems, including rules for eligibility, and the practices of street-level bureaucracy, transitional housing users in Los Angeles and Tokyo are largely excluded from accessing levels of welfare benefits sufficient to allow them to exit homelessness immediately. In this process of exclusion, transitional housing users were disciplined to varying extents through messages about the unfavorable nature of welfare receipt, sometimes with psychological and emotional costs. Most conceded to competing for income in the labor market in order to purchase rental housing during their stay in time-limited programs. For those who were unsuccessful in finding employment, obtaining welfare benefits was possible only with the help of skilled advocates. Also, several interviewees in Los Angeles were able to move into subsidized housing, but this too required an inside tip about an opening, along with quick action and often advocacy by an NPO staff person. These findings highlight the persistence of street-level bureaucratic practices, rather than simply formal criteria, in determining eligibility for state welfare benefits. Given that state welfare benefits represent a final safety net preventing literal homelessness, this discretion in eligibility determination calls into question the fairness of state welfare systems that are supposed to allocate benefits and services based on universal criteria rather than access to a dedicated and resourceful person willing to help them overcome exclusionary tactics.

But the ways that welfare systems and street-level practices interacted to exclude people varied between the two cities. In Los Angeles, those who felt they were eligible for SSI because of disabilities were often trapped in a bureaucratic labyrinth for years as they appealed rejections. Even those who relied on GR benefits described struggling to meet paperwork and workfare requirements to avoid termination. Thus in Los Angeles, exclusion from sufficient state aid was done through bewildering processes of entanglement. In contrast, in Tokyo exclusion from state welfare benefits was more clear and direct, with most interviewees having already internalized a distaste for welfare and a perception of ineligibility, with welfare office caseworkers steering interviewees into a second tier of aid that included emergency and transitional housing. None of my interviewees who went to Tokyo welfare offices by themselves were able to even submit applications for benefits due to steering or, in a few cases, outright berating by caseworkers at the mere request for help.

Despite this general exclusion, some interviewees were able to obtain benefits through the aid of an advocate. Although advocacy was necessary to obtain benefits in both cities, the process of advocacy also reflected the different mixes of system structure and street-level bureaucracy. In Los Angeles, one's advocate for SSI also had to fight through a troublesome bureaucratic process by drawing on professional knowledge and experience, a process often lasting several months if not years. Even in the shorter process of obtaining subsidized housing, an inside tie was necessary to jump the line on the waiting list for a precious resource in Skid Row. In Tokyo, advocacy was necessary to penetrate the rigid but clearer barriers to obtaining *seikatsu hogo*. Once advocates were able to get caseworkers to accept welfare benefit applications, the Tokyo welfare offices conformed to their legal obligation to provide a result in two weeks. Advocates were also able to pressure caseworkers to find housing for applicants as they waited for their results. But it is important to note that having an advocate was not without costs and did not always result in a durable exit from homelessness. The "poverty businesses" that have proliferated in Tokyo in recent years are often criticized as simply warehousing and exploiting dislocated men for a portion of their welfare benefits. Similarly, the fairness of lawyers in the United States receiving a portion of back payments when SSI appeals are accepted is questionable.

Moreover, the effectiveness of a system that steers people into transitional housing initially, only to reluctantly grant them welfare benefits later, can be questioned. Those who struggled to find employment while in transitional housing had been disciplined to accept that welfare aid from the state would not be forthcoming. Urban ethnographer Javier Auyero (2012, 2) describes the forced waiting by the poor implemented by state bureaucracies as a "temporal process in and through which political subordination is reproduced." Indeed, many of my interviewees conceded to substandard aid in the form of transitional housing in the process of exclusion and to waiting for more substantial forms of state welfare aid. While waiting for relief from the state, not only were their expectations of aid reduced through discipline and domination but there were other costs. In their liminal state, many experienced stress not only at being turned down for employment but also due to the constant threat of termination from the programs for even minor rule infractions. This was compounded by the difficulties of group living with others going through complex situations. Sometimes this produced camaraderie and the sharing of information about jobs and housing, but it also produced conflicts and the danger of termination. For some, their physical and mental health deteriorated as they lingered in limbo while waiting for benefits. For a few others who did not benefit from an advocate or family, the failure to find employment in the face of exclusion from welfare benefits resulted in a return to literal homelessness.

So in the face of general exclusion from welfare benefits, how did transitional housing users trying to exit homelessness fare in labor and housing markets? What barriers did they face in the polarized markets of Los Angeles and Tokyo? How were they able to overcome these barriers? How did these barriers and strategies differ in the two global cities? These are the questions I turn to in Chapter 3.

SEARCHING FOR WORK AND HOUSING

In the exit stories that opened this part of the book, Michelle and Tsukada-san exited homelessness with savings from low-skill service sector jobs at the bottom of global city labor markets—Michelle as a security guard working at amusement parks, concerts, and other high-end special events and Tsukada-san as a custodian for a downtown office building. But both struggled to find work, overcoming myriad barriers such as health problems, age discrimination, human capital mismatch, and lack of transportation. With varying degrees of success, they both tried investing in their human capital, Michelle through her pursuit of degrees related to social work and Tsukada-san by taking simple workshops on skills useful in custodial work. Although both worked in the low-wage service sector of their respective cities, they varied in the extent to which they were able to use income from work to buy housing on the rental market. Michelle was unsuccessful getting help to move into a subsidized SRO, so she augmented her low income with savings from her stay in the transitional program to pay for a room in unsubsidized SROs. But the grim conditions were taxing on her and the "twenty-eight-day shuffle" forced her to change rooms frequently while denying her residency rights. She moved into an apartment at the very margins of Los Angeles's rental market and was only able to stay over the long term with forced concessions from her slumlord. Also, she only very slowly paid down her debts. Tsukada-san, however, with his full-time job, albeit earning only slightly over minimum wage, received overtime pay and other benefits such as payment into pension and health insurance systems. Thus, amid Tokyo's more forgiving rental market, he was able to limit his rent payments to less than one quarter of his income and, albeit after declaring bankruptcy and while living austerely, quickly pay down his debts.

Michelle and Tsukada-san's experiences with labor and housing markets reflect some general patterns among the transitional housing users I followed in Los Angeles and Tokyo. In Chapter 2 I showed how neoliberal globalization interacts with more local conditions, such as racial stratification, deinstitutionalization of the mentally ill, welfare reform, mass imprisonment, and a drug epidemic, to produce a larger homeless population in Los Angeles than in Tokyo. In this chapter, I turn to the question of how these contextual differences affected the labor and housing market experiences of persons attempting to exit homelessness through transitional housing in the two global cities.

Human Capital Mismatch

In both Los Angeles and Tokyo, many interviewees stated that they lacked the education and skills needed to make them competitive in the local labor market. In Los Angeles, nearly all of my interviewees had at least a high school education. The two exceptions were Barry, a forty-one-year-old white man from Rhode Island who dropped out of the eighth grade after he was bullied for being a "narc," and Carlos, a fifty-year-old Mexican American who dropped out after the tenth grade to contribute income to his large and poor family of farmworkers. Four Los Angeles interviewees had bachelor's degrees and a few had attended college, junior college, and vocational schools. All of my Tokyo interviewees had completed compulsory education in Japan (junior high school), with eight going on to high school and three earning their high school degrees. Two Tokyo interviewees had also completed vocational school—Murata-san, a fifty-three-year-old from Hokkaidō who trained in electronics, and Andō-san, a fifty-three-year-old from Nīgata who completed a program in data management. So, although almost all interviewees in both cities had completed compulsory education, very few had advanced beyond that, disadvantaging them in labor markets that increasingly placed a premium on higher education. Also, considering that many interviewees in both cities grew up in low-income households and neighborhoods, the quality of that education may have been below average, especially for those who grew up in more highly segregated Los Angeles.

In contrast to popular perceptions of homelessness, most of my interviewees in both cities had worked for the greater part of their adult lives, generally in economic sectors that have contracted and, especially in Los Angeles, have seen increased competition from immigrant workers in areas such as manufacturing, construction, warehousing, and retail. In both cities, only a few interviewees had substantial experience working in an office environment. Also, the limited possession of education and marketable skills was exacerbated by experiences of homelessness, which often coincided with the deterioration of skills and mental and physical health. There were a number of Los Angeles interviewees who had lengthy gaps in employment, mostly due to addiction, illness, and incarceration. Walter, a fifty-four-year-old African American former computer operator from Detroit, was battling a substance abuse problem and coping with the tragic death of his wife while trying to find work from the transitional housing program. He had been clean for three months and looking for work mostly via publicly funded Workforce or One-Stop employment agencies, but he found that his skills had become outdated. He said, "I got a call from the Long Beach School Board. Yeah, the agency told me about the job. The guy wanted to hire me, the feedback to me was, man, he liked me. But the only problem was I didn't have *recent* computer experience because I had been out there using. Now I could have been trained. Or I could have lied and said, "Well, I know it." But see by me being clean and sober now, I can't lie. I got to run a honest program about everything. And he's directing me and gonna see everything. But after it was said and done I wish to hell I had, because it [paid] like about $19 an hour." Though it ran counter to the principles he hoped to stick to in his loose following of a twelve-step program, Walter lamented that he had not embellished his work history to get a well-paying job.

Many interviewees in Tokyo also found that they had few skills to offer the current labor market. Yamada-san, the fifty-five-year-old introduced in Chapter 1, completed junior high in nearby Chiba Prefecture and came to Kawasaki City near Tokyo at age fifteen as part of "group employment" (*shūdan shūshoku*)[1] for Toshiba Electronics. He obtained a high school degree through a correspondence (*tsūshin*) course during his two-year training period but quit Toshiba to take a live-in contract job. He did this type of work through his late forties, changing jobs when they no longer suited him. For the most part he worked hard for long hours and lived in small and sometimes shared quarters, and never was unemployed for very long. But eventually he found it difficult to find work.

> It's not so much that work using a lathe (*senban*) has decreased. Well, it has decreased, but, it's my skills, my arms, you could say they're bad (*ude ga warui*). Normally, someone in their fifties should be a specialist or a master of something. They should be like a boss (*oyakata*). They've gotten good at something. They should have taken things to the next level. But I didn't. And lathes are computer operated now. I could learn it if I had the chance, but I always put working first. As a contract worker,

you learn a little as you work, but things like getting qualifications are put off for later. I know that I don't have any skills so I've only been looking for work in cleaning and security. But it hasn't gone well. For security, you need two guarantors.

So in addition to lacking skills for nonstandard employment in manufacturing, he had no one who could serve as a guarantor for a low-skill service-sector job as a security guard.

There were also a few transitional housing program users in Tokyo who had licenses that would likely have been useful in their job searches, but they lost them in the process of falling into homelessness. Kikuchi-san, a forty-one-year-old from the southern prefecture of Fukuoka, had worked in manufacturing and construction, obtaining licenses to operate a crane and bulldozer. However, when he lost his housing he stored them in his duffel bag in a locker at a train station. He did not have the money to get it out, so eventually his bag was disposed of. He was fed up with the instability of work in the construction industry anyway, so he did not bother to get his licenses renewed while in the transitional program.

Some transitional housing program users in Los Angeles were constrained in their job searches by mental health issues, including substance abuse, in addition to their limited education and skills. Although Walter, the former computer programmer discussed above, moved in and out of spells of addiction and homelessness before entering the program, a few others in Los Angeles had been addicted and out of formal employment continuously for up to two decades. Thus, although they were in a transitional housing program that required them to have income and aimed to help them find employment, they were more focused on recovery from substance abuse. A job search was something that they would engage in more actively in the future; their daily life was centered on attending twelve-step meetings and other treatment in order to ensure that they did not relapse and return to homelessness. Here, Jill, the forty-nine-year-old African American introduced in Chapter 1, explains her plans: "I will look for work, but not now. I'm still thinking about teaching because I'm only going to do eighteen months here. This is my first and only program. Because I know I'm kicking it. I have that much confidence in myself. And then because I'm ready to go on my own I don't want to go stay with no sisters no more. They say, 'Well, you can come here when you get out of there.' No. They ask, 'You gonna stay downtown?' If I have to, yes. I want my own foundation, something that's mine, my own. If you want, give me a little help; *if* it's necessary, I'll take it. But I'm going to try to do it by myself." This could be seen as strategic labor market withdrawal, not actively searching for work in order to focus on her health, but with a plan to return to the labor market. Others, such as Sinee from Thailand and Evan from South Central Los

Angeles, did not have substance abuse problems but had diagnoses of anxiety/ bipolar disorder and schizophrenia, respectively. Thus, they also did not actively search for work but focused on stabilizing their mental health.

In Tokyo, those with physical and mental health issues that would prevent them from working were supposed to be screened out of transitional housing programs and diverted to welfare facilities. However, in addition to those with physical limitations noted in Chapter 2, there were two men in my sample who felt that they needed mental health treatment in order to effectively secure and keep a job. Nakamura-san, a thirty-five year-old who had been involved in organized crime (*yakuza* or *bōryokudan*), had served five years in prison for murdering a rival gang member. Subsequently, he was diagnosed with alcoholism and depression. However, he felt that the treatment he received in emergency and transitional housing was focused more on providing him medication than the counseling he needed. Andō-san, the former computer operator from Nīgata introduced in Chapter 2, complained that the intake process was more of an inquisition into his background, and his mental health was never evaluated. He thought that undiagnosed depression was behind his inability to appeal to employers in interviews. Unlike in Los Angeles, both men had very little time to improve their mental health once in the transitional housing program, with only two months to find full-time employment in order to obtain a two-month extension.

In contrast to Los Angeles, by far the most common barrier faced by transitional housing program users in Tokyo was age. This was a problem for older men looking for work in cleaning, construction site security, manufacturing, and construction. Here, Andō-san, fifty-three years old, responds to my question about his job search: "As soon as I went to the public employment office (*shokuan*), I knew that things were going to be tough because of my age. The only reason there are ads for older workers is because the Hello Work [public employment office] is telling them to advertise for older workers. In reality, they are hiring younger workers." Although he was unable to apply for jobs that specified an age limit below fifty, even those that he was eligible for preferred younger workers. He mostly looked for work in cleaning because over a decade had passed since he had last worked as a computer operator, and he had an aversion to construction site security (*gādoman*)[2] work given a previous negative experience directing traffic on a winding mountain road in Nīgata. He had a few licenses for welding, handling hazardous materials, crane operation, and crane slings (*tamakake*) that he had obtained through special publicly funded training programs in San'ya that provided short-term housing and a small stipend. However, he had no experience working in construction, failing at his lone attempt to work day labor. Many cleaning jobs that seemed to be open to older workers were part-time jobs that would not qualify him for an extension in the transitional housing program. Andō-san, with an eye to the encroachment of neoliberalism into Tokyo's labor market, said, "Now at the employment office, almost all of the jobs are for contract workers, just like America—one-year contracts." He had an interview during each of his first three weeks in the program, two for cleaning jobs and one in a laboratory tending to guinea pigs, but he received no offers. He was not exactly sure why but thought that there was tight competition, about twenty applicants per job by his estimate. As noted in Chapter 2, he did not get help for his depression and returned to an encampment along the Sumida River.

Even those in their thirties who had previously worked in restaurants and *pachinko* parlors felt that their age prevented them from finding work in these sectors. Takagi-san, the thirty-eight-year-old Ibaraki native whose exiting vignette appears at the beginning of this book, was unable to find restaurant work while in the program, despite nearly two decades of experience: "Even restaurant (*inshoku*) work has an age limit, about forty-five or so. But there are places that only hire workers in their twenties. It's not because they work better, but for the atmosphere of the place."

Stigmatized Statuses and Spaces

Transitional housing program users in both Los Angeles and Tokyo reported discrimination from potential employers, but the source of stigma differed. In Los Angeles, a number of transitional housing users had criminal records, mostly for violations related to substance abuse disorders and from living in high-poverty neighborhoods that have a strong police presence. Many with records found that employers used background checks and felt that prior convictions prevented offers. Although in interviews with me, Los Angeles transitional housing users seldom described being discriminated against directly on the basis of race in job searches,[3] employers of low-skill workers in urban areas often have an aversion to black workers, especially those with criminal records (Wilson 1996). In Tokyo, there were far fewer interviewees with criminal records and none racially or phenotypically distinct from mainstream Japanese.[4] But many transitional housing users in Tokyo felt that they were discriminated against simply based on an address that could reveal they were in a government-funded housing program for the down-and-out. Conversely, very few transitional housing users in Los Angeles described their residence in a Skid Row program as potentially being viewed negatively by employers, despite having an address in a neighborhood reputed to have the country's highest concentration of homelessness and relief organizations. These differences in stigmatized statuses and spaces reflect differences in how national welfare regimes interact with local urban contexts. The Japanese welfare regime's reliance on male breadwinners stigmatizes unemployed men who must rely on government aid. The American welfare regime's response to increased social insecurity has been a punitive approach to poverty and substance abuse. This has been concentrated in Los Angeles neighborhoods where poor blacks and Latinos predominate, entangling many of my interviewees in the penal system and saddling them with conviction records that are then visible to employers who seek them out.

For Marcos, a forty-eight-year-old former accountant from Puerto Rico, the conditions of his parole and his criminal background interacted to put him in a precarious position of virtual exclusion from the labor market and in danger of being sent back to prison. During a period of unemployment after moving his family from New York back to Puerto Rico, his dabbling in the use and transport of cocaine escalated. Eventually he was arrested and convicted of participating in a cocaine trafficking conspiracy, serving five years in prison. He obtained parole in California by using the address of a woman he had met while in prison. However, she became anxious about the arrangement and backed out, leaving Marcos homeless upon arrival. His parole officer required him to enter the transitional housing program and find full-time work or be sent back to prison. Although he was college educated and had worked in the finance department of a small private college in New York, he found that his felony record obstructed his ability to land a job. He applied to accounting jobs at local community and private colleges and sales jobs at retail establishments and car dealerships but was unable to secure employment, even when the employer was willing to hire a felon. He said, "I had a job offer as an auto salesman but I got turned down by the state. They would not give me the auto salesman license because I have a recent criminal conviction. The guy was very, very kind. I told him, 'I am on parole. I do have a felony conviction for drug conspiracy. It happened in 1996. It doesn't have anything to do with my professional skills or my professional jobs that I've had in the past. I'm looking forward to getting a second chance.' I did a sales pitch on him. He said, 'You got it.' But then the state turned down my license, so I couldn't take the job."

Amid this catch-22, Marcos found himself scrambling to meet such program requirements as attending job preparedness courses; trying to help a new girlfriend he sent for in Puerto Rico obtain welfare benefits and housing for herself and her child; and looking for full-time work that would meet his parole requirements. The job preparedness instructor threatened to kick him out of the class for repeated absences, and Marcos feared this would result in termination from the program, a parole violation, and a return to prison. Additionally, he was frustrated about being repeatedly drug tested, both in the program and by his parole officer. He became extremely anxious but was calmed down in counseling sessions by the on-site clinical psychologist. However, when he was mugged outside the program on the streets of Skid Row, he began a frantic effort to get out.

Some transitional housing program users in Los Angeles had accumulated records of violations and convictions for problems not related to substance abuse, but driven by their long-term experience of concentrated neighborhood poverty. Oneita, the twenty-four-year-old African American from South Central Los Angeles introduced in Chapter 2, described herself as being "on a natural high" and never interested in drugs. She moved between the homes of her parents and relatives as a child, changed schools often because of disciplinary problems, and had a few close friends and relatives killed in gang violence. She came to transitional housing after fleeing an abusive boyfriend. She had a high school degree from a continuation school and had taken community and vocational college courses in accounting, computer software, and child development. She had experience in low-skill service-sector jobs like retail, security, and customer service. But she had also been arrested and jailed a few times for what she saw as minor offences. Once she was stopped for jaywalking and arrested because she had a warrant out for failure to pay a ticket for riding the Metro Blue Line without payment (she said that a friend's child she was babysitting threw out her train ticket). Another time she was arrested for illegal possession of a concealed firearm, but the case was thrown out by the District Attorney's office. Oneita said small children in her housing project told her that her boyfriend had stashed a gun in a mailbox. When she went to move it away from the children, someone saw her, called the police, and she was later arrested when she would not say that it belonged to her boyfriend. While in the program she completed a job preparedness course and actively searched for work, openly explaining her record when asked by potential employers. She was never told directly that she was denied employment because of her record, but she felt that she did not get a job offer from a legal aid office because she was unable to clear a background check.

Although far fewer interviewees in Tokyo faced the stigma of a criminal record,[5] a few found that their delinquent debts reduced their options in some sectors of the job market. Tsukada-san from the exiting vignette preceding Chapter 2 said his delinquent debt limited his job options by preventing him from applying to construction site security (gādoman) jobs: "I have only been asked about debt once in an interview. They are really strict on construction site security so that is why I can't work in that area. If you've been exempt from responsibility for the entire amount, you can get hired. But between filing for bankruptcy and being cleared takes two or three months. You can't get hired during that period." A few other interviewees in Tokyo who had substantial debt felt ambivalent about finding work and moving into an apartment since that would often bring them unwanted attention from aggressive debt collectors. Some, including Tsukada-san, were linked to legal assistance by emergency and transitional housing programs and were either told that a statute of limitations (generally five years) had passed on their debt or they made plans to slowly pay the debt back. A few interviewees with debt did nothing. In contrast to the well-noted fears of many indebted men who endure homelessness outdoors rather than use transitional housing (Gill 2012), only one interviewee (Hirota-san) who accumulated new debts reported being hounded by debt collectors after moving into an apartment. Debt collectors repeatedly called his employer, causing him to get fired and eventually return to homelessness.

But more than the stigma of criminal records or delinquent debt, many Tokyo transitional program users found their program address to be a barrier in their search for employment. This problem was particularly acute for those who went to the transitional housing program in Taitō Ward. Due to NIMBY (not in my backyard) opposition from local residents, the prefabricated building housing the program had to be located in a parking lot in Ueno Park. Thus, the address that program participants used on their proof of residence (*juminhyō*) used in job searches and other application materials read "Ueno Park," a place known more for blue-tarp tents and flopped out men than conventional residences. Kikuchi-san, a forty-one-year-old former factory worker from the southern city of Fukuoka, said, "They look at my application and ask, 'Is your address really Ueno Park?' Then I have to talk about the self-reliance support center, and the conversation goes no further. They'll say, 'Oh, I see . . .,' and the tone gradually sinks." While in the program Kikuchi-san looked for work every day at the public employment agency, each week bringing five or six job ads to the employment specialists, of which two or three would meet program requirements of full-time work and pay. He started off looking for work as a security guard, but since he was out of contact with friends and family, he lacked a guarantor. So he applied for cleaning jobs, went on nine interviews, but received no offers. After a short stint in a live-in job with a company receiving government subsidies to employ people experiencing homelessness, Kikuchi-san found himself earning little money so he left and began living outdoors in Ueno Park again.

Even interviewees in other programs who disguised transitional housing programs with names like "Heights" and "Co-op" to sound like residential apartment buildings had problems with their address. Andō-san, the fifty-four-year-old former computer programmer from Nīgata, said, "When I went on an interview, they looked at my address and they could tell because they got several people from the same address. They know it's the self-reliance support center address. They usually don't turn you down when you call for an appointment. It's when you bring them your resume and they see your address. But one time I called

Seibu Tetsudō [a private rail company] about a part-time job. They asked, 'Where do you live?' When I told them my address, they said, 'Oh, is that so? Um, sorry but that place is . . .' and they hung up on me." For Andō-san, experiencing a rejection and his anxiety about the possibility of more rejections because of his address, compounded by his age, caused him to see little hope and give up on his job search. In contrast, my Los Angeles interviewees did not say that potential employers used their residence in a Skid Row program as a basis for discrimination, but they felt that most employers simply did not recognize the program address. Rita felt that since more young professionals are living downtown as the area gentrifies, employers did not find the program address suspicious.

Localized Time-Space Compression

David Harvey (1990) argues that globalization has coincided with time-space compression, a phenomenon in which spatial borders are increasingly crossed by people, goods, and capital at heightened speeds. In earlier chapters I have described this process as contributing to deindustrialization, the restructuring and polarization of labor markets, and the erosion of affordable housing, creating sizable populations vulnerable to homelessness in global cities. In this section I use the term to organize the last set of barriers that my interviewees faced in trying to secure employment. However, in contrast to the term's conventional use in highlighting processes of globalization, the barriers I describe in this section had strong local origins. For example, the major form of time compression facing Tokyo interviewees was the two-month time limit they faced from when they entered the program to when they had to request a two-month extension, which was contingent on full-time employment. This contrasts with a much less compressed time frame for my Los Angeles interviewees who had two years to stay in the program, and GR benefits were accepted as meeting the program's income requirement in lieu of employment. However, transitional housing users in Los Angeles did face a barrier that could be linked to space compression—that of competition from workers who migrate across borders. Last, a different, much more local spatial barrier that actually worked as time-space *expansion* in Los Angeles—a sprawling urban labor market and limited access to transportation—interacted with the other barriers to limit the capacity of transitional housing users to secure employment.

Ishimura-san, a thirty-seven-year-old former hostess club (*mizushobai*) staff person from the northern prefecture of Hokkaidō, felt that the short time limit and pressure from staff caused him to hastily take a job that did not offer him long-term stability. When we first met at the emergency shelter, Ishimura-san wanted to take skills training (*ginō kōshū*) courses in computers and try to find some semiskilled work in building maintenance. His backup plan was to do a course in cleaning and find a job in that sector since it did not require many specific skills, and job opportunities were available even though the work was low paid. He completed both courses, but after moving into the transitional housing program he was worried about finding work within two months. Ishimura-san was offered a job after his first interview and he took it, despite being a little suspicious of the business's small-scale and somewhat unprofessional atmosphere. He thought that it was hardly the time to be selective since he needed to save enough to move into an apartment before his four months (once granted a two-month extension) in the program expired. Unfortunately, the job conditions ended up being different than advertised. Also, he caused an accident at work and was forced to pay the company for damages, with the cost garnished from his wages.

> If I hadn't had a problem at work, I wouldn't be in this situation. And the first place they sent me to, it was a different company, not their own. And I didn't know anything. That would make anyone uncomfortable. I had a little less than ten days off the first month but then the second month there wasn't much work. They had me off for four or five days straight. The job was supposed to be on a fixed salary of 200,000 yen [about $1,794]. But then, since there were so many days off, they started paying me on a daily basis. Since then I haven't gotten a decent month's salary. I only made about 140,000 yen [about $1,256]. I ended up leaving the program a little before my [second] two months were up because I had saved up money. The staff told me to leave, but there is no sense in staying longer anyway. They are always saying, "Hurry up! Hurry up!" They rush us. They have their targets to meet.

Ishimura-san persisted on his job, was able to accumulate savings, and with 130,000 yen (about $1,166) in financial assistance from the program, moved into a small, six *tatami* mat (about 108 square foot) apartment with a kitchen, private bath, and toilet renting for 50,000 yen (about $449) per month. After his move, he was able to earn enough to barely cover his basic needs but accumulated no savings and wondered how he could look for a new job effectively with his low-paying and unreliable work schedule.

Although transitional housing program users in Los Angeles benefited from more time to search for work, they faced more competition for low-skill work from immigrant workers than their counterparts in Tokyo. However, as with racial prejudice, interviewees were unlikely to see competition with immigrants as a barrier in their efforts to find employment. Oneita, the twenty-four-year-old African American from South Central Los Angeles, described feeling somewhat uncomfortable applying for jobs in workplaces dominated by Spanish speakers. Here is how she responded when I asked her about recent job applications:

> The only one I gotta turn in now is for Auto Zone. I ain't even filled it out. Because the one I went to, it was like a gang[6] of Hispanics in there. I understand what they be sayin' but I can't talk. I be like lookin' at them, "Um, okay." When I came in, as soon as they saw me, they'd be like, "What?" "Over there." "What?" "Over there!" [indicating limited communication]. It seems like it's not mandatory that you know how to speak Spanish. It's that most of the customers that come to this spot right here are all Hispanics. I've been going back and forth past that Auto Zone store since I was like thirteen years old. My brother got killed in that parking lot. So that's how I know that many black people don't go through it. But I should apply. It's a job. I'll work there if I get an offer.

Oneita noted that the potential of being the lone African American working at the store would not keep her from pursuing the job but wondered how well it would work out over the long run. Her comment that her brother was killed in the parking lot highlights the extent of violence she was exposed to growing up in a high-poverty, high-crime neighborhood. Also, it is important to note that some immigrant interviewees, such as Peter, a thirty-one-year-old Asian Canadian, lacked documentation to work, denying them access to all but the most marginal forms of employment.

Although it is hard to assess the extent to which Los Angeles transitional housing users were affected by immigrant competition in their job searches, it is clearer that poor access to transportation limited their job searches. Many described difficulty accessing jobs spread throughout Los Angeles's sprawling metropolis away from the core downtown area where the program was located, despite it being a public transportation hub. For some, even when there were job interviews in locations accessible to them by public transportation, they were limited by their own low incomes and program practices for allocating bus tokens. Like nearly all Los Angeles interviewees, Rita, the forty-nine-year-old former administrative assistant, was completely reliant on the public transportation system to get to interviews and said it was difficult to access it. Not only did the public transportation system have limited capacity to traverse the sprawling labor market, many of those who found the system to be efficient for the immediate area could not afford it since most only had $55 per month in discretionary funds from their GR benefits. Those who did not sacrifice other needs to purchase a bus pass generally had to procure bus tokens from staff who had limited supply. Rita said, "You can't get any bus tokens from case managers. If you're a 'job search,' you get them from there. If you're not, then you have to find other programs around in the area to get them [from]. Before, you had a couple of options, you could get them from your case manager, you could get them from job developers, you could get them even from the clinic, they would give you some. And all those dried up now, you can't get them from anybody."

In addition to limited access to bus tokens, the job searches of Los Angeles interviewees were disrupted by a strike of Metropolitan Transit Authority bus drivers and mechanics during the time of my research. Peter, the thirty-one-year-old Asian Canadian, described its effects on his attempt to get work as a production assistant and paid audience participant across town in Hollywood: "The bus strike affected me big time. There was like a month where I couldn't get anywhere. I went to like a few jobs using the Dash Line. But the problem with that is that it stops running at six and the train stops running at eleven and I would have to walk back to the Metro Line. That was a long walk. I went a couple of times, but it was too much of a hassle trying to get back." Although the bus strike did not completely shut down the local public transportation system, for thirty-five days the already limited mobility and job searches of transitional housing users were further impaired.

Leveraging Human Capital

Whereas many of my interviewees in Los Angeles and Tokyo faced formidable human capital deficits, several of those who succeeded in finding work were able to leverage human capital by drawing on work experience or existing skills or gaining new skills through education and training. This differed in the two cities, with transitional housing users in Tokyo having less severe deficits, and thus more human capital resources on which to draw. Conversely, transitional housing users in Los Angeles had more time to invest in education and training. However, for some interviewees in both cities, their human capital deficits were severe enough to make the available investment strategies appear futile. In Los Angeles, Sinee, the fifty-one-year-old documented immigrant from Thailand with bipolar and anxiety disorders introduced in Chapter 2, while caught up in the SSI appeal process, participated actively in her job preparedness course, learning Microsoft Word and Excel. However, sometimes she would get confused discussing simple topics, suggesting she would face difficulty completing a job interview, let alone maintaining a full-time secretarial job. In Tokyo, Andō-san, the fifty-three-year-old former computer programmer, had numerous licenses to work in construction that he had accumulated in public training programs, and he participated in the cleaning training program while in emergency housing. But his complete lack of experience in construction, along with his age, program address, and what he felt were undiagnosed mental health issues, prevented him from leveraging these skills into a job.

Despite limited skills, age discrimination, stigmatized addresses, and a short time limit, a majority of my Tokyo interviewees found work, some through leveraging human capital that they already had prior to entering transitional housing. Higashi-san, the fifty-six-year-old carpenter from the southern prefecture of Kyūshū introduced in Chapter 1, was in this group. After receiving treatment in emergency housing for a severe cold he had caught on the street, Higashi-san moved into transitional housing and began searching earnestly for work. Highly outgoing and personable, Higashi-san knew many people around Ikebukuro (where his transitional housing program was located) that worked in the construction industry. One former coworker happened to walk by the outdoor seating area of a McDonald's where we were talking, and they exchanged greetings. Immediately afterward, he told me he felt he would lose face if he asked these old contacts for work as an unskilled laborer (*dokō*) since he had worked with them as a skilled carpenter (*shokunin*). He did not bother doing any training courses while in emergency housing since he already had a driver's license and certifications related to construction work (welder, electrician, and so forth).

Soon after his arrival in the transitional housing program, Higashi-san found an advertisement for construction work at the local public employment agency and had the employment counselor at the program arrange an interview. The young foreman who interviewed Higashi-san was impressed by his carpentry experience, which fit in perfectly with the company's ongoing internal renovation of a school dormitory. However, the company had a policy of only hiring workers in their thirties for full-time jobs.

> They had an advertisement at Hello Work under "interior construction," and I found it. The most important thing I learned at the transitional housing program was "If you want to find work, you need to search using an age at least five years younger than your own." I first looked using my age, fifty-six, and there was barely anything. Then I tried fifty, and the jobs came one after another. So I went for an interview. The boss (*shachō*) was young and when I told them I could do any kind of work, he said that he couldn't hire me as a full-time employee (*seishain*) but asked if I would work as a subcontractor. So I asked them to let me work for fourteen days. And I earned 278,000 yen [about $2,493]. That's about 20,000 yen [$179] per day. Well, it is the same work that I did in the past, so it was simple.

Together, Higashi-san's hard and soft skills helped him persuade his employer to take him on as a subcontractor rather than just turn him away at the interview.

When I visited his apartment several months later for a meal and drinks, he showed me the floor plans, contracts, and receipts for work he had done. Proud of how far he had come in one year after living on the streets, he downplayed his carpentry and business experience, as well as his networking skills, boasting, "Do you know why I got this far? My determination is twice as strong as [that of] the average person."

Others in Tokyo were able to find employment in areas that used skills bolstered in training courses while in emergency housing, although it was not clear they would not have got these jobs without the training. For example, there were a number of interviewees like Yamada-san, Ishikawa-san, Tsukada-san, and Nakamura-san who took a course that taught the basics of cleaning work (*seisō ginō kōshū*) and later took jobs in cleaning. But most of these interviewees downplayed the role of the training programs. Yamada-san, the fifty-five-year-old former contract factory worker from neighboring Chiba Prefecture, described how the training program helped him find work: "I'm using the skills I learned in training a bit. About 10 percent of it was useful. It's not really skills, it's much less than that, smaller things. Like, how to wring out a mop, you know, the kind you spin around? I learned how to do that—also, the different kinds of cleaners. That is about it. The rest of it will change from job to job so I don't know if I will use it." Like others who took the cleaning course, Yamada-san felt that the course did not so much provide him with valuable skills as with basic knowledge and the simulation of a workplace, helping him to prepare mentally to reenter the low-skill workforce. Some interviewees complained that the more-intensive training programs they wanted to pursue, such as a home helper certification course or a driver's license course, were too long, or there were simply not any slots open when they applied.

Although transitional housing users in Los Angeles had more human capital deficits, they did have more time (up to two years) to pursue opportunities to acquire skills and education. A few interviewees were able to take advantage of these opportunities to invest in human capital and were successful to varying degrees in using newly acquired skills to secure employment. For Michelle in the exit story above, her investment had yet to translate into clear financial gains, and she remained working and living at the margins of Los Angeles's labor and housing markets. Rita, the forty-nine-year-old African American former administrative assistant who had been laid off twice due to corporate mergers, was the Los Angeles interviewee who was best able to translate an investment in human capital into stable employment that paid a living wage. Once in the program she was eager to reenter the workforce and begin saving money to move into her own housing. Given that she had a degree from a vocational school, some community college course credit, experience in a corporate environment, and cultural capital from growing up primarily in a middle-class, predominantly white suburban neighborhood, she did not suffer from human capital deficits and stigmatized statuses to the same extent as many other Los Angeles transitional housing users. So, from early in her stay in the program, she was able to find more job opportunities. In her first months in the program, she was offered a live-in, twenty-four-hour on-call job at a local nonprofit SRO hotel. But the job paid only $14,000 annually and in the long term she wanted to move out of Skid Row, so she turned it down. Her case manager encouraged her to take her time finding the right job, and she was interested in courses in medical billing at a nearby trade school so she could make a transition into the growing field of health care administration. However, she got along so well with the instructor of her job preparedness class that she took more computer classes with her to brush up her Word and Excel skills and participated in job search activities.

The instructor, dispatched from the Los Angeles Unified School District, recognized Rita's skills and began mentoring her to apply for a job with the district. A unionized public-sector job appealed to Rita given her past experiences with corporate mergers. However, the job required first passing an aptitude test, submitting documents, and then applying to and interviewing for jobs at specific schools. Rita prepared hard for the test and passed but had a difficult time getting records from her high school since she had graduated over thirty years before. She finally submitted her transcripts and was given eligibility to apply for specific jobs with the district. With the advice from her teacher, she printed and sent out letters, and over almost eighteen months she interviewed at about a dozen schools. She turned down one job offer because she had a bad feeling about the safety of the school and the capability of the administration, and another offer because the school was about twenty miles away in Pacific Palisades.

When she could not find a job with the district that suited her, she faced pressure from job developers at the program to take a minimum-wage job at a coffee shop or in telemarketing. She took a temporary secretarial job that was supposed to be long term, but it only lasted one week. Then she interviewed again with the district, this time finding a job in their administrative office downtown, paying about $20,000 per year. But by then her time limit in the program was close to expiring and she had only a few hundred dollars in savings since her GR benefits were occasionally terminated. She had to move into a pay-by-the-day shelter, an SRO, and then another, much more strict transitional housing program. She endured commuting to work from the program (concealing brown bag lunches of bologna sandwiches marked with a large "32," her bed number) for five months to save money. She found a room in a four-bedroom house renting for $500 per month, with a $250 deposit, moving into her own apartment a few years later. Rita passed an exam to become a "senior office technician," increasing her income, but then changed jobs numerous times amid what she described as the school dis-trict's "budget-musical-chairs job dance." When we communicated in early 2014, she was still working for the school district and living in her apartment.

There were also two transitional housing users in Los Angeles who could be classified as "institutionally adapted" (Snow and Anderson 1993), given that they found work within the homeless services industry rather than the outside labor market. However, they could also be seen as securing returns on an investment in human capital since volunteering led to full-time employment. Sally, the thirty-six-year-old white woman from Long Beach introduced in Chapter 1, was ter-minated from transitional housing after a conflict with housekeeping staff about storage of her belongings. She checked into the mission across the street. While she was there she did workfare jobs for GR, about forty hours per month shred-ding paper at a health center, but her benefits were terminated multiple times for missed paperwork and meetings. After staying several months at the mis-sion, Sally began a formal program there in which she took courses on accessing benefits and housing, healthy relationships, and life skills. She also enrolled in a program called Dignity through Service in which she received an $850 monthly stipend for six months working in the shelter and a free medical clinic, mostly answering phones, escorting residents to classes, distributing bed tickets, and completing some basic medical billing. She developed a tight relationship with her case manager, who helped her secure a full-time, live-in position as a staff as-sistant at a program the mission opened in a suburban location for families and persons with disabilities. Although Sally was unable to break into the mainstream labor force, she was able to draw on her knowledge of homeless services and a volunteer-to-staff program to secure employment within the "homeless services archipelago" (Gowan 2010).

Also, influenced or at least reassured by some job developers' encourage-ment of transitional housing program users not to take minimum wage jobs that would render them susceptible to returns to homelessness, a substantial number of interviewees in Los Angeles tried to learn new skills on their own or pursue entrepreneurial endeavors. However, most of these efforts did not seem realistic and failed to pan out. For example, Peter, the thirty-one-year-old Asian Canadian who lacked documentation to work and access public benefits, spent most of his time at the Los Angeles Central Public Library self-learning computer programming and working on a screenplay. He hoped that he could find some fake paperwork so he could get hired to do simple computer repair to get out of homelessness. He also was holding on to his dream of selling his screenplay and using the revenues to fund his training to become a mixed martial arts fighter. Vernon, a forty-nine-year-old African American with roots in the South and Midwest, volunteered at a local promotion company and in Skid Row nonprofit

arts community activities in hope of eventually establishing his own promotion and management company. Evan, a thirty-eight-year-old African American
with schizophrenia, drew on his degree in economics from Howard University,
brief, entry-level work experience on Wall Street, and access to computers at nonprofit organizations in Skid Row to produce a single-page financial newsletter.
The newsletter included basic information on exchange rates and stocks, and
Evan made a halfhearted and futile attempt to obtain sponsors. Barry, the forty-
one-year-old white man from Rhode Island, had long worked day labor jobs
distributing flyers in residential areas but was trying to start his own business by
setting up a website to get distributing contracts directly from businesses who
needed advertisements and coupons distributed. Even though all of these transitional housing users in Los Angeles were dedicated to these activities, none of
these investments in human capital and entrepreneurial efforts translated into
employment or substantial income. These efforts could be seen as unsuccessful strategic labor market withdrawal, a last-ditch effort to exit homelessness
through work in an environment full of barriers to employment such as human
capital deficits, stigmatized statuses, limited transportation, immigrant competition, and a labor market offering few opportunities for stability.

Job Leads from Program Peers Rather Than Staff

Although some transitional housing users received useful advice from employment specialists in the programs, in both Los Angeles and Tokyo many of my
interviewees stated that these staff persons were not able to provide leads on
jobs of which they were not already aware. Commenting on the "job developer"[7]
she was working with, Rita, the forty-nine-year-old administrative assistant, said,
"I like Francisco but I don't think I'm getting any help because everything that
they're suggesting I can do on my own. I can get jobs from CalJOBS [a job-
search website of the California Employment Development Department], you
know." Despite having the title of job developer, many of these staff persons in
Los Angeles would just recommend jobs to clients that were advertised on the
state employment website, which program participants were already checking on
their own. In Tokyo, transitional housing users looked for work at local public
employment agencies, the same agencies that dispatched employment consultation staff (*shūrō sōdan-in*) to the programs. As in Los Angeles, the employment
specialists generally did not provide job leads beyond those to which program
participants already had access. Ishimura-san, a thirty-seven-year-old former
hostess club staffer, said, "Staff doesn't really help us with our job search. Staff
just calls you in to see if you are doing it or not. It's more like, 'You can't do this or

that. You can't take a job lead from a friend.'" According to Ishimura-san, rather than providing specific job leads, the main function of the employment special-ists was ensuring that program participants were searching for what the program defined as valid employment. In staff interviews in Tokyo, many claimed that they discouraged program participants from sharing job referrals because if one caused problems at work others could be fired, and with multiple applicants with the same address, it would be easier for employers to discriminate based on residence in the program.

However, it was not unusual for my Tokyo interviewees to share information on jobs and even obtain work through leads from acquaintances in the program. Kitajima-san, a fifty-four-year-old former sushi chef from the city of Sendai north of Tokyo, took a job on a tip from a fellow program participant. Realizing that his prospects in restaurant work were dismal because of his age, he decided to look for work in cleaning and security at the local employment agency, receiv-ing minimal assistance from the job search counselors at the program. Another man in the program that he had gotten to know told him that the construction site security guard (*gādoman*) dispatch company he was working for was hiring. Kitajima-san applied to the company, which sent around 450 employees to large construction firms throughout Tokyo. He took the job and worked five to six days per week, paid weekly according to the number of days worked. With some overtime, he earned about 250,000 yen ($2,242) per month. His employer once commented on the fact that he and two other employees shared the same address, but Kitajima-san felt that the employer did not think much of it. The man who recommended the company to Kitajima-san quit suddenly for a higher paying job at Expo 2005, the world's fair held near Nagoya in Aichi Prefecture. Despite the fears of staff, this had no impact on Kitajima-san's employment. He was able to save 100,000 yen (about $897) and with an additional 100,000 yen in aid from the program, moved into a six *tatami* mat (about nine by twelve feet) apartment with a shared toilet, a coin laundry next door, and a public bath about one hun-dred meters away, using a local nonprofit organization as his guarantor. His rent was 35,000 yen per month (about $315).

In Los Angeles, however, job leads from other transitional housing users more often led to extremely precarious and low-paying employment at the very fringes of Los Angeles's labor market. David, a thirty-five-year-old from Mexico with American citizenship, worked thirty-five hours per week as a telemarketer but only earned about $200 every other week, unable to bring in commission. The in-come helped him stay in a pay-by-the-day SRO when he was terminated from the program, but he was eventually fired for lack of productivity. Frustrated with his lack of success in Los Angeles and becoming increasingly emotionally distressed, he used what little money he had to buy a Greyhound ticket to New York where he stayed in an emergency shelter. Marcos, the forty-eight-year-old Puerto Rican who faced the catch-22 of a felony record and a parole requirement of full-time employment, learned about a telemarketing job by word of mouth from another program participant. The job was in the distant suburb of Riverside, but that was exactly where Marcos was planning to soon move with the financial help of his family. Under an immediate deadline from his parole officer, he quickly took the job, in which he cold-called people and tried to set up appointments for a promotional event selling time-shares. It paid $8 per hour, but his earnings could increase if his appointments actually showed up. At first, Marcos was confident in his ability to make the job work: "To tell you the truth, I could make anywhere between $500 to $600 in a week, eventually. Because I'm a hustler. I'm gonna be working hard to get the money. I know I can make the money there. It's just to comply with my parole, I have to work forty hours. Being that I'm gonna produce, they are gonna have me work forty hours." His family loaned him money to rent an apartment and purchase a car, but the job did not provide him with long-term stability. About a half year later, he was in an accident without insurance; his car was impounded, and he was saddled with hundreds of dollars in fines. He was still working the telemarketing job, but only twenty-five or thirty hours per week, and he had yet to hit the target that would increase his wage and give him commission. So he took on another telemarketing job that paid $7 per hour but quit after a few weeks when it did not pay enough to cover his gas. He was trying to find more lucrative and stable work, but his felony record prevented him from finding anything in accounting, sales, or collections. His monthly income from telemarketing varied but never exceeded $650 per month, leaving him still dependent on his family and a live-in girlfriend who was receiving CalWORKs benefits.

Despite myriad barriers, some interviewees in both cities were able to find employment. However, outside of the rare cases like Rita and Higashi-san who were able to draw on human capital to secure relatively well paying work, most of my interviewees who found employment worked in low-skill, low-wage, and precarious service-sector employment. For those in Los Angeles, this barely allowed them to purchase minimal housing on the rental market, and even after exiting homelessness, many remained vulnerable to falling back into the predicament. Interviewees in Tokyo were better able to find affordable housing, but their job conditions were often still unstable. This highlights the expanded precariousness of labor markets in globalized cities like Los Angeles and Tokyo. In both cities, some interviewees benefited from opportunities to train to learn new skills, but these programs often did not lead directly to jobs and sometimes were inaccessible because of limited time, transportation, and an immediate need for income.

Although the medicalization of homelessness has obscured the role of the labor market in producing and potentially ameliorating homelessness, my findings show that training and educational programs could be useful if they address these barriers. Also, my findings show the need for more skilled job developers, those who network to find new job leads they can share with program participants who already have access to job leads through mainstream channels, such as public employment agencies.

But the specific barriers, strategies, work, and housing procured differed greatly between the two cities, highlighting the uneven nature of globalization and the persistent importance of local structural conditions. Whereas twelve of seventeen transitional housing users in Tokyo earned at least the equivalent of a monthly income (122,120 yen or $1,095) by working at minimum wage for forty hours per week for two months prior to leaving the program, only one of seventeen transitional housing users in Los Angeles (where the comparable monthly income was $1,161) was able to do the same. Los Angeles's labor and housing market has polarized to the point where it was nearly impossible to exit homelessness to rental housing through income from employment. As I argued in Chapter 2, higher unemployment and income inequality in Los Angeles are influenced by the mix of the U.S. liberal welfare regime's deregulated and racialized labor markets and processes of globalization such as increased competition from immigrant workers. There were very few transitional housing users in Los Angeles with enough income even to begin looking for housing on the rental market, and the few who did either had to depend on friends or relatives for help or ended up in very marginal forms of housing. The lack of affordable housing is the result of a mix of rising income inequality, high migration, speculation in the real estate industry, and insufficient production of low-rent housing. The difficulties of navigating the labor market were exacerbated by the human capital deficits of mental health problems, especially substance abuse, and the taint of criminal records among transitional housing users in Los Angeles. These limitations themselves should be seen as a product of U.S.-style structural inequality, since the crack cocaine epidemic, the punitive response to rising social insecurity, and cuts to social services for the mentally ill have most negatively impacted predominantly poor black and Latino neighborhoods in Los Angeles and other U.S. cities. Thus, none of my interviewees in Los Angeles were able to follow the straightforward process of finding employment, saving income from employment, and purchasing housing on the rental market. Some even strategically withdrew from the labor market to address health issues or invest in human capital, with some developing far-fetched entrepreneurial plans amid dismal conditions in the wage labor market. These last efforts were bolstered by staff encouragement to avoid minimum wage employment since it would not lead to durable exits out of homelessness. These "rags-to-riches" entrepreneurial dreams could also be seen as reflecting the U.S. welfare regime's emphasis on rugged individualism and the Los Angeles urban regime's entrepreneurial stance, both of which de-emphasize state responsibility for aiding poor and vulnerable populations.

In contrast, a substantial number of my interviewees in Tokyo were able to use earnings from the low-skill labor market to purchase simple housing, a pathway encouraged by the transitional programs' rigid and lean approach to aid. Japan's welfare regime places primacy on male breadwinners, props up employment through "work-mediated welfare," and generally uses very lean social spending. Also, Tokyo is less of a magnet for foreign workers; thus its labor and housing markets face less pressure than those in Los Angeles. Transitional housing users in Tokyo faced the barriers of age discrimination, stigma of program addresses, and limited time to find work, but they still found work much more readily than Los Angeles transitional housing users. Also, rents in Tokyo found by interviewees were generally lower (median rent of about $375) than those found by the very few in Los Angeles who were able to rent (median rent of about $550). Apartments in Tokyo were very small and simple, some requiring use of a public bath, but unlike Michelle's apartment they were in buildings that were not neglected. Although they benefited from more forgiving labor and housing markets, most Tokyo transitional housing users worked in very precarious jobs that left them vulnerable to unemployment and subsequent returns to homelessness.

Amid such precarious market conditions and limited aid from the state, as shown in Chapter 2, what other resources can transitional housing users draw on to escape homelessness? In the following part of this book, I explore how social resources were accessed to different extents in the two cities to counteract or exacerbate the uncertainty of market conditions and state welfare in efforts to exit homelessness.

Part III

EXITING HOMELESSNESS IN LOS ANGELES AND TOKYO

Social Ties

Exit Stories: Venetia and Sawa-san

Venetia

Venetia Cheatham, an African American woman from Inglewood, first experienced street homelessness at age fifteen: "My mother died when I was twelve years old. My father at that time, he would drink. He used to beat on my mother all the time, you know? So I felt like an unwanted person because he used to beat on me, too. When I was fifteen, he remarried. My stepmother used to beat on me, me mostly. It was me and my brother, and she had two kids. One day she went to hit me with a belt. I grabbed the belt out her hand and told her, 'If you hit me again, I'm gonna hit you back.' But I ran away. I stayed gone. I ended up pregnant. They had an APB [all-points bulletin] out on me because I stayed gone for a year. They couldn't find me. So I ended up in juvenile hall and then a foster home." In foster care she earned a GED and began working part-time. She moved back in with her father and worked first as a file clerk at the Los Angeles County Department of Water and Power. But she wanted to follow in her mother's footsteps as a registered nurse, so she worked at a doctor's office without pay for the experience. She was later able to get a job as a medical assistant at the County Medical Center and by her late twenties was raising two children and living in an apartment.

However, her dabbling in marijuana, pills, and cocaine on weekends progressed into a more regular crack cocaine habit when the cheap and addictive drug became popular in her neighborhood. This began almost two decades of hardcore crack addiction and precarious housing during which she sent her children to live with their paternal grandparents. Venetia did what she needed to survive and lived "pillar to post"—staying in and around dingy MacArthur Park, motels, shelters, jail, prison, with men who were also addicts, and with family or friends. In 2002, at the age of forty-nine, she "got tired" of addiction and the harshness of street life. As she had done a few times before, she checked herself into a detoxification program in Skid Row. But this time she felt confident that she was going to beat her addiction. She was not just physically tired. Venetia said, "I was tired of me. I was tired of who I'd become—someone who would manipulate others and do almost anything to feed my addiction."

After detox, Venetia moved into transitional housing, where she bonded with her case manager, Margaret, a white woman in her thirties. One day as we sat on cold plastic chairs in a dimly lit, drab room in the program facility, Venetia said:

> When I got here, I met Margaret. I was in my room one day and for some reason—I don't know what was wrong with me—I woke up cryin', scared to death. I ran downstairs because I felt I needed to talk real quick. She told me to come in and sit down. And I just broke out crying and I told her, "I don't feel right. I'm scared." There was crack cocaine pulling me this way and me wantin' to do the right thing by going this way. I call it being fooled by the devil. Temptation, temptation was on me. I had to fight if I really wanted to stay clean. While I'm cryin' and talkin', Margaret is on the computer, on the phone. She sent me to mental health treatment because I needed help. She knows what she is doing. And she's never been there before but for some reason she can relate to us.

Despite coming from a different social background, Margaret's willingness to listen and sympathize, as well as her professional skill in identifying and accessing appropriate services, earned Venetia's trust and helped her avoid a relapse.

After about eleven months in transitional housing, Venetia moved into an apartment in a high-poverty South Central Los Angeles neighborhood managed by someone she had met at her weekly Cocaine Anonymous meetings. She was awarded a Section 8 voucher after over a year on a special waiting list for people experiencing homelessness, so her apartment was subsidized. Still, she paid $150 of her $221 in monthly GR benefits for rent. She also received about $200 per month in food stamps but she scraped by, sometimes selling bar candy out of a cardboard box when visiting the transitional housing program in Skid Row. At this time, Venetia felt her job prospects to be dismal and sought out a higher and more stable income by applying for SSI benefits. While addicted, she had been shot in the face, beaten into a coma with a baseball bat, hit by a car, stabbed, raped, and regularly beaten by a long-time boyfriend. This left her without sight in her left eye and without a kidney. She also had arthritis, leg pain, and was diagnosed with bipolar disorder in addition to her substance abuse disorder. Despite these numerous documented ailments, her application for SSI was rejected four times. When I asked her why she was rejected, Venetia stoically replied, "They do that. As long as they can, they will."

Fortunately, she heard about a lawyer who helped her friend get SSI benefits. This lawyer, a former judge who once ruled on SSI appeals, took Venetia's case, and her appeals were finally approved more than a year later. Her health and disabilities had not changed, but the lawyer was able to navigate the appeals process. Venetia was awarded approximately $10,000 in "back pay" for the benefits she was denied, but one-fourth went to the lawyer for compensation, and the county was also reimbursed for the GR benefits that they had paid during the same time period. Still, for Venetia, the SSI benefits were "big money" because of a higher monthly allocation ($560) and, unlike GR, no time limit. When I visited her small one-bedroom apartment behind a duplex in South Central, Venetia brought out the approval letter from the Social Security Administration. We sat down to talk at her small kitchen table, and she welled up with tears saying, "I bought me a big ol' steak, Matt. And I'm not even a big meat eater." She was relieved and exhilarated that she was going to have more stability and proud of how far she had come. By chance she had reunited with her daughter at the program and was hoping that some tough love and nurturing would help her daughter kick her own drug addiction.

A few months later, Venetia moved with an old boyfriend, also a recovering addict, into an apartment in the same neighborhood, with both of them on the Section 8 contract. He was using crack behind her back, sometimes becoming physically and emotionally abusive. When reflecting on this time, she felt that she was in denial, or that deep-seated self-esteem issues made her feel she did not deserve any better. One day he did not turn up to a Cocaine Anonymous meeting, and she rushed home to find him smoking crack in their bathroom. He taunted her by blowing crack smoke in her face and she relapsed to temporarily escape the turmoil. Amid an argument a few weeks later, he punched her in the face and threw her up against a metal bed rail, and Venetia had to be hospitalized. This time she had had enough. She called the police multiple times, had him arrested, and he served a month in jail. The police officer who responded to her call found that Venetia had multiple warrants, mostly for unpaid jaywalking tickets. However, Venetia pleaded that she was going back to transitional housing to focus on her recovery. She called Robert, a former case manager, and when she told the officer that there was an opening, he told her to go to the program.

She hid her relapse from SSI administrators, feeling that they would terminate her benefits, but moved out of her subsidized apartment and back into transitional housing. Venetia persisted in her recovery, helped by steady emotional support from Robert, an African American from South Central Los Angeles who was about her age. In addition to providing emotional support, he helped her get warrants cleared through a "homeless court" on Skid Row that dismisses minor offenses of people in programs. Serena, her job preparedness instructor, required Venetia to volunteer at a nearby drop-in center that provided short-term beds and helped people access services. Venetia threw herself into the work and earned a job starting at $10.30 per hour, forty hours per week, that even provided medical and dental insurance, allowing her to move off of SSI benefits. She started dating a parking attendant ten years her senior, a recovering addict of eight years whom she met at a weekly karaoke event at the Central City Community Church of the Nazarene in Skid Row. Within a year they married in front of family, friends, and transitional program staff at a small South Central church and moved into a modest apartment subsidized through Section 8. As of nine years later, in 2014, they were still happily living together. They purchased a four-bedroom home in Watts with help from HUD's Family Self-Sufficiency program. Venetia was focused on taking courses at Southwest College to earn a certificate

Venetia outside her home in Watts with her new car

in drug and alcohol counseling in hopes of moving into case management at the drop-in center, although she had already been promoted to shift leader. Venetia was still trying to help her daughter overcome her addiction and had initiated the process to get custody of her grandson.

Sawa-san

Sawa-san, originally from a rural area in Kyoto Prefecture, was fifty-seven years old when he entered transitional housing. As a young man, he moved to the northern prefecture of Iwate to join Japan's Self-Defense Forces (SDF). He worked as a cook for the SDF, married a local woman, and had two children. When his daughters were still young, his wife convinced him to be a guarantor on a loan for a family friend. When the friend went delinquent on the loan, it became Sawa-san's responsibility. He took the case to court, but it was decided that he was responsible as the guarantor. He sought help from his oldest brother in Osaka, but his brother's wife objected to getting involved. So, he resigned his duties with the SDF and used his severance pay to cover most of the amount due. As we stood and talked one day on a narrow San'ya Street, Sawa-san said, "Because of that, my wife and I were like this [crossing his index fingers, making an "X" and indicating conflict]. It became uncomfortable for both of us. Then, it was bad for my kids, but that is how it went. I had no other choice, so I came to Tokyo." Consistent with the tendency for fathers in Japan to leave all rearing responsibility to mothers after separation, Sawa-san felt his only choice was to fend for himself in Tokyo.

Like many migrants coming from the north to look for work in Tokyo, he arrived at Ueno Station on Tokyo's east side. With nowhere to stay, he lay down for some rest on a park bench, only to have his bag holding most of his savings stolen. But he met someone in the park who offered him part-time, pay-by-the-day work separating packages at Nippon Express (Nittsū), the shipping company. After a while, he began staying in Tokyo Station, where he lived for about seven years while holding the part-time job. We would meet and talk often during this time, since we were both regular volunteers at Sanyūkai, a free medical clinic in San'ya. Eventually, a severe leg rash and encouragement from a street outreach volunteer prompted him to give transitional housing (*jiritsu shien sentā*) a try.

As required, he first entered emergency housing to get treatment for his leg. He stayed there for almost three months because transitional housing was full, but he was thankful to have more time to heal and to take training courses in cleaning and computers. In his two months in transitional housing he went on three interviews, two in cleaning and one for a job as a live-in cook, but he did not receive any offers. When a friend from the program was going to a legal office to get help with debt, Sawa-san tagged along thinking he could get some help for his own debt as well. He learned that his debt was cleared because it had been over ten years since the money was borrowed, and he had no ability to pay. But he was still unsuccessful in finding work. When the legal aid office staff learned he would soon be timing out of transitional housing and likely heading back to live in Tokyo Station, they took him to the welfare office to advocate on his behalf.

> So there is a lawyer and a paralegal at the legal aid office, Endō-san and Kusano-san. The paralegal, Kusano-san, came with me and talked to my caseworker. At first the caseworker said it was too late in the afternoon [to process an application] but then when Kusano-san came, it went smoothly. At first they fought about *seikatsu hogo* but then *sensei*[1] [the paralegal], he didn't say anything about suing them, but he put some pressure on them and they changed their tone. Then, we all three met, and I said clearly that I would work as a condition to get on welfare. *Sensei* pleaded more, and then they put me in the flophouse (*doya*), and I got on *seikatsu hogo*.
>
> [MM: Do you know why they did not put you on *seikatsu hogo* from the beginning?]
>
> For example, if I went there alone, I would be "turned away at the gate (*monzenbarai*)," to put it bluntly. They won't listen to you (*aite shite kurenai*). And, then there is my age. I'm fifty-eight now. Normally you can't get *seikatsu hogo* until you are sixty-five. If you are really ill, then it's another story. I'm still healthy and young. So, in reality, I shouldn't be on it. If I went on my own, they would not have put me on. But by chance I met the *sensei*, and he helped me out. I think I'm lucky.

Although he never attempted to obtain *seikatsu hogo* on his own, Sawa-san believed that he would have been turned away without the paralegal's advocacy on his behalf. The caseworker was initially resistant but finally relented when the three sat down and Sawa-san promised that he would not sit idle on benefits but would look for work. Sawa-san was put in an SRO in San'ya and began receiving benefits. He shared a three *tatami*-mat (about fifty-four square feet) room with a man in his seventies, with two beds and a little room for a television. He did not feel comfortable using his roommate's TV, so Sawa-san sometimes would watch in the small air-conditioned lobby between 4 and 11 p.m. He said that since he was on welfare, he should not be drinking, but he and other residents would sometimes drink together discreetly, chatting and sharing simple snacks like *edamame*. His leg still bothered him, so he received treatment at the free medical clinic where we had volunteered, just steps away from his *doya*.

However, even after exiting homelessness, he never reached the point of contacting his family. When I asked why, he said, "It's the countryside (*inaka*), right? It is in the north [Tōhoku]. They probably would say, 'Don't come to us with that [a request for help or contact after several years]!' So I don't call. Of course I can't go back there. There would be all sorts of complaints. So absolutely under no circumstances will I call them." He also had no contact with his three brothers or his parents since leaving for Tokyo. He bumped into an old friend of his wife who had come to Tokyo to look for work and learned that his mother had died a few years after he left Iwate. He knew that his eldest brother was living in Osaka, and another brother was in Ishikawa Prefecture near Kyōto, but he did not know the whereabouts of his younger brother.

> I'm completely cut off (*zetsuen*) from my brothers. So there is nothing for me there. But it's not like I want to see them, either. My older brother, since he married, it is like I am a stranger. Of course, that's only natural, but then I can't really say anything to him. If I get in the middle of things, it is not good for his wife. It's been almost ten years. I caused him some problems too in the past, so it is hard for me to call him. I know he is in Osaka, but if I went there, I would be turned away immediately (*monzenbarai*). So, I don't call at all. It is probably better that way anyway. It's like that for my wife, too. But, if I called, I don't know if my kids would answer. They probably know that I am in Tokyo but don't know exactly where I am. If I am here in Tokyo, at least there is some work, but in the country there is no work. In the past there was but now there isn't so everyone comes here for work. I've screwed up once before and I am not going to do it again. But, being here [at the free medical clinic], there are a lot of young people that come here to volunteer, right? Basically, I speak to them in the same way I would my daughters.

Sawa-san felt that it was better to live independently than to get mixed up in the messy relationships that he had fled before. In invoking the cultural frames of *zetsuen* (complete separation) and *monzenbarai* (literally, being turned away at the gates), he spoke as if his brother had completely cut him off because of the problems he brought them when he was trying to deal with the debt he had taken on for his wife's friend. Fortunately for Sawa-san, he had developed relationships with a number of staff and volunteers at relief NPOs outside of the transitional housing program that served as a temporary surrogate family. These ties provided crucial aid in exiting homelessness and avoiding a return, helping him procure welfare benefits as he rehabilitated and began looking for work.

A few months later, by chance Sawa-san bumped into his old boss from Nippon Express in the 7-Eleven at the Namidabashi intersection in San'ya and was asked if he wanted to work his old job separating boxes. Sawa-san said, "I thought, 'I promised the guy at the welfare office, right?' He said, 'If you don't work, I'm going to cut you off.' That was a condition from the beginning. I couldn't start in April so I told them clearly that I could start in May. Now I turn in my receipts for work to the welfare office. So you never know who you are going to meet and where, but right now I am blessed by good people. That is what I feel. Right now, my work is going well. I have friends here. If anything happens or I need to consult on anything, *sensei* said I can call him whenever. So, now things are great for me." He had paid into the national pension system (*kōsei nenkin*) for about twenty years while working as a cook for the SDF, so when he turned sixty in two years, he planned to start receiving payments early at a reduced rate and maybe move into an apartment.

While Sawa-san was living in cramped conditions in a stigmatized neighborhood, he felt much better than when living in Tokyo Station.

> You can tell the color of my face is different now, right? It's better than before. Everything I have now is because of everyone's help. I am one of the more blessed. Up until now, I've been sleeping like this [motions to ground], putting a piece of cardboard down. It's okay in summer, but winter is cold. The ground is cold. I was inside the station, right?

Sawa-san outside of Sanyūkai, the free medical clinic at which he volunteers

It's concrete, right? That gets chilly. No matter how many layers you wear and how bundled up you get, you can't sleep because it's too cold. So you walk 'round and 'round the streets for that time. You don't get enough sleep. Then you have to go to work. Of course, I did my job. Then, it's so cold, you can't even feel the effects of alcohol. No matter how much you drink, you can't feel it. You don't get drunk. Now, I can totally relax without worry, by myself, for example, because I have a room. Psychologically, it's different. Physically, it's different, the fatigue. Over there [at the station], if you lie down too early, then the JR [Japan Railways] staff is going to get mad at you. Then they'll get mad if you have your stuff all spread out. Now, when I've finished work, I just go home. As long as I am there before the curfew, the manager will not say anything. Maybe I have it a little too easy. My work is going well. It's like "the moon and a turtle" (*tsuki to suppon*) [a phrase meaning "black and white"]. I'm very thankful to my boss at work, and my friends here [at the clinic]. They are all good people.

TIES WITH ORGANIZATIONAL STAFF

The experiences of Venetia and Sawa-san underscore the impactful role of staff in transitional housing and other programs designed to help people experiencing homelessness secure employment, welfare benefits, and housing. This role has been demonstrated in research where program staff are portrayed in their interactions with program participants alternatively as benevolent saviors whose actions are critical in successful efforts to exit homelessness and cold, power-wielding nemeses who ultimately prevent people from improving their situation.[1] Similarly, in my fieldwork in Los Angeles and Tokyo, I have found support for both perspectives—good, trustful relationships with program staff can combine with other factors to help people out of homelessness, and poor, distrustful relationships with program staff can combine with other factors to prevent people from exiting homelessness. However, there has not been a balanced examination of what causes these relationships to take on a helpful or harmful nature. Part of this imbalance is due to the general lack of comparison between housing programs with substantial differences in structure, philosophy, and practices, and how they either promote or discourage facilitative relationships between program users and staff.[2]

This chapter focuses on the organizational level of analysis to understand how characteristics of transitional housing programs can affect the amount of trust that clients place in them and their staff, and thus to understand the potential of staff-client relationships to mobilize a variety of resources. I use data from transitional housing program staff and client interviews to describe the specific organizational contexts that influence whether relationships between staff and clients take on a facilitative nature. I interviewed staff persons in the transitional housing programs (eight in Los Angeles and fifteen in Tokyo)[3] who interacted with and attempted to aid my program client interviewees. In both cities, my staff interviewees covered direct-service roles including intake, case management, employment assistance, and housing placement, as well as program development and management. Many of my interviewees in Los Angeles, as reflected in the stories throughout this book, developed positive relationships with transitional housing program case managers that were crucial in their exits from homelessness, but this was less common among my Tokyo respondents. Staff helped program users access material and instrumental resources, such as clothing, health (including dental and mental health) care, legal assistance, and basic assistance in securing employment to similar extents in the two cities, but staff in the Los Angeles program more often provided *affective* resources. These included critical emotional support, encouragement, and facilitation of normative change such as learning how to manage and save money, dress appropriately for employment and for maintaining self-esteem, set long-term goals, and avoid arguments and violence. Certainly there were cases that defied this pattern in both cities. In Los Angeles, college-educated David's repeated clashes with a job preparedness instructor and his case manager over a required mock-interview contributed to his termination from the program and a downward move to emergency shelters. Higashi-san, the highly sociable and skilled carpenter in Tokyo, said that staff greeting him with "*Itte irasshai!*" (Have a good day!) and "*Okaerinasai!*" (Welcome home!), as well as asking about his day at work, made him feel like he had a family and motivated him to succeed in renting an apartment. Thus, specific organizational characteristics can promote or deter trusting and beneficial staff-client relationships, but certainly not determine them.

In this chapter I use the concept of *organizational culture* (predominant rules, norms, understandings, frames, scripts, and practices within an organization), rather than national culture, to understand the source of these differences (Hallet 2003; Schein 1992). I show that the organizational culture of the Los Angeles program, compared to that of Tokyo programs, was characterized by a higher prevalence of three key principles of care: holism, flexibility, and homophily, or social similarity. Rules, norms, understandings, and practices imbued with holism, flexibility, and homophily tend to promote staff-client trust. In social capital research, trust is seen as the lifeblood of social ties (Smith 2005, 2007). Simply knowing someone is not sufficient for social ties to mobilize resources, but trust is generally necessary for social ties to be activated. I extend this understanding to "organizational ties" (Small 2009b; Small, Jacobs, and Massengill 2008), or the relationships between people and organizations and their staff. Organizational ties have become a growing focus of research on urban poverty, which highlights how these ties with bureaucratic organizations have become increasingly important in urban society, especially when one finds that ties with family, friends, and neighbors are unable to help them endure or escape poverty (Marwell 2007; McQuarrie and Marwell 2009).

However, given my focus on how social contexts at multiple levels affect the process of exiting homelessness, I also examine how extraorganizational social conditions shape the different organizational cultures in Los Angeles and Tokyo. Organizational cultures are hardly immune from the influence of social conditions beyond their walls, being shaped but not determined by broader *welfare regimes* and *urban regimes*, especially key funding and administrative bodies. National and local governmental bodies responsible for distributing funds to transitional housing programs in Los Angeles allowed a more extensive scope of aid to be provided and encouraged more linkages with other relief organizations, thus promoting a more trust-building organizational culture in comparison with their counterparts in Tokyo. My broader fieldwork in the two cities, including persons using additional programs, supports my claim that differences in the mobilization of resources among transitional housing users are due to organizational factors rather than merely national cultural differences. For example, Tokyo respondents such as Sawa-san described, and I have observed, programs operated by private NPOs largely outside the influence of the Tokyo Metropolitan Government that had organizational cultures and mobilized resources similarly to the Los Angeles program I studied. Also, Los Angeles respondents described, and I have observed, NPO programs there that had organizational cultures and problems with trust similar to the transitional programs in Tokyo. This could be seen in Rita's story in Chapter 3 where she commuted from a highly disciplinary program to her job with the school district. Whereas she had abundant beneficial relationships with staff at the transitional housing program, at the other program she had no such organizational ties. This also shows that welfare regimes, urban regimes, and organizational cultures are "loosely coupled," thus influencing but not determining organizational ties.

Organizational Culture and Trust in Los Angeles and Tokyo Transitional Housing Programs

Holism

The holism principle is rooted in staff demonstration of a broad, social understanding of the causes of poverty and homelessness, with limited emphasis on purely individual causes, thus rendering appropriate a variety of forms of aid. Counter to this understanding, many staff in both cities widely described clients as possessing myriad individual moral and behavioral deficiencies, especially a lack of desire to obtain conventional employment and housing. Staff described barriers to employment primarily as the result of deficits in human capital such as education, job skills, and employment history, as well as low aspirations. However, the assumption that participants' problems were based on their own individual failings was noticeably more pervasive, extreme, and absolute among staff at the Tokyo programs. A Tokyo housing specialist dispatched from a local realtor to one of the transitional housing programs observed the following about clients:

> Of course, in every country there are issues with finding work when you are old or in a bad economy, but speaking truthfully there are a lot of people here who are in their twenties and thirties. If you buy an *Arubaito Nyūsu* [a magazine for part-time job seekers] for 100 yen, there is plenty of work. There are plenty of job openings. But the reason they aren't working has got to be part of the individual, that is a big part. That is my impression here. In international terms, I don't think Japan is a country with a high unemployment rate or anything like that. So really, if someone has the desire, they will absolutely achieve self-reliance [work and an apartment] here. With all that we do for them, they should achieve self-reliance. But, even when we are kicking their asses and forcing them to get self-reliant, only 30 percent or so do, right? So the success rate is very low. This means that most people do not have the desire to be self-reliant. So, to tell you the truth, we need brainwash education here, something like Aum [the cult responsible for the 1997 sarin gas incident in a Tokyo subway] would be fine—when they were told to spread the gas around, people did, right? You can brainwash people like that. I think we should have someone like that come in and brainwash residents, telling them "Stop loafing around!" You shouldn't bother with your research, you should come here and try to brainwash these people.

Although this housing specialist was rather extreme in his focus on individual moral flaws, his quote reflects the stronger tendency in the Tokyo programs to focus on individual-level problems. This contrasts with an approach that employs a "social imagination," highlighting social causes of poverty and removing blame from individuals for their situation as a way to gain program participant trust (Rowe 1999).

Statements by staff in Los Angeles did often point to clients' individual flaws, but they were tempered by somewhat higher levels of social imagination and holism. Whereas staff in both cities described clients' work orientations as flawed given a focus on quick cash from low-skill, short-term jobs, Los Angeles staff generally saw this as more than simply an individual moral flaw. A bilingual (English-Spanish) case manager stated, "I've had a couple of clients, maybe, where they make their working environment uncomfortable for themselves because they think, 'Oh, I've been discriminated against all my life, and I've been knocked on.' I say, 'Well, why is that you see things in that way?' And then you realize that they've had history of their parents telling them that they're a certain way, and that they're believing it subconsciously. And then it just runs with them their whole life. And that's when, you know, counseling is really imperative, I think, to the client." Like this case manager, Los Angeles staff tended to point to impoverished and challenging family backgrounds and traumatic experiences such as rape, domestic violence, and betrayal as producing normative and behavioral issues such as substance abuse and low employment aspirations. In contrast to the bombastic suggestion to turn to brainwashing by the Tokyo housing specialist, this Los Angeles staff person said she usually makes references to professional counseling to help clients deal with issues that could have resulted from coming from a disadvantaged background.

Because staff in both cities viewed clients as individually flawed, they also tended to feel that clients were trying to manipulate the program for its material resources. Staff in both cities described sharing information and monitoring clients to prevent manipulation of resources and to promote cognitive and behavioral change, a form of "network closure," for the purported benefit of the client. Information about specific clients was shared through centralized databases, formal meetings, and informal exchanges. In Tokyo, this monitoring took a strong disciplinary tone by seeking out and punishing transgressions. Regarding persons apparently lagging in their job searches, a Tokyo frontline caseworker stated:

> I ask what they have been doing. If it is a proper reason [being sick, and so forth], then nothing can be done. In those cases we already have the necessary information to verify. Other than that, it has to be the participant's dependence on the program. In those cases, I tell them sternly, "If you have no desire to work then you can pack your bags and leave." Then I check what employment consultation they have done to see if they have been introduced to jobs and if they have missed opportunities. If they are looking but not finding appropriate jobs, I suggest changes like widening their occupational choices or lowering their minimum salary for which they are willing to work. Then I talk to them about any worries they have. After hearing their stories, if they are just slacking off, I let the thunder come down on them. I observe them

carefully. I look very closely at their faces when they come back from looking for work. Then I have them come sit down in the office and talk.

Given an intense emphasis on a lack of desire to work in the Tokyo programs, efforts to address individual problems were often manifested in regular and accusatory questioning. Other forms of monitoring included making clients keep a record of when they accomplished program tasks, checking how allowances were spent down to the last yen, contacting employers about attendance, and patrolling the facility, with one program utilizing video cameras.

In the Los Angeles program, monitoring took more of an evaluative form consistent with holism, emphasizing the identification of needs and referral to specialized services. The lead case manager of the Los Angeles program described how she addressed a problem client lagging in his job search. "He is almost going to be here for two years. When working with a client for so long, you get to know if there's some barrier there. So let's kind of determine what that is and, because I don't specialize in that area, I'll send 'em to a specialist, which is the clinical therapist on site. And then from there, I mean, they just become a different person because they're working on those issues. They say, 'I'm actually dealing with these issues. And it's making me feel better about myself. So I could get to point B, which is to employment.'" Although still focused on individual and oppositional behavior, this approach is less accusatory and disciplinary. Enabled by the two-year time limit of the Los Angeles program, this staff person helped clients identify and address the sources of some of their problems via professional mental health treatment, rather than simply scolding them. All case managers in Los Angeles reported frequently turning to an array of nearby organizations to refer clients with varying needs.

The experiences and interpretations of my client interviewees toward these differences in holism among staff understandings and practices contrasted sharply between the two cities. Although a few in Tokyo appreciated the regular monitoring as a demonstration of concern, more described it in negative terms. Murata-san, the fifty-three-year-old who was "restructured" after thirty years of working for Hitachi in the northern prefecture of Hokkaidō, felt distrusted because of the regular questioning by staff. Though he struggled to find work because of his age and the stigma of the program address on his applications, he eventually found a part-time cleaning job. Even so, his case manager continued to ask him about work, namely whether or not he would get more hours.

"There are some people who go to staff for help," Murata-san told me. "When I am called, I answer their questions, but that is about it. The other day a staff person came and said to me, 'You haven't been going to work very much. Do you think you will get more hours?' I told him that it looked like I would and he said, 'Okay, well then I guess we will see how things go.' So, they come at us with doubts like that, but there is nothing I go to them for help about. Well, he has his own position. He has to increase his numbers in terms of the percentage of clients working full-time. So, since we're in different positions, even if I wanted to go for help, I couldn't really." Murata-san eventually rented an apartment, but he generally avoided staff and exited homelessness without any help beyond the basic aid provided by the program. Although Tokyo staff may have intended to focus their efforts on participants who appeared to be lagging, their intense monitoring often extended to participants who were working and on track to move into a rental apartment, sometimes making them feel doubted by staff.

Although for Murata-san and others this monitoring eroded their trust of staff and prevented them from seeking aid, Nakamura-san experienced a more direct negative effect of this monitoring. A native of Tokyo and thirty-five when he entered the transitional housing program, he was trying to start a new life after a stint in prison, severing ties with *yakuza* (mafia), and bouts with depression and alcoholism. Given his youth, he found a cleaning job relatively quickly and was saving money and on track to move into an apartment. However, his case manager had become his adversary, often berating him for being in the program at such a young age as well as for his lack of job experience, repeatedly making him rewrite his resume during his job search, and meticulously monitoring his spending to ensure he did not buy alcohol.

Like most Japanese workplaces in December, Nakamura-san's employer had a small party to forget the troubles of the past year (*bōnenkai*). As is customary in such celebrations, they began with a group toast, and then coworkers took turns pouring each other small glasses of beer, thanking each other for their hard work. Happy about finally being part of a mainstream work environment, Nakamura-san actively participated in the event, drinking despite his attempt to recover from alcoholism and the transitional housing program's ban on drinking. Nakamura-san did not feel very drunk and thought that staff at the program would not smell any alcohol on him since he took a long walk back to the facility. However, his nemesis was close to the door when Nakamura-san returned and noticed that his face was reddened. His case manager quickly got in his face, smelled the alcohol on his breath, and reprimanded him. Nakamura-san exchanged harsh words with the staff person, using the rough and intimidating language he became fluent in while in organized crime. When Nakamura-san woke the next morning he was told to gather his things because he was being terminated for drinking. Luckily for Nakamura-san, his caseworker at the welfare office who initially referred him to the transitional program was able to find him short-term housing. Although he eventually moved into an apartment and exited homelessness, the close punitive monitoring by his case manager almost derailed his progress.

Though a few participants in Los Angeles also expressed distrust in reaction to staff monitoring, most described staff as sympathetic and helpful given their willingness to provide a variety of forms of aid to meet their needs. Like Venetia, Jill, the forty-nine-year-old woman from South Central Los Angeles recovering from a twenty-year crack cocaine addiction introduced in Chapter 1, formed a tight bond with her case manager, Margaret. She said, "You couldn't make a better case manager. Margaret is the bomb! She's Johnny-on-the-spot! She helps me, she always helps when something's wrong, and she asks me if anything is wrong, and what can she do, and what do I need. She gets involved with her clients. She has a personal rapport with each client." Jill's trust evolved over time as Margaret helped her identify problems she was grappling with and think about how to address them, with each interaction leading to more trust and aid. This included linking Jill with professional mental health care when she was in crisis after a breakup with a boyfriend and on the verge of a relapse. Subsequently, Jill described Margaret as teaching her how to manage her emotions, "how to be a lady," and how to listen before taking action—all skills Jill described as helping her avoid conflicts and progress smoothly through the program.

Sinee, the fifty-one-year-old immigrant from Thailand introduced in Chapter 2, who was suffering from bipolar and anxiety disorders, was supported by an array of community organizations in Skid Row. She was referred to many of them by her case manager at the transitional housing program. She had been working as a live-in caretaker for a disabled elderly woman and her infant grandchild but left the job thinking she could find less grueling work. After about three years of shuffling between emergency shelters throughout the county and sometimes sleeping in her car, she made her way into the transitional housing program. She had been married and divorced twice, and she had a child from a third relationship. Though she was in regular contact with her four children by phone, they were living far from downtown Los Angeles. Even though she was a bit worried about being terminated from the transitional housing program for rule infractions, she felt that the program staff there was much more helpful than the staff in the shelters. She looked for work, but given her mental health issues her prospects for employment were bleak. Also, the density of poverty and street violence in Skid Row made her anxious, exacerbating her poor mental health. So, her case manager, in addition to ensuring that she got proper treatment (counseling and medication) at a local mental health clinic, encouraged her to stay socially active and referred her to a variety of community organizations in Skid Row. In addition to completing the required job preparedness courses, she helped prepare meals at a local mission, participated in Bible study at another mission, went to church each Sunday, worked on her computer skills at a nearby school for adults, frequently visited a women's center where she would help clean the facility, and regularly participated in a weekly community karaoke event. Here is how Sinee described her case manager:

> I'll tell you, Robert is my backbone, you know. I can tell you why I'm really happy and successful here. You must bond together. Like, you have to communicate well with your case manager. And my case manager, he is always willing to help 100 percent. You know, he never refuse when I ask him, like, I need to go see a legal attorney. He will refer me. I need eyeglasses, he refer me, and dentist. You know he helps all the way down with even counseling. I'm in the dorm, anybody give me a hard time, let him know. He will try to clear the problem for [me], and to him it is not just work. He's dedicated to you to make you successful and to get out of homelessness.

With greater stability, eventually Sinee was able to reestablish contact with her former boyfriend and his parents, who were taking care of her daughter in the outer suburbs. They invited Sinee to move in with them and help them with their small furniture business and household, thus helping her exit homelessness and move away from the stressful environment of Skid Row.

Flexibility

Flexibility in implementing program rules and services according to the diverse circumstances of the client, rather than rigidly applying them in a uniform fashion, encourages client-staff trust and thus the likelihood of organizational tie activation. In contrast, rigid implementation of rules, especially sanctions for transgressions, promotes client disengagement with staff. Program staff in both Los Angeles and Tokyo described a degree of flexibility in the implementation of some rules, especially regarding substance use or drinking, usually not terminating clients for the first infraction. However, the flexibility of the programs diverged in the extent to which clients were allowed to establish and pursue their own goals. Although Tokyo staff paid homage to meeting individual needs, in describing their actual practices they depicted more of a conveyor-belt approach with predetermined tasks concerning how goals are established and how subsequent support is delivered. A case manager in one of the Tokyo programs described how she works with clients upon program entry:

> In the packet we give to each client, there are detailed planned dates for each goal and dates of completion so we have them write the dates of when they plan to do each and when they have finished we have them write "completed" and fill in the date. There may be a lot of people who

aren't that good at putting things in order, but it is unclear if we do not put things down in a way that they can see them. I think that having a "paper trail" is a very effective method. So we have them promise to complete each task one by one and we agree to confirm each thing and we go through that again and again.

The predetermined goals and tasks for the program included registering the center as the participant's address with the local authorities, registering with the local public employment office, completing a resume with a photograph, searching for employment, saving funds for apartment move-in, and obtaining assistance in dealing with debt. Although having a clear path set out and detailed attention from staff may benefit many clients, intensive micromanagement of those with ample job search experience and inflexibility with those whose needs do not fit the predetermined program can alienate clients. Indeed, many Tokyo case managers saw a need to be more flexible and to create a variety of pathways out of homelessness for clients, but did not see it as practical given the short time limit of the program.

In contrast, the program in Los Angeles strived to work with participants to identify their goals and create individualized plans to achieve them. Here, Robert, a popular veteran case manager, describes how he encourages program participants to identify and prioritize their goals:

> I try to stay away from telling them what their goals should be because if I tell them what I think they should do then what I'm really doing is making them a cripple. I can assist them in trying to figure out what they should be doing, what they want to do, and when it's too vague I'll go through a little exercise. I call it "the cup." I use one of those boards back there and draw a cup and ask them what the cup is for. And they'll say, "It's to drink water. And you need water to live. And you don't want to die." And then I put layers in there. "What would make you happy? What's the next thing that will make you happy?" And the next thing, the second half of the cup, I ask them what things about themselves they think they need to change. And then at the top I put for everyone that's homeless that that's what it takes to get through the program. And then I go back through what they gave and I use that to show them that they know what they need to do.

The case manager notes that frequently residents do not have specific goals established so he has had to come up with a creative way to help residents identify them. Robert's use of "the cup" lesson allows residents to identify for themselves a specific goal that they want to achieve, with the case manager chiming in to help them determine how goals should be prioritized to lead the resident out of homelessness. He can then draw on a variety of services available in-house and through referral that will help individuals achieve their goals.

The difference in degree of flexibility in the programs in the two cities is also clear in the guidance subsequent to the establishment of client goals. Despite staff acknowledgement that many Tokyo clients had long worked short-term contract or live-in work and that older clients may not have other opportunities, program rules and staff guidance largely restricted job searches to full-time, non-live-in, "standard" employment. Also, since the employment assistance staff of the program was dispatched from the public employment office, participants were strongly encouraged to not use periodicals or referrals from friends. Although some staff stated that they did not force participants to use the employment office to find full-time standard employment, they also said that clients who strayed from this course were not eligible for additional program benefits. This limited and ambiguous flexibility is also visible in other practices. For example, staff stated that clients were not forced to submit their bankbooks, but clients reported fearing being held suspect and subject to more monitoring if they did not.

Although the program in Los Angeles had some specific requirements of all clients, case managers were often able to adjust these requirements on an individual basis. Requirements that in the abstract may seem to be for the benefit of all clients but in specific cases impede individual progress could be sidestepped. The lead case manager in Los Angeles said the following about a requirement to take a job preparedness class:

> I would say about 75 percent are really reluctant, because they've been through other agencies that provide a week's worth of job training. So that's when I meet with a lot of them. They go through their appeal process, "I want to appeal this; I don't want to go to this class." And we get a compromise going. "You know what? Give it two weeks, let me know if it's working out. Give the instructor a chance to actually show you something. And if you know it all and you really don't need to be there, then I'll talk to the instructor and we'll meet and we'll pull you out." And they usually come back in two weeks, "Oh, no, I need this. This is perfect."

This case manager pointed out that by acknowledging clients' ability to appeal, she was often able to convince them to give the class a try. Other staff in Los Angeles reported taking a "let them learn for themselves" approach that allowed clients to try to find work on their own, but many were unsuccessful and came back to request the course.

Many Tokyo client interviewees perceived the staff practice of predefining and limiting appropriate goals and means to attain them as negative and discouraging. Some clients were frustrated because staff would often focus on what clients could not do (such as take part-time jobs or use their savings as they wish). Shimada-san, the twenty-four-year-old from the northern prefecture of Hokkaidō who found work in a *pachinko* parlor introduced in Chapter 1, described staff as seeing their responsibility as being limited to the formal supports of the program:

> They talk like nothing is their responsibility. They should do their consultations with a little more kindness and affection. That's why there are so many people that just disappear [from the program]. For example, I hadn't paid my residency taxes, about 60,000 yen [about $538], so a letter came from the City of Yokohama. But when I tried to get some help on that, the staff person said, "I have nothing to do with it" and "That is your problem, deal with it yourself." You know, that isn't really "consultation." So in the end you have to do it yourself. The staff's attitude is like at the level of elementary or junior high school. It's like an assembly line. They need to get more involved.

Given his view of staff as uninvolved and solely concerned with bureaucratic responsibility, Shimada-san withheld his trust and did not approach them when in need. Amid anxiety about additional debt and repeated mistakes and criticism from his superiors at work, he quit without consulting with staff and returned to a Ueno Park.

Takahashi-san, the fifty-five-year-old skilled and veteran day laborer from Tokyo introduced in Chapter 2, was also unable to fit neatly into the conveyor belt approach of the program. Before entering the transitional housing program, he spent about two years circulating between live-in construction jobs, pay-by-the-day flophouses (*doya*), emergency shelters, and the streets around Asakusa. Once in the program, he struggled to find full-time work through the local employment agency as required. He had one interview at a Buddhist temple for a job that would involve carrying and cleaning large, heavy incense holders. With a bad back, he worried about being able to do the job over the long term, and before he heard the result of the interview he took a day labor job he negotiated at a construction site he passed on his way back to the program. He got paid 15,000 yen ($135) per day in cash laying concrete (*tekkinkō*). However, since the program did not acknowledge day labor as employment, he was not allowed to eat meals at the program and was required to leave after only two months, rather than get a two-month extension. He saved what money he could and moved back into a *doya* in San'ya, hoping that his turn would come up on the waiting list for public housing. However, his luck ran out first and his job ended, putting him back on the streets and wondering whether his predicament could have been avoided if the program had recognized his day labor as employment.

In contrast, the greater flexibility of Los Angeles staff encouraged clients to see them as professionally competent, understanding, and helpful. In the exit story that opened this book, Carlos's case manager, Marisol, exhibited flexibility by referring him to a special jobs program when he was unable to pass his GED, and then to assistance in applying for SSI when he was unable to work. Rita, the forty-nine-year-old woman from suburban and South Central Los Angeles who found a school district administrative job after a lengthy and trying job search, also benefited from staff flexibility. After staff helped her emerge from a funk resulting from living in the Skid Row program and her inability to find viable employment, she said, "I'm beginning to see the light at the end of the tunnel. The things that I've thought about in my mind are materializing. I'm beginning to see that I can go to school if I want to or I can get retrained in something else I want to, or there are so many options to me right now." When I asked what she felt helped her get through her down times, she said immediately, "Having professionals that are really helpful and concerned, and open." A number of staff provided Rita with extensive assistance to ensure that she ended up in a job that would provide her long-term stability, flexibly applying program requirements to her benefit. When she was depressed about her appearance, her case manager bent rules and allowed her to take money out of savings to purchase clothing and have her hair done. An instructor for the job search class, herself a school district employee, encouraged her not to accept offers for low-wage jobs and provided extensive guidance through the test taking and interviewing process.

Marcos, the forty-eight-year-old former accountant from Puerto Rico introduced in Chapter 3, avoided a particularly dismal outcome thanks to staff flexibility. His employment readiness instructor berated his outdated "dinosaur" job skills and threatened to terminate him from the program given repeated absences while he was out searching for work. However, his case manager and a professional counselor at the program cooled him down to prevent an overt conflict and convinced the instructor not to seek his termination, which would cause Marcos to risk possible rearrest since his participation in the program was a condition of his parole. The flexibility of the program, despite his violation of its rules, allowed him to stay until he eventually received critical aid from family that allowed him to exit homelessness.

Homophily

The principle of homophily, that "similarity breeds connection" (McPherson et al. 2001, 415), can also fuel organizational ties via encouraging client-staff trust. Homophily is generally manifested in similarities in experience and social status (race/ethnicity, class, gender, and so forth) between program staff and clients, promoting trust by limiting social distance. Although generally limited in both cities, homophily was more prevalent in the Los Angeles program. Here Robert, a case manager, describes how he uses his social similarity with clients to build trust.

> I used to sleep in theaters so I kind of know from experience and sometimes in groups, my men's groups, one guy asked me, "Well, how do you know what we're going through, you ever been homeless?" I said, "You know, nobody ever mentioned that before," I said. "Yes." And I talked about a place in Vegas where I used to sleep, and there were two guys that knew the place that I was talking about, so it changed the perception. Some people I tell, some people I don't right up until they leave the program. I've even had my twin brother come down and talk to them before. Because he's been on the streets for a long, long, long time. My brother went through the local detoxification program. My uncle went there, too. I see people in there that think I'm my brother. I see people I went to school with and I've seen them on the streets outside. I used to do work for Labor Ready [a day labor agency] and a guy today was working there, so we had a nice little chat. He said, "If I get myself back together, I'm going to go into counseling."

The case manager notes that when he selectively informs his clients of his past experiences of homelessness, their suspicions of the appropriateness of his advice seem to be largely alleviated. The extent of homelessness in his family not only reflects how the epidemic has disproportionately affected certain neighborhoods around South Central Los Angeles, but serves as a resource that he can draw upon to demonstrate empathy with his clients.

Another form of homophily likely in operation in the Los Angeles program was that of shared ascribed characteristics such as race, ethnicity, and gender. The racial and ethnic makeup of Los Angeles staff generally matched that of the participant population, although African Americans were slightly underrepresented among staff. In interviews, program participants very rarely mentioned shared race or ethnicity explicitly as facilitating their relationship with staff, but this could be due to social desirability to be seen as "color blind" or hesitancy to discuss race with a white researcher. Although I was not able to directly observe given my inability to speak Spanish, shared ethnic status likely played a role in positive relationships between Spanish monolingual immigrant clients and bilingual 1.5- and second-generation Latino staff. Beyond their language ability, these staff stated that their knowledge of "Latin culture" and their own families' experiences with immigration helped them understand and sympathize with the struggles of their immigrant clients. Also, as Robert described, the program in Los Angeles held gender specific meetings that many client interviewees described as helpful.

Different racial/ethnic demographics and discourse in Japan render a different meaning for racial/ethnic homophily in Tokyo's transitional housing programs. As mentioned in Chapter 2, a pervasive ideology that Japan consists of a single, pure race has been criticized as a "hegemony of homogeneity" that masks diversity and inequality (Befu 2001). For social science research, this often prevents collection of information about race and ethnicity. There are no systematic data on the percentages of persons experiencing homelessness in Japan that are part of the roughly 5 percent of the national population that is resident Korean or Chinese, descendants of feudal outcasts dubbed *burakumin*, Okinawan, indigenous Ainu, or immigrants (Sugimoto 2010). Nevertheless, given the ideology of homogeneity, staff and clients in Tokyo's transitional housing programs are generally assumed to be "pure," "Yamato"[4] Japanese. Since everyone is assumed to have a homophilous relationship along race/ethnic lines, a small minority of clients is denied the possibility of a racially/ethnically homophilous relationship with staff.[5]

Although homophily in terms of gender and age was prevalent between some staff and clients in Tokyo programs, generally there was social distance, especially in terms of class and experience of disadvantage. The employment counselors dispatched from state employment offices were in later stages of their careers and thus middle aged or older men, like many of their client counterparts. However, the middle-class backgrounds of career bureaucrats differed greatly from that of their clientele. Other caseworkers and guidance counselors were much younger and included women, rendering them generally socially distant from an older, all-male clientele. In terms of experiences of disadvantage, no Tokyo staff reported experiences of homelessness, but one young male case manager described being sympathetic to clients given an experience of prolonged unemployment. Overall, opportunities for significant homophilous relationships between staff and clients appeared to be much scarcer in Tokyo than in Los Angeles.

My interviewees in Los Angeles pointed to the fact that some staff persons had experienced unemployment, poverty, and homelessness as demonstrating that they understood their situation and could offer insightful advice. Vernon, a forty-nine-year-old African American, described how a job preparedness teacher's shared experience bolstered her appeal: "I balked at [the job preparedness class] until I got into the program. And it's not the program. It's the teacher. She's the reason why. This woman has taught me things that I never knew. She has a complete realistic take based on experience and knowledge. She has, like, two degrees—in economics and something else. Plus, she herself has fallen upon difficult times similar to ours and had that background to draw upon." Vernon pointed to the fact that the instructor experienced prolonged unemployment but was able to get back on her feet again and thus she has practical knowledge and advice to share. The homophilous relationship erased his initial skepticism and replaced it with trust in this staff person, enabling receipt of job search assistance and encouragement.

However, it is important to note that some Los Angeles client interviewees pointed out that staff who had never experienced homelessness or addiction were still able to demonstrate sympathy and earn their trust. In the vignette preceding this chapter, Venetia's case manager, Margaret, earned her trust through willingness to listen and be sympathetic, as well as through such holistic and flexible practices as referring her to mental health treatment and being patient when she struggled multiple times to fight off relapses. Also, given that some interviewees had conflicts with security guards at the entrance of the program, it should be noted that another limitation of homophily has been identified in cases when former clients are placed in frontline security positions in shelters and other programs without adequate training (Dordick 1997).

In contrast to a generally positive reception to similar social status in the Los Angeles program, some program participants in Tokyo complained that social distance from staff impeded their ability to trust, communicate with, and receive advice from staff. Murata-san, the fifty-three-year-old former factory worker from Hokkaidō, felt that he could not relate to his case manager who was in his twenties and from another generation. Yamada-san, the fifty-five-year-old former contract factory worker, generally thought that staff were reasonable, well-intentioned people, but he also felt that the age difference was a significant barrier to seeking out advice from staff:

> I do feel like I can go to them for help, but they're really too young. And if they are too young, even if they know the bureaucratic stuff, the appropriate laws and all of that, it's kinda like they don't really understand. So, if there is no work, or if I can't find anything because of my age, or I don't have skills, even if they say they understand, there is nothing they can do about it. They won't find you a job, give you a guarantor, and employ you as a security guard. There is no real way to get help from them. I kind of think that I am old, I have a lot of experience, and I understand my position, so there is no point in going to them. It is kind of an individual thing, like developing a personal connection with someone.

Whereas for Yamada-san and Murata-san age was a barrier to the trust needed to seek out aid, for a few others this combined with the fact that the case manager was female. A man I met who was living in Shinjuku Central Park but had once been in one of the Tokyo transitional housing programs said he had trouble taking direction from a female case manager in her twenties, referring to her as "the coldest woman I have ever met." But a few client interviewees did point out that having their screening interview conducted by a female social worker while in emergency housing before the transitional program made it easier for them to talk about troubling experiences that brought them to homelessness.

Others felt that a difference in social class served as a major barrier to trusting and communicating with staff. Ishimura-san, the thirty-seven-year-old from Hokkaidō who worked a cleaning job, felt that his case manager did not grasp the situation of clients, given his middle-class background.

> They don't know about "life below." They can't provide consultation about anything. There is a difference in talking to people here and talking generally. So they don't match. Staff only speak with common intellect. There are people here that cannot think with common intellect. In other words, there are people here who cannot understand that one plus one equals two. There are people who cannot write. There are people who cannot converse well. I don't get along with my case manager. He is the type that I hate the most. He's uppity and has a quibble with everything. A person who hasn't worked construction won't understand construction. If they have, then they can say, "You should do this." But, if they haven't, then they can't. They are messing with us. Staff people here are just young. They have something like a manual, right? They just memorize that and don't know about the real world.

The different class backgrounds of staff eroded Ishimura-san's trust. Thus, like many others in Tokyo, when facing problems on the job both during and after the program that threatened his housing stability, he did not turn to them for assistance but fended for himself.

Welfare Regimes, Urban Regimes, and Trust in Los Angeles and Tokyo Transitional Housing Programs

Scope of Aid

As evident in a number of quotes in the previous section, the much shorter time limit (a maximum of four months in Tokyo versus two years in Los Angeles) on the programs in Tokyo constrained staff ability to engage in holistic and flexible practices. The time limits originated from, but were not determined by, the major funding sources of the programs. The program in Los Angeles received the core of its funding from the U.S. Department of Housing and Urban Development's Supportive Housing Program (SHP), a program that was created by the McKinney-Vinto Homeless Assistance Act of 1987. Funding guidelines for this program placed a maximum of twenty-four months on stays in transitional housing. Given the difficulties in securing stable income and housing for persons experiencing homelessness, the program in Los Angeles, like many that receive HUD SHP funding, allowed for the full twenty-four months of stay. Although national policy and legal development were an impetus for the Tokyo programs (namely the 2002 "Homeless Self-Reliance Support Act"), time limits and other specific aspects of the program were determined at a more local level. A representative of the TMG Welfare Division responsible for Tokyo's homeless self-reliance support system stated in an interview that there was not a standard for such programs at the time and the "two plus two" time limit was established after discussion between TMG and ward welfare representatives.

However, the differences in time limits are not simply due to the individual opinions of national and local bureaucrats. According to the head of the TMG's homeless self-reliance support system, since public funds pay for the programs, TMG needed to create guidelines that the public would accept. The head stated that the Japanese public would simply not accept a program that was too cushy. Many of the Tokyo program staff, even those who pointed out problems posed by the short time limit, felt the limit was appropriate given the danger of giving participants more time to abuse resources. Thus, the constraints posed by the short time limit can be seen as reflecting dominant cultural views in Tokyo at the time. This is also reflected in Japan's particular welfare regime that gives the state a very limited role in supporting individuals, with more responsibility placed on the labor market and families (Estévez-Abe 2008; Miura 2010; Schoppa 2006).

Both staff and clients of the programs in Tokyo observed that the "two plus two" time limit pressured clients to find work quickly, thus limiting their ability to be selective about the jobs they took and to pursue long-term plans. Many staff reported encouraging clients to find work as soon as possible, even well before the two-month deadline, to ensure that they had enough savings to move into an apartment after four months. Here, a case manager explains how the pressure to beat the clock encouraged extensive and intensive monitoring:

> Up until now, even I have tried a variety of approaches like "noninterventionism." But since there is so little time, if we just leave it to the pace of the individual, then even if they aren't really thinking of just messing around, if they have some problems, then their time will be up

before they know it and it will be too late when they realize it. So, I think part of our purpose is to become their pacemaker. We work with them so that they can get things done on time. The process will vary by the individual, but we will take about a week to observe them, then there are times we will say something like "How are things going?" or we try to have them promise to go to the public employment agency every day and meet other criteria, so we will say, "What? Aren't you supposed to be out today?" Then sometimes they will say, "The weather is bad," or "I have a cold." After that, they tend to start moving, so we try to be sure to say something to them.

In addition to the pressure to engage in intensive monitoring, the time limit also has prevented this case manager from what she called "noninterventionism." It is likely that the time constraint also prevented analogous hands-on and time-consuming practices associated with flexibility, such as molding self-identified goals and "letting the participants learn for themselves."

By encouraging practices antithetical to holism and flexibility, the short time limit in Tokyo was experienced negatively by participants. Here, Ishimura-san, the thirty-seven-year-old from Hokkaidō, describes how he was rushed to find employment and ended up in a low-paying and unstable job: "I would have two, three, four, five ads and look for the job that looked best. But I would be told 'Hurry and wrap it up!' But finding a job is something that you can't rush, if you are looking for somewhere to stay for a long time. You need to look slowly and examine things. I didn't want to take the job I have now, but I was in the program and I had a few jobs chosen for me [by employment counselors]. In the end, I went on my own. But, you can't [have your job] chosen by other people." Clearly rushed into a job that he did not want, Ishimura-san was able to save money and exit homelessness, but the job did not offer him many prospects for long-term stability. Soon after moving into his apartment, he was already anxious about his ability to make ends meet over the long term. Unlike Los Angeles program participants, he did not even think to contact the program to consult with them about how to improve his situation.

Interorganizational Linkages

The operation of the Los Angeles program by a private nonprofit organization (NPO) that was networked tightly with myriad aid organizations in close proximity promoted holistic, flexible, and homophilous practices. As in the case of time limits, major national and local funding and administrative bodies shape the organizational linkages of transitional housing programs, most directly by requiring referral and collaborative relationships. These bodies also determine what type of organizations (private nonprofit, private for profit, governmental, semigovernmental organizations, and so forth) can receive their funds to administer programs. These types of organizations can vary not only in the extent of their connections but also in their experience in working on homelessness; knowledge and understanding of the causes and practices to address homelessness; and professional background, experiences, and other characteristics of staff.

In Los Angeles, transitional housing and other homeless programs are largely administered by private, nonprofit organizations that are required to demonstrate a high level of interconnectedness. HUD allows a variety of organizations to apply for funding to administer programs including states, local governments, other governmental entities such as public housing authorities, and private, nonprofit organizations. Interconnection between organizations is encouraged by requiring programs to demonstrate the extent to which they have leveraged resources and coordinate with other programs. HUD also requires localities to coordinate programs and services into a Continuum of Care when applying for funding. Locally, this is led by the Los Angeles Homeless Services Authority (LAHSA). In 2009, LAHSA listed seventy programs within the county's Metro Service Planning Area (which includes the program in this study), all but one of which are private nonprofit or faith-based organizations.[6]

In Tokyo, the transitional housing programs and other publicly funded services for persons experiencing homelessness are largely administered by semigovernmental "social welfare legal entities" (*shakai fukushi hōjin*). These organizations are contracted by the "Special Ward Personnel/Welfare Rehabilitation Affairs Union" (abbreviated as Tokujinkō), a body that has provided social services for the TMG since the early postwar period. *Shakai fukushi hōjin* are private, not-for-profit organizations, but they have largely maintained a subcontracting relationship with the TMG. They stand in contrast to NPOs in Tokyo that have incorporated since the passing of the NPO law in 1998 and emerged largely from grassroots voluntary and advocacy organizations that provide emergency aid to persons on the streets. Although national legislation and guidelines do allow NPOs to operate programs, the TMG has generally relied on its subcontracting relationships with the Tokujinkō. In a rare exception, one self-reliance support center in Tokyo subcontracted NPO staff to provide case management. Only a few other NPOs and volunteer groups provide supportive services like legal aid, guarantors for apartments, and welfare consultation directly to Tokyo's self-reliance support system. In my observation at one of these NPOs, clients from the self-reliance center subcontracting casework to an NPO made up a substantial proportion of their referrals. In an interview, the Tokujinkō staff person in charge of overseeing the centers expressed aversion to expanding services through referrals to NPOs and stated that additional services would only encourage dependency and abuse. Additionally, many NPO leaders have strongly opposed government measures (or inaction) to address homelessness. They are critical of the operators of the self-reliance support centers who are seen to be tightly tied to the government, further complicating cooperation (Hasegawa 2006; Watanabe 2010).[7]

This rift impeded the ability of Tokyo staff to connect clients with diverse services, likely eroding clients' trust that they would be linked with services that meet their individual needs. For example, despite pointing out that the biggest problem in finding housing for clients was a lack of guarantors for rental agreements, a housing specialist presented an array of reasons why he did not refer these clients to an NPO that provided guarantors: "I think they understand that if they are guarantors for anybody unconditionally, they will have problems. They won't help out people who aren't young or who aren't earning 180,000 yen [about $1,614]. Also, they help people out for a low fee, right? So, speaking frankly, if they were to help everyone out, they can see that they would go under." Although these reasons have surface validity, my observation at the NPO suggests that he is providing euphemisms for the lack of a more cooperative relationship. Contrary to his claims, the organization very rarely refused to provide a guarantor, and had no age or income criteria (other than that the individual must have enough income to cover their rent). The practices of this NPO's staff were much more holistic (addressing instrumental and affective needs), flexible (supporting employment, welfare benefits, or both as appropriate), and homophilous (with consultation staff who had experienced homelessness).

In addition to the direct effects of funding restrictions from state regulators, the difference in level of interconnection between programs in the two cities was also fostered by a greater geographic concentration of services in Los Angeles, a product of local spatial politics. The Los Angeles program's location is Skid Row, east of downtown, where single room occupancy (SRO) hotels, missions, shelters, substance abuse programs, and other services have been concentrated for about a century (Wolch and Dear 1993). The concentration is often criticized by residents and organizational staff as a "jail without bars" isolating the extremely poor. Indeed, many of my interviewees in Los Angeles expressed a firm desire to get out of Skid Row as soon as possible. But spatial proximity can enable convenient access for clients and encourage referrals. This is perhaps most evident in the experiences of Sinee, the Thai immigrant grappling with bipolar and anxiety disorders, but buffered by an array of connections with community groups. These ranged from professional mental health care to Bible study to a weekly community karaoke event. She was referred to many of these organizations by her case manager, but she found others through word of mouth or while walking around the neighborhood. Although confined to the "service ghetto" of Skid

Row, where she often worried about exposure to drugs and violence, Sinee noted that her anxiety was abated by keeping busy in a variety of community organizations, all within walking distance.[8]

Although Tokyo has a district that contains a concentration of NPOs and voluntary groups serving persons experiencing homelessness, local spatial politics promoted the dispersal of transitional housing programs and emergency shelters. Somewhat similar to American skid rows, districts dubbed *yoseba* or *doyagai*, found in many major Japanese cities, have traditionally been concentrations of flophouses for day laborers (Marr 1997). After the bursting of the economic bubble and the onset of recession in the early 1990s, voluntary groups increased in San'ya, Tokyo's major *yoseba*, with the expansion of unemployment, homelessness, and welfare receipt (Hasegawa 2006; Watanabe 2010). As these groups have increased capacity with their incorporation as NPOs and growing public support, they have expanded their range of aid to include permanent supportive housing, short-term housing, employment training programs, alcohol and gambling addiction treatment, and counseling. However, facing a NIMBY (not in my backyard) reaction, the TMG distributed the programs across the metropolitan area, promising to demolish the prefabricated buildings holding them and rebuild them elsewhere every five years. Thus, compared to Los Angeles, geographic dispersal in Tokyo impedes staff contact with other programs and the ability of participants to walk to get referral assistance.

The sizable research literatures on urban homelessness in the United States, Japan, and other countries has shown that relationships with program staff can have an important impact on trajectories of homelessness, either obstructing access to key resources necessary to exit homelessness or helping people obtain these resources and get out of the predicament. My comparison of transitional housing programs advances this knowledge further by showing how these relationships develop. Importantly, I identify organizational culture as a key influential factor explaining why some organizations can promote trust and mobilize a variety of resources for clients whereas others can stifle trust, contact with staff, and mobilization of resources. Thus, aid organizations for people experiencing homelessness and extreme poverty should be seen in a differentiated fashion, rather than lumped together as homogeneous. Organizational cultures abundant with holistic, flexible, and homophilous understandings and practices are more likely to promote trust and the tendency of staff to serve as key allies rather than as nemeses for clients. But organizational cultures are also strongly shaped by extraorganizational factors, namely key funding and regulatory bodies embedded in welfare and urban regimes. Thus these national and local bodies should be aware of how their requirements affect delivery of aid on the ground.

The urban welfare regimes in the two cities operated transitional housing programs through two different approaches: Los Angeles followed a more neo-liberalized model through maximizing use of the strengths of private, nonprofit organizations, whereas Tokyo used a developmental model tightly controlling semigovernmental organizations. Although I argue that the differences in trust and mobilization of resources between my interviewees in Los Angeles and Tokyo are primarily the result of different organizational, urban, and national conditions, I oppose the simplistic interpretation that overall Los Angeles has a more effective approach to addressing homelessness than Tokyo. Homelessness and responses in Los Angeles are much larger in scale and longer in history. More salient trust-promoting practices among staff at the Los Angeles organization have emerged over a longer period of organizational and field-level learning and development. Also, given Los Angeles's much larger homelessness relief sector, people experiencing homelessness in Los Angeles are more likely to have contact with relief organizations and be socialized to use the social services system and ties with staff for subsistence. Nevertheless, I argue that the specific organizational-level principles of care and urban and national regime-level conditions do promote trust and mobilization of myriad resources. Given that state-funded transitional housing programs in Tokyo operate amid somewhat better labor and housing market conditions and show effectiveness in delivery of instrumental resources, their performance could be bolstered through the adoption of more trust-promoting organizational-level practices and field-level conditions. This would likely increase emotional support, normative change, and contact with staff after program exit, outcomes noted as necessary but lacking in interventions in Japan that focus narrowly on pushing people into the low-wage labor market (Tamaki 2002; Terao and Okuta 2010; Watanabe 2010; Yamada 2009). Since my fieldwork between 2004 and 2006, administrators of Tokyo programs have taken measures to promote more flexibility, now allowing some participants to follow a "half-work, half-welfare" course out of homelessness. This was impossible for my interviewees, who were in the programs when they supported only the path of full-time employment. As I showed in Chapter 2 and in Sawa-san's case, for a select few of my interviewees, this was only possible after failing to find work and when they secured help from a skilled advocate.

However, in its implementation of a new style of transitional housing programs beginning in 2013, the Tokyo Metropolitan Government and Tokujinkō did not extend the time limit on transitional housing programs. Even though the short time limit of the housing program was a clear barrier to holistic and flexible understandings and practices of Tokyo staff in my analysis, there are potential positives to minimizing time spent in institutional, group-living settings. First, long stays in housing programs may increase the likelihood of clients becoming "institutionally adapted" (Snow and Anderson 1993). As shown in Chapter 3 in the cases of Sally and Venetia, this does happen, but nearly all of my interviewees in both cities had no desire to remain in transitional housing programs, expressing a strong distaste for group living under the potential threat of termination for rule violations. Considering this and a need to better ease people into independent living, the new Tokyo system is trying to move employed clients out of the dorms early on and into subsidized, scattered-site apartments.

In the United States, given the high cost of transitional housing programs and the potentially negative effects of institutionalization, more federal funding has been directed toward homeless prevention and "rapid rehousing" of at-risk and recently dislocated persons. My research suggests that these newer, less-institutional models could be successful in addressing the limitations of institutional approaches. However, they should also encourage staff to be readily accessible to clients living in subsidized housing in a way that maximizes holism, flexibility, and homophily. This is crucial because, as I note throughout this book, exiting homelessness and achieving long-term stability requires not only material resources but also social, informational, emotional, and normative resources. Although some people experiencing homelessness or severe housing precariousness may have family and friends to turn to, many must rely on organizations and their staff for aid. Improving the organizational contexts of social service delivery is particularly important for transitional housing users in Tokyo, who I show in the next chapter to be largely cut off from networks with family and friends. Cases from Los Angeles show that organizational ties with staff can combine with family ties to promote durable exits from homelessness.

TIES WITH FAMILY

Venetia's and Sawa-san's stories depict different ways that relationships with family can affect and be affected by experiences of homelessness and exiting the predicament. Venetia was in touch with her brother and father amid her addiction and homelessness, until her father died. She was reunited with her daughter by chance when she too checked into a housing program. An old abusive boyfriend sabotaged one exit from homelessness, but a new boyfriend who became her husband served as support, helping her avoid relapses and returns to homelessness, and helping her eventually become a homeowner. Sawa-san, in contrast, was completely out of contact with family while he dealt with homelessness. His conflict with his wife over responsibility for a friend's debt caused them to break up, and he saw it as natural that he would have to leave her and their children to fend for himself in Tokyo. He had been away from his brothers for several years and he was unable to get help from them when he was dealing with the debt issue, so he felt that suddenly contacting them when he became homeless was out of the question. So, for Venetia, family served as a constant but not completely reliable buffer to homelessness, and for Sawa-san, family was hardly even conceived of as a source of emotional and material assistance.

Ethnographic and other research on homelessness has depicted different roles of family members in serving as a source of myriad forms of assistance. Some studies, focusing on the low levels of social ties among people experiencing homelessness, have emphasized two processes: as people—especially those with vulnerabilities like substance abuse and mental health issues—fall into homelessness. they exhaust the help of family and friends (Wiseman 1970); and people who become homeless most often come from disadvantaged or abusive families and thus hardly have a base of support to tap (Burt et al. 2000; Tsumaki and Tsutsumi 2011; Wagner 1993). Other studies have noted that depictions of complete social isolation amid homelessness are overstated, and that many people do maintain contact with family (Snow and Anderson 1993). However, this contact is socially and culturally patterned. Eliot Liebow (1993) found that most women living in an emergency shelter outside of Washington, DC, maintained contact with a sister or mother, highlighting the central role of women in poor and working-class families. Philippe Bourgois and Jeff Schonberg (2009), in their fieldwork among mostly homeless heroin injectors in San Francisco, found that black and Latino street addicts were in much more frequent contact with family, parents, siblings, and children than white street addicts, who felt a sense of shame and outcast status in their families.

Although my findings include bits of support for all three of these perspectives, they ring particularly true with the last. I found a considerable amount of contact with family and friends amid homelessness and various forms of assistance in exiting, but contact and assistance was conditional on social and cultural factors. The differences between Venetia's and Sawa-san's contact with family exemplify patterns across my samples in the two cities, with families playing more of a supportive role in exits out of homelessness in Los Angeles, and being more distant and limited in experiences with homelessness in Tokyo. So why are people experiencing homelessness in Tokyo generally not in contact with family members? Also, if many Angelenos who fall into homelessness have contact with family, how do their families help them get out of their situation? In this chapter, I address both of these questions by exploring the role of cultural and other factors in shaping the extent of contact and tie activation that my interviewees had with their housed relatives and, to a lesser extent, friends.

Some classic American anthropological work on Japan suggests that a "culture of shame" (Benedict 1948) would drive a stronger stigma of failure and homelessness there, in particular in how the larger society (*seken*) views one's family, thus limiting the ability of people in the predicament to draw on family members for help. Hideo Aoki (2006), a longtime scholar of homelessness and urban marginality in Japan, presents a nuanced version of this theory. Aoki suggests that through the practice of intergenerational "shared poverty," Japanese families serve as a crucial mechanism preventing homelessness, with family members likely to provide housing or economic support to vulnerable relatives. This can be seen as related to the tendency for Japanese families (*ie*) to encourage an indulging dependence (*amae*) on the family unit for material and emotional support. Thus, if a son or a daughter accrues debt and defaults, it is likely that another family member, often the father as household head, will pay off the debt to protect the child and avoid additional problems. This is partially motivated by the family's concern about the eyes of society around it and its need to preserve its reputation in order to function and survive in a social world. The family fears being ostracized from the outside world (*murahachibu*) should it be made known that a member is not reputable and the family cannot provide for all. However, once an individual sharply deviates from familial or societal norms, as in the case of a man's being unable to sustain the breadwinner role or through participation in disreputable activities such as organized crime, and once these violations become visible to the outside world, the family's tolerance level is exceeded, and the offender may be excluded by family members or may remove and distance himself from family (*zetsuen*). This is because of the pressure on the family for acceptance from the outside world, in which it is assumed that having a member experience homelessness is unacceptable. Thus, if a family member does become homeless, it brings shame to the family (*ie no haji*). So this cultural tendency simultaneously encourages families to serve as a mechanism to prevent homelessness *and* to push members out once norms are transgressed and discourage (re)engagement with family once one becomes homeless. Aoki sees increases in homelessness in Japan in the 1990s as evidence of the weakening of the subsuming nature (mutual aid functioning) of Japanese familism under economic globalization, and he sees the lack of contact with family amid homelessness as a pathology of Japanese familism.

However, critical scholars of Japan point out that sweeping portrayals of a homogeneous national culture in Japan exoticize and essentialize, underappreciating how Japanese culture varies over time and space and is shaped by important social institutions and conditions (Befu 2001; Cave 2011). Also, cultural sociologists note that culture does not operate monolithically as a unified system of values homogeneous within national, ethnic, or class boundaries, and neither does it trap generations of people in poverty (Small, Harding, and Lamont 2010). They call for more empirical specification of how cultural frames and scripts (predominant understandings and practices) that make up cultural tool kits can affect critical life choices (Harding 2010). In this chapter, I draw on these critical insights to guide my assessment of the extent to which a "culture of shame" approach explains the limited ties among my Tokyo interviewees. I also explore the cultural dynamics of families' aiding exits from homelessness among my Los Angeles interviewees.

I find some evidence for the culture of shame theory but argue that rather than a static, free-floating national culture, the distinct welfare regimes in the two countries promote different structural conditions and cultural frames regarding family responsibility, driving these differences in familial contact amid homelessness. Whereas in Japan's welfare regime full-time paid employment of a male household head supported by a (increasingly part-time working) housewife is central, it leaves little room in the family for an adult male who is a financial burden on the family. Along with lean state outlays for welfare benefits, this tends to encourage accumulation of debt for male members of a household and divorce after unemployment. Also, divorce law in Japan encourages only one parent, almost always the mother, to take custody of the children, and child support requirements are few and hardly ever enforced, thus promoting termination of contact with former spouses and children after divorce (Feuss 2004). All of these effects are exacerbated by familial separation driven by the widespread practice in the postwar miracle economic growth period of group employment (*shūdan shūshoku*) in which young people from the countryside were employed directly out of junior or senior high school by firms in central urban areas like Tokyo. In contrast, the more liberal welfare regime in the United States generally requires financial contribution from a diversity of household members, allowing room for both unemployed men and women to be financially supported by spouses and other family members. However, a strong sense of individualism, independence, and privacy often intersects with the limited financial capacity of family members to discourage cohabitation of multiple generations and households. Also, given high divorce rates and a punitive approach toward poverty in the United States, decisions about maintaining contact and seeking aid from family when trying to exit homelessness often cannot be made without consideration of legal issues. Thus, rather than claiming that a dysfunctional culture of poverty transmitted intergenerationally traps people in poverty, I show how welfare regimes can impact cultural and other aspects of social tie activation amid poverty.

Attempting to Exit Homelessness amid Social Isolation in Tokyo

Although in both cities interviewees described a degree of embarrassment and shame about their condition of homelessness, my interviews suggest that these feelings obstructed the use of familial and friendship ties for assistance in exiting homeless to a greater extent in Tokyo than in Los Angeles. First, Tokyo interviewees were much less likely than their Los Angeles counterparts to discuss in depth their relationships with family and friends and the circumstances that surrounded their loss of contact, perhaps indirectly reflecting greater shame and embarrassment. In Tokyo, a common response was to flatly respond that they had not had contact with family since coming to Tokyo, and when probed about reasons for lack of contact, many used vague phrases like "There was a lot going on" (*Iroiro jijō ga atte*) without revealing any specifics of those circumstances. However, interviewees in Los Angeles frequently openly described details of the unflattering circumstances of their relationships with family, including details of domestic violence and betrayal of family members or friends amid addictions. This may be because of more frequent contact with professional counselors addressing homelessness and addiction in Los Angeles's larger social service system, which would encourage them to talk about personal problems that may have contributed to their homelessness. However, a greater pervasiveness of silence and lack of response to probing in Tokyo suggests that talking about such circumstances would be embarrassing and uncomfortable. But this is only very modest support for the idea that a stronger sense of shame surrounding homelessness prevents contact with family members and friends among Tokyo's transitional housing users.

More direct support for the culture of shame hypothesis should include stories of exhausting the support of family in the fall into homelessness and then refraining from contact or being coldly turned away when seeking aid. Only one of my Tokyo transitional housing interviewees, Shimada-san, the twenty-four-year-old from the northern prefecture of Iwate introduced in Chapter 1, described being rebuked by family when seeking help. Shimada-san left home for Tokyo to pursue his dream of working for the Tokyo Metropolitan Police. However, he was unable to get through the very competitive application process and subsequently worked a series of low-paying jobs. This intersected with an emerging gambling addiction, and Shimada-san sunk deep into debt (about 2,000,000 yen or $17,940 to his parents and about 1,600,000 yen or $14,352 to predatory lenders). Shimada-san's failure in Tokyo, along with the financial and emotional drain it caused his family, rendered him unwelcome when he returned to Iwate for help: "I don't know how it is in America, but in Japan people in the country really worry about the outside world (*seken*). You go to the country, and you hear that the son of a family has come home. The population is small so everyone knows. It's especially embarrassing for parents. My parents said to me in the end, 'Die!' Those words show you just how hard we fought but they said, 'At the very least, just disappear.' I was like 'What?!' We fought and they just said, 'You only come around when you're in trouble.'"

Shimada-san's experiences with his family closely resemble the "Janus-faced" theory of the support role played by Japanese families put forward by Aoki (2006). At first his family provided him with financial support while he was struggling in Yokohama, showing a tendency toward indulging dependence (*amae*). However, when his financial problems continued to grow, and his failure in the big city became visible to society (*seken*) around his family in Iwate on his return, he was excluded and told not to bring his troubles on the family. So, with the last ties of his social capital shredded, he returned to Tokyo, enduring a few weeks on the streets around Ueno Park and a few weeks in live-in construction work before making his way into the transitional housing system.

Whereas Shimada-san's family turned him away because he had become a substantial financial burden and had brought them embarrassment and shame, a more common pattern in Tokyo was for separation to precede homelessness by many years, sometimes decades, and for homeless men to refrain from any contact with family or friends amid their predicament. A few initiated the separation from parents and siblings when they felt their involvement in illicit activities would bring problems (including shame in the eyes of *seken*) to family. For example, Kitajima-san, a fifty-four-year-old from the northern city of Sendai, fled to Tokyo in his early thirties amid threats from gangsters since he was not paying them compensation when he was operating a prostitution ring from his restaurant. He was already alienated from his family due to this activity, but he refrained from contacting his parents and younger siblings because he did not want to cause them problems. He entered transitional housing about twenty years later after losing a live-in job—he felt because of his age—as a sushi chef. He lived in a park for a few weeks until he was beaten badly in a fight, prompting him to enter the self-reliance support system after his discharge from the hospital. When I asked why he did not get in touch with his family for help, he said, "It's been over twenty years since I had been in contact. I don't even have their phone numbers."

From transitional housing Kitajima-san was able to get a job as a construction site security guard (*gādoman*) and move into a simple apartment. Since moving to Tokyo, he had made male and female friends with whom he would drink and gamble on horse races offtrack in the east side entertainment district of Asakusa. However, he refrained from contacting them while experiencing homelessness, only getting in touch after he had moved into his apartment.

> I have friends here [in Tokyo], but my one friend, she is a strong-willed woman (*ki no tsuyoi onna*). So I hadn't been in contact with her. If I told her I had gone there [transitional housing program], she would say all sorts of things. Up until now, how should I say it, people have helped me, but of course I hadn't ever been taken care of by the government. She would say things like, "You think it's okay to do something so embarrassing?! You don't think it is shameful to eat off of the pity of others?!" Even though I couldn't help it, I am the only one I know who has done something like that [become homeless and had to rely on government aid]. It's strange for me to say this, but until now I hadn't lived such a poor life. All of my friends were middle class or above. I'm a little vain so I didn't want to see anyone. I didn't want anyone to see me fall

so low. I don't know what will happen here on out, but I want to live
my life as I want to, and to never have to be taken care of like that again.

So, while the shame of homelessness and his need to rely on government aid
prevented Kitajima-san from contacting his Tokyo friends, his separation from
family was even more durable. We would meet up occasionally for a drink in
Asakusa when I was in Tokyo, but about three years later, Kitajima-san's landlord
returned a letter I had sent from Los Angeles. The letter informed me that he had
had to be hospitalized in the fall of 2008 at the age of fifty-eight. Kitajima-san
was diagnosed with cancer and passed away soon after. His landlord contacted
his mother who brought his remains back to Sendai and provided him with a
proper Buddhist memorial service. So although Kitajima-san fended for himself
at various times of crisis throughout his life to avoid being a burden on his family
and friends, his mother ensured that he would not be alone in the afterlife as a
"disconnected soul" (*muen botoke*).

For many of the older men, separation occurred when they migrated to Tokyo
from rural areas for work and lost contact over time. Yamada-san, fifty-five years
of age when he entered one of Tokyo's transitional housing programs, came to
Kawasaki (near Tokyo) from nearby Chiba Prefecture when he was fifteen after
graduating middle school as part of group employment (*shūdan shūshoku*) for
Toshiba Electronics. He quit the job soon after his two-year training period and
did live-in contract work in manufacturing for three decades until his late forties. During this time he lost contact with his parents and never really had stable
work that would allow him to marry and start a family. In the program he found
a low-paying and physically taxing job as a janitor at a small college and exited
homelessness, using a private firm as a guarantor for his apartment. When we
last met a year after he had moved into his apartment, he worried that Japan's
declining population would cause his employer to go out of business and, with
no one to turn to for help, leave him unemployed and facing homelessness again.

For most Tokyo interviewees who had been married, complete severance of
ties (*zetsuen*) with the families they had formed began at divorce and continued after they had become homeless. Four out of five of the Tokyo interviewees
who had been married described their divorce as resulting in total separation,
including halting contact with children. Of the three interviewees in Tokyo who
disclosed having children, none were in contact at all over the course of our
interviews, compared to five of seven interviewees with children in Los Angeles. Indeed, only one Tokyo interviewee had been in contact with his child after
separating from his wife, but this contact ended as he fell into homelessness.
Higashi-san, the fifty-six-year-old highly sociable and skilled carpenter introduced in Chapter 1, migrated to Tokyo for group employment as a teenager from

Miyazaki Prefecture on the southern island of Kyūshū. He later began working as a carpenter and married a girlfriend with whom he had been living. They separated and ultimately divorced because of conflicts that arose when they went 7,000,000 yen ($62,790) in debt to start a small restaurant. Also, they had disagreements about how they were raising their daughter. Immediately after their separation, Higashi-san lived with and took care of his daughter, then a middle school student, while doing subcontracted carpentry. One evening she found her father collapsed in a pool of blood in the kitchen. Higashi-san was exhausted from full-time work and parenting, developed a severe stomach ulcer, and had to be hospitalized for about a month. After being released, he resumed taking care of his daughter, who had temporarily stayed with her mother, but he could not get work in construction because of his health. So he took a commission job selling newspapers.

The job provided an apartment where he could live with his daughter, but he struggled to make ends meet. This is how he described his separation from his daughter when we first met at an emergency shelter in Tokyo:

> I sent my daughter to live with my wife for summer vacation. I sent her there every year, so I sent her again and we've been separated since. I know my daughter's phone number. But I haven't called because I am in this situation. Even if I got her back, I can't even take care of myself so I couldn't provide for her. I could have gone to the government for help and it would have been okay—they would have done something for me because I have a kid, but I didn't really think of that [laughs]. I knew that I could get welfare, but I thought it wouldn't be good for my kid. I would have done it if my [ex-]wife wasn't around, but I was in contact with her and I knew she would take care of our daughter. If my wife went on welfare, it would be easier for a woman, right? I'm a man, so if I am on my own, I'll somehow survive, right?

Higashi-san essentially saw family, especially his child, as people he cared for emotionally and had an obligation to take care of financially, rather than a potential source of support. However, Japanese gender norms that he saw as embedded in the public welfare system prevented him from turning to public aid to support his daughter. His impression that welfare offices "are easier" on women contrasts with research demonstrating stigmatization and heavy work requirements for single mothers on welfare in Japan (Aoki and Aoki 2005), but it is consistent with research showing that women are more likely to be awarded benefits at welfare offices (Maruyama 2013). Indeed, it was only in 2010, long after Higashi-san's predicament, that single fathers were officially recognized as eligible for *jidō fuyō teate*, a welfare benefit cash supplement, in addition to livelihood protection (*seikatsu hogo*) for single parents, that previously had been reserved for single mothers.

As described in Chapter 3, while in transitional housing, Higashi-san got well-paying work as a freelance carpenter. But even several months after moving into an apartment, he still had not contacted his daughter. He felt that he would like to see her, but since he knew she would be upset with him for disappearing, he did not quite know what to say.

> I don't care much about my [ex-]wife, but I don't know what my daughter would say to me. My wife separated from me so I have to think for myself. So, as long as they don't come to me, I can't take care of my daughter. Even if I were able to live with my wife again, I don't know what my daughter would say. I cannot decide on my own. I want to give everything to my daughter. I want to give her everything I have. I always think of seeing her. They are in Chiba [adjacent to Tokyo]. But, if I called they would be like, "What are you doing!?" They have it tough, too. I am sure they are struggling with money and they can't talk about having to turn to the government for help. In a month or two when the weather gets better, maybe I can go see her. I wouldn't be trying anything funny. My daughter is very important to me.

So, unlike Sawa-san and others in Tokyo with children, Higashi-san did not see himself as having completely cut off ties with his child upon divorce. As his own income and housing became stable, he began to try to formulate concrete plans to reunite.

Attempting to Exit Homelessness amid Social Isolation in Los Angeles

Although the majority of interviewees in Los Angeles maintained fairly regular contact with family, there were some whose contact was much more limited. Carlos, the Mexican American whose story began this book, was completely out of contact with his former wife and children in Northern California since he had been in prison and on the streets in Texas and California for nearly two decades. However, he was in almost monthly contact with his brother, a truck driver who would come through Los Angeles. The other men who had been married were focused on reestablishing contact with children but faced difficulty largely due to legal and substance abuse issues. Thus, even the experiences and perspectives of these few individuals in Los Angeles with the least contact with family differ from the larger group in Tokyo who had cut off ties. Although a few interviewees refer to being cut off from some family members, rather than espousing frames of complete severance and scripts of refraining from contact in order to avoid being a bother to the family amid their homelessness, Los Angeles interviewees more often used frames of responsibility to contribute to their child's upbringing and scripts of pursuing contact, even if it involved difficult interactions with former spouses and fighting in the courts.

Vernon, a forty-nine-year-old African American, had migrated to Los Angeles as a young adult from Tennessee and Florida, where he had spent his youth and junior college days. Largely due to conflicts with his disciplinarian, military veteran father who abused him physically and emotionally, Vernon had a turbulent upbringing, first experiencing homelessness as a runaway when he was sixteen. He moved between various relatives, sometimes staying in abandoned buildings, but eventually he graduated from high school. He completed some college, majoring in music, before being kicked out and arrested when he got into a fight with another student whom he stabbed in the neck. After coming to Los Angeles he "finagled" his father's first wife, whom Vernon had not met before, into letting him stay in a group home that she ran. He exhausted his welcome with her and drifted to Skid Row where he lived in an unsubsidized hotel. From there he worked as a security guard and commuted to a business college where he met a girl whom he married when she became pregnant.

Since he wanted his son to have an extended family, he resumed contact with his parents and two younger sisters. He dreamed of working in the film and television industries but only occasionally got paid work as an extra or production assistant. Since he was unable to bring in a steady income, his wife worked full-time, and Vernon was the primary caregiver for his son. He and his wife had disagreements about money; they grew emotionally distant, and she had an affair. When he served his wife divorce papers in an effort to obtain half of the household's resources, Vernon claimed that she trumped up a domestic violence charge and had him arrested. He vehemently denied his guilt in court and demanded a full trial, so he ended up spending four months in jail until he finally pleaded no contest. He was out for a month but then spent four more months in jail for violating parole when he went to his ex-wife's garage to retrieve some of his possessions and she called the police. While in jail, Vernon made a futile effort to maintain contact with his mother. He said, "The last time I spoke with my mother was Christmas morning. And at that time she told me what a failure, what a loser I was, and she never wanted to hear from me again. And that's the end."

Although he was rebuked by his mother and felt viciously betrayed by his ex-wife, Vernon remained focused on reuniting with and serving as a source of guidance and support to his fifteen-year-old son, even amid legal restrictions and homelessness. He left jail with a three-year restraining order that prevented him from visiting his son, was levied a several hundred dollar monetary penalty, and was required to attend fifty-two weeks of domestic violence classes. Upon his release, he applied for GR and stayed two weeks in an SRO hotel room on an emergency housing voucher and a few days at a Skid Row mission. There, he heard about the transitional housing program, applied, and soon moved in. Seeing his employment prospects as dismal due to his conviction record and parole requirements, he subsisted on his $221 in monthly GR benefits while he tried to start up his own public relations business in the emerging downtown arts scene using a prepaid cell phone, a website he created using a free hosting service, and Internet access at local libraries and nonprofit organizations. He would call his son periodically, but Vernon felt that his mother had influenced him to be distant and disengaged.

Vernon's public relations venture failed to bring in revenue, so he got some part-time work collecting surveys for a nonprofit organization. But he still did not have enough income to rent a private market apartment. Then his stay in the program became tenuous when a conflict with his roommate was brought to the attention of staff. Case managers intervened and tried to resolve the issue, warning both that if the conflict persisted they both would be terminated. Subsequently, the two got into a heated argument and Vernon had to leave the program immediately. Vernon sought refuge at a nearby mission, but he was unable to meet their requirement to prove he had had a TB test, and he spent a few nights on the streets before he was admitted. His application for a subsidized SRO room was eventually accepted and he lived there for at least three years after the transitional housing program, struggling to earn a living in the downtown arts scene, but mostly surviving off of GR. His housing stability coincided with his son's turning eighteen, thus allowing Vernon to contact him without the intervention of his former wife. He was worried about his son's not having much of a direction in life and his being interested only in playing video games, so Vernon tried to coach him to develop and pursue an interest that could lead to a career. The two were communicating, but his son was not very receptive to his advice: "He's done the exact opposite of everything that I've planned his whole life. Everything. And I have no idea what to do so it's best just to leave him alone. So that's what's happening here. I'm not the only person going through stress with their kids, so I don't feel as bad as I used to, it's just it's still my kid. You know everybody wants their kid to do well. I don't want him to wind up like me, God knows."

Exiting Homelessness with the Aid of Family in Los Angeles

Although interviewees in Los Angeles described strained family relations, which were often related to substance abuse and other problems connected to their fall into homelessness, they maintained these ties and drew on them selectively for mutual assistance that proved crucial in their exits from homelessness. Marcos, the forty-eight-year-old Puerto Rican parolee introduced in Chapter 3, was one of two Los Angeles interviewees whose relatives could be described as literally pulling them out of homelessness by arranging a place for them to stay more or less over the long term. While in transitional housing, Marcos had trouble finding work in accounting and sales because of his felony conviction, and he was under pressure to meet a parole requirement of full-time work. When Marcos was scraping by in a low-paying and unstable telemarketing job, under threat of being terminated from the program for missing required classes, and he was mugged on Skid Row, his son intervened to get him into his own housing. Marcos's son, who was working as a car salesman, signed a lease and covered move-in costs for a small one-bedroom apartment in an outer suburb that rented for $795 per month. He also loaned Marcos money to buy a car and pooled funds with a sister living in Texas and an uncle in New York to help cover subsequent rental payments. When I commented on how crucial his family was in helping him, Marcos simply said, "Oh, yeah, they've been very, very helpful. That's one thing I appreciate. They've been there for me." For Marcos, his family "being there" for him was as natural as "cutting ties" (*zetsuen*) was for many Tokyo interviewees.

There were more Los Angeles interviewees who had regular contact, but they were not quite able to rely on family to pull them completely out of homelessness. Although they did not contribute much in the way of material and financial assistance, these contacts provided crucial emotional support and sources of connectedness that contributed to exits from homelessness. This was the case with Oneita, the twenty-four-year-old black woman from South Central Los Angeles introduced in Chapter 2. Before entering the transitional housing program, Oneita fled an abusive boyfriend she was living with and first tried to go stay with her aunt. "I was gonna go back with my auntie but then I was like, oh, because two of my cousins had just got outta jail. The males in my family, besides the ones that's done something for themselves and got outta here, they jailbirds. They get out, they go straight home to mama. My female cousin had just had a baby and she was there and her boyfriend was staying there. My auntie's boyfriend was staying there. My uncle Ray was staying there. It was only a two-bedroom house. Everybody else slept in the living room and it was like way super crowded." Although Oneita describes extensive mutual aid in her family, there is also widespread unemployment and incarceration and ultimately a limit to their capacity to help out a needy member. Thus a family friend helped her apply to the transitional housing program on Skid Row.

But in a later interview, she framed her ability to turn to family somewhat differently, noting that she also had the option of moving in with her stepfather and mother who had moved to the outer suburbs. "See right now if I really wanted to—but I don't like depending on nobody—I could be living in Rialto with my daddy [her stepfather] right now. I don't want to. I'm already spoiled that bad. Like if I don't get myself out from under his wings, I ain't never gonna accomplish nothing. He still call and ask if I need anything." Here she sees herself as having a responsibility to secure her own income and housing and not take up her stepfather's offer to put her up. But while she was in the program, her stepfather, a freelance carpenter and former gang member, was shot in an incident in which her uncle was killed. Adding punishment to injury, his "congregating" with other gang members was a parole violation, and he was given time, but Oneita was unable to visit him in prison given her arrest record. Also, she pointed to "bad chemistry" with her mother, overcrowding similar to the situation at her aunt's house, and the demands that her family would put on her as also preventing her from moving in with her stepfather and mother.

> I think the kids out there [are] driving my mom crazy. 'Cause she takes care of all my sister's kids. She got six. My momma got custody of five. I'd rather go straight to my daddy or I go jump off my momma and go to my auntie or somebody. My momma's so mean. 'Cause if she help you—whatever she help you with you've got to give back to her double. My mom and them help me out when I need it. I try my hardest not to ask my momma for nothing. If I go out there, I gotta quit my job. I can't constantly continue to put my life on hold to go help them out, because every time I do that, I lose.

Rather than being a source of housing or financial assistance to immediately end her homelessness, family, for Oneita, were a source of periodic help, for which there were sometimes heavy expectations for reciprocity. For Oneita, given pervasive poverty, contact with family members sometimes turned into a burden, with her mother expecting her to help take care of her sister's children. As she notes, this would require her to quit the job she found at a Skid Row mental health clinic while in the transitional housing program, as well as her broader pursuit of self-sufficiency. So although she did not go stay at her stepfather's or her aunt's house while in the transitional housing program, she spoke to one of her sisters by cell phone several times a day, visited another sister at her home at least once a week, and had weekly Sunday dinners with her extended family at her aunt's house. She would talk to them about issues she faced in the program and visit them as a means of stress relief from living on Skid Row. Ultimately she was able to move into a subsidized SRO and continue her pursuit of education at a junior college and employment in medical administration, all the while remaining in daily contact with family.

The kinship network of Raymond McPheters,[1] a fifty-year-old African American with some Cherokee heritage from East Los Angeles, was not as plagued by poverty and criminalization as Oneita's, but it similarly served as a source of intermittent mutual aid and a constant source of emotional support. He had worked for the U.S. Postal Service for sixteen years, but he had to quit due to nagging lower back pain that had worsened over the years. Physically unable to do manual labor, the only work he knew, he moved to Oklahoma, where for over seven years he lived with and helped take care of his elderly mother. When a Social Security Administration (SSA) office worker in Oklahoma told him that he would qualify for a higher SSDI benefit level in California, the state in which he had worked for most of his life, he decided to return to Los Angeles. He applied for disability benefits but was denied because the doctor he was sent to deemed him physically able to work, so he began the lengthy appeals process.

Initially staying with his sisters and their families back in Los Angeles posed no problem, but they began quibbling after a few months. He would try not to stay too long with any particular sister in order to avoid exhausting his welcome, but this proved unsuccessful. "You know, I don't like everybody in my business. And my sisters, they all gossip between each other, 'Rob's doing this and Rob's doing that.' Then they call my mother and say, 'Rob's doing this with his SSI.' I don't need all that drama." When his sister complained about his eating too much and running up her grocery bill, Raymond could no longer tolerate the living situation. He decided to pursue his own housing to preserve his privacy and autonomy. Since he was without a source of income, he went to the local Department of Public and Social Services, applied for GR benefits, and was given a fourteen-day voucher to stay in emergency housing on Skid Row. The temporary housing was in the same building as the transitional program, and when he learned that he could stay in that program for up to two years while looking for work or going to school and pursuing his SSI case appeal, he applied at a nearby drop-in center.

While in the transitional program, Raymond maintained daily contact with his family and the few friends from his old neighborhood that were able to avoid drugs, crime, and early deaths. When we met up one day, he was carrying a small, frilly pink dress on a hanger wrapped in plastic. I asked if he had seen his family recently and he replied, "Oh yeah, I go over there. I went a couple of days ago, Monday, to one of my sisters' house and my niece's house. That is what this dress is for. My baby, she's my grandniece, she just turned a year old. They're giving her a little birthday party. But I see my sisters every weekend. When I visit, I stay maybe four or five hours and I come back this way." Not only would he visit his family often while in the transitional program, Raymond would talk to his younger sister a few times per day by phone. The ties that Raymond maintained with family and friends provided limited material aid while in the program, with Raymond often giving what little cash he had to children in his extended family. However, these ties supplied him with a sense of connectedness and purpose that helped him sustain his efforts to secure income and housing.

Eventually Raymond got frustrated with the paperwork and conflicting requirements with his GR benefits, so he dropped his SSI appeal. Despite his bad back, he applied for warehouse jobs but did not get much response. Eventually he took a street cleaning job from a Skid Row nonprofit organization recommended by a fellow transitional program participant. It paid $6.75 per hour, and Raymond took triple doses of Motrin to work through the pain. He began dating a nurse who was living in a Skid Row hotel after relocating to Los Angeles. A few months later, when his case manager refused to let him use some of his savings to buy winter clothing and help pay his daughter's tuition, he took his savings, left the program, and stayed in an unsubsidized SRO in Skid Row, paying $137 per week. Through a tip from another man he met in the transitional housing program, he took a higher paying job as an on-call driver for Amtrak. He would drive maintenance staff to and from trains, and he earned up to $2,000 per month after taxes, depending on his hours. Raymond and his girlfriend moved into a one-bedroom apartment near MacArthur Park that they rented for $1,300 per month. They married a few years later in 2007. He took a better paying job as a flatbed tow truck driver for the American Automobile Association and worked until his back pain became unbearable yet again. When we spoke in the summer of 2010, he had not been working for two years, and his SSI application had been rejected another two times, despite his lengthy paper trail of documentation. Still calm and cool, Raymond said, "If they [the Social Security Administration] need the money that bad, they can have it. I go to church every week and have my family so I am fine." Soon after, Raymond and his wife moved to Oklahoma, where he was able to get disability benefits and a lower spine fusion. As of early 2014, they were living in his grandfather's old house, and he was still in regular contact with his sisters, nephews, nieces, children, grandchildren, and great-grandchildren in Los Angeles.

Even those without family members in the Los Angeles area maintained contact with family living out of town, which served as emotional support at least, and in some cases also material and financial assistance. Throughout his homelessness, Peter, the thirty-one-year-old Asian Canadian introduced in Chapter 2, was not in contact with his parents but would frequently communicate with and sometimes get financial help from his sister in Washington, DC. David, a thirty-five-year-old whose father was American but who grew up in Mexico, was in daily e-mail contact with his mother in Mexico City. In our conversations he referred to her frequently as a source of emotional support.

Raymond in his apartment with family pictures

Exiting Homelessness with the Aid of Family in Tokyo

Although most interviewees in Tokyo did not have contact with family and often deployed frames of complete severance (*zetsuen*), there were a few who were in touch with family while they were homeless. Takagi-san, the thirty-eight-year-old whose exit story preceded the introduction, had his mother send clothes to the emergency shelter and, after a great deal of hesitation, asked her to serve as a guarantor when he rented his apartment. However, he did not discuss the details of his homelessness with her. Even the others who had contact maintained a degree of distance, and the extent of aid provided to the interviewee did not come close to that provided to Los Angeles interviewees. These Tokyo interviewees generally framed their limited contact with relatives amid homelessness as being appropriate given their inability to contribute financially to the household, almost a diluted form of *zetsuen*—occasional contact without any obligations on either side.

Murata-san, the fifty-three-year-old former factory worker introduced in Chapter 2, regularly phoned his former wife in Hokkaidō and sought help from his older brother there in his effort to get out of homelessness. After being "restructured" after twenty-nine years from a factory job at Hitachi Electronics, he came to Tokyo in search of work. However, because he was unable to find a job, he decided to give up his obligation to support his wife, and they divorced, even though they still got along. Here is how he explained the circumstances of his divorce:

> First, of course, is because of finances. In other words, in Japan there is an obligation to support dependents (*fuyō gimu*). For example, I have an obligation to provide support to my wife. I have to bring in some earnings, right? That and, well, my wife is a nurse. She told me, "I'll work so let's try real hard together." But my pride would not allow that. The possibility of me providing support was gone. That was the biggest reason. I thought of bringing my wife to Tokyo, but she has her parents, and we had both been taking care of her parents. We were living together [with her parents], and I was even supporting them financially and I just did not want to support them anymore. But once we had talked about it, she said, "I don't want to cause you any more problems, so it would probably be easier for you if you lived your precious life on your own." So it wouldn't be a burden anymore, the obligation would go away. "I don't want to cause you any more problems" is what she said. I said, "Okay, then let's part ways."

Aside from finances, Murata-san's relationship with his wife did not become problematic and, unlike the rest of the divorced interviewees in Tokyo, he remained in contact with his wife throughout his homelessness, albeit without telling her that he had spent time on the streets. After their divorce, he said he and his wife were good friends but not responsible for taking care of each other financially. His brother initially agreed to be his guarantor after he got a job and moved out of the transitional program, but his sister-in-law intervened and opposed the arrangement, causing him to temporarily move in with an elderly neighbor he had befriended. After a hospitalization, he was able to get welfare benefits and move into a new apartment in the western ward of Nerima, augmenting his benefits with part-time work in building maintenance. As of several years later when we met in the summer of 2011, he was receiving pension benefits and was still working part-time, but his contact with his ex-wife had become less frequent.

The experiences and interpretations of my interviewees provide moderate support for the idea that a "culture of shame" prevented contact with relatives amid homelessness to a greater extent in Tokyo than in Los Angeles. This includes the greater reluctance to discuss their separation from family and more framing of relationships with family as severed ties (*zetsuen*). However, the motivation for *zetsuen* was not always merely the failure of homelessness or a disreputable status from involvement in criminal activity. In many cases, Tokyo interviewees had been separated from their natal family since late adolescence because of group employment (*shūdan shūshoku*). Also, some had divorced and completely separated from former spouses and children many years before becoming homeless, often amid unemployment or debt. Given a lack of legal and cultural support for shared custody and child support payments, as well as a welfare regime modeled on male-breadwinner-led households, most Tokyo interviewees saw any contact with former spouses and children as troublesome to all parties involved. Thus, the greater prominence of the severed tie script should not be seen as solely driven by a free-floating, national "culture of shame" but as more the result of generational factors, such as group employment's moving young men away from families, and of Japan's welfare regime, which leaves little room in a household for an economically unproductive male adult or for shared custody of children after divorce.

However, my findings do not suggest that families play less of a role in addressing homelessness in Japan than they do in the United States. As Aoki (2006) argues, shared poverty and intergenerational households likely contribute to Japan's relatively low rates of homelessness compared to countries with liberal welfare regimes such as the United States. Multigenerational households, although on the decline, are more prevalent in Japan than they are in the United States, where single-member households are more common (Rindfuss et al. 2004). This, along with much lower levels of immigration, could contribute to Japan's lower rate of homelessness because fewer single-member households means that a smaller stock of housing is needed, and larger households have more members to pitch in during a crisis. However, in the future, lower birth rates in Japan will contribute to a continuing decline in household size and an increase in the number of elderly—who are less able to provide aid for other members—in the household. A declining and aging population also puts strain on pension and welfare budgets; this fact has been used to argue for cutbacks on pension and welfare outlays in Japan.

Also, understanding the institutional underpinnings of the lack of social ties among people experiencing homelessness in Tokyo has relevance for rising debates in Japan about the responsibility of family members to provide support before state welfare benefits are granted. As welfare rolls have risen to record highs amid higher unemployment during the post-2008 global economic crisis and the aging of Japan's population, including many people who do not qualify for pensions sufficient to cover all living costs, conservative critics have been advocating stricter enforcement of the legal requirement that relatives of welfare applicants be unable to provide support in order for benefits to be awarded. In the summer of 2012, a popular comedian confessed that his mother remained on welfare despite his financial success, and the media brought this debate to the public. My findings, especially the strong desire among Tokyo interviewees not to be a burden on family, show that rigidly enforcing this type of legal requirement could prevent eligible persons from applying and actually fracture families and encourage separation. If it is expected that relatives will provide financial assistance, an individual in need may avoid seeking aid from the state because they do not want to be a burden on their family. Also, being contacted by the welfare office for financial assistance may cause family members to cut off ties to the individual in need.

For the United States, it is important to consider the extent to which a punitive approach to poverty affects the ability of families to support vulnerable members. Laws and regulations on visitation that prevent contact between felons and family members erode the capacity of social networks to buffer the effects of poverty and to help felons get out of poverty. As critical urban scholar Loïc Wacquant (2009) notes, neoliberal approaches to poverty are hardly hands-off and laissez-faire but are expensive and invasive. In addition to the direct costs of imprisoning masses of poor people, there are indirect costs, including constraints on the ability of people to turn to broader familial networks for aid, especially when there are problems related to substance abuse, with little rehabilitation. Also, an emphasis on individualism and separation from family households upon adulthood in America's welfare regime may prevent cohabitation amid need. Understanding these cultural dynamics of familial support is crucial amid the more frequent and prolonged recessions of late capitalism, as more people become vulnerable to homelessness and turn to shelters for help (HUD 2011).

In conclusion, my analysis in this chapter elaborates the sociological literature on social tie activation among people experiencing homelessness. Some of my interviewees in both cities had worn out their welcome amid their descent into homelessness, and some had disadvantaged upbringings that left them with very few or no relatives to turn to for aid. However, the differences in experiences and interpretations between my interviewees in Los Angeles and Tokyo show how familial assistance in exits from homelessness is socially and culturally shaped. Most important, I show how this process is shaped by the institutional context of welfare regimes.

Part IV

ENDING HOMELESSNESS IN GLOBAL CITIES

Exit Story: Kobo

Tanaka Kobo was born in April 1945 amid the American firebombing of Tokyo at the tail end of the war in a working-class neighborhood in Tokyo's "downtown" (*shitamachi*) on the eastern side of the city. He, his parents, older sister, and a brother seventeen years his senior survived the bombing, which was especially destructive in *shitamachi*'s dense residential neighborhoods of wooden homes. However, in October of the year he was born, Tanaka-san's father and older sister were killed in a traffic accident with a jeep of the American occupation forces (*shinchūgun*). His mother received no compensation but managed to send him to high school with the help of his older brother who had become an accountant. Tanaka-san saw the United States as helping Japan emerge from the war and grow economically, despite the tragedy and burden caused to his family. "In the '60s, when Japan's economy was on the rise, America really helped us out. Young people these days always say that America is a bad country. That's wrong. In our generation, it wasn't like that. America always helped. Americans came, and there were some bad things, but there were many more good things. That is why I like Americans." He never left Tokyo until he was married and moved to Chiba, the prefecture immediately east of the capital. When he was twenty-two years old, he began working at a friend's all-night café and five years later opened his own. His café was successful and benefited from Japan's slowed but still strong economic growth of the 1970s and early 1980s.

However, Tanaka-san developed a penchant for gambling, mostly on horse racing, boat racing, and *pachinko*. He accumulated a considerable amount of debt, borrowing from gangsters (*yakuza*). When he was unable to pay them back, he feared for his life and the safety of his family. So he divorced, closed his business, and left his home and three children in 1984. Unsure where to go next, Tanaka-san phoned a friend who had moved to Los Angeles ten years before to consult about his situation. His friend told him to come to Los Angeles and they would figure something out when he got there. So, in 1984, at thirty-nine years of age, he boarded a plane at Narita Airport and flew to Los Angeles on a six-month visa. He worked for a few months at his friend's video store in Little Tokyo, near Los Angeles's downtown, where Japanese firms were soon to begin buying up property, fueled by profits from exports and Tokyo's real estate bubble. He worked there for about half a year and then found a job at a produce market in Little Tokyo; the employer was willing to hire him despite his lacking a green card. He rented a small apartment for $400 per month just west of downtown and the 110 freeway.

But in 1986, the Immigration Reform and Control Act was passed by Congress and signed by President Reagan, granting amnesty to undocumented immigrants who had lived in the United States continuously since 1982, but increasing enforcement of penalties on employers of undocumented immigrants not amnestied. Kobo, as Tanaka-san came to be called in the United States, fell into this latter category, and his employer, fearing a penalty, let him go. Other employers in Little Tokyo were unwilling to hire Kobo because of the new legislation, and he struggled to make his rent. Eventually he moved out of his apartment and began to stay sometimes on the street but usually at the Union Rescue Mission, Midnight Mission, Gravy Joe Mission, and other shelters scattered throughout the Skid Row district immediately south of the Japanese commercial neighborhood.

He made some friends in the missions, and since he was not a drug user he was trusted to do small jobs in some of the shelters in exchange for more regular access to a bed. A Latino immigrant he became friends with introduced him to day labor jobs distributing flyers. He would gather at the intersection of 4th and Crocker streets in Skid Row starting at 3:30 a.m. with around a hundred Latino day laborers and a handful of African Americans for a chance to be taken to walk the streets and distribute flyers in residential neighborhoods throughout Southern California. A day's work would last three to four hours for which he would be paid $25 to $30. He learned a little Spanish, which helped him find work and negotiate pay. For about ten years, Kobo moved from mission to mission, given the time limits of around thirty days, working as many days as he could to try to save money for when he would become physically unable to work. The drivers who hired day laborers liked Kobo because he was fast and dependable. But his savings would dwindle when he gambled at the Commerce Casino near the 105 freeway and the Bicycle Club near the 710 freeway.

In 1999, an organization called Volunteers of America opened a drop-in center on San Julian Street in Skid Row that also included beds for eight-hour sleeping shifts. This fit well with Kobo's work schedule and, unlike the missions, the drop-in had no time limit, so he used it as his residence from which he would commute to day labor jobs for another three years. In 2002, the rules changed to limit use of beds to every other day, so Kobo would alternate sleeping in a bed one night and in a chair in the drop-in-center's open-air waiting area the next night for about a year. Over time, Kobo became a public character on Skid Row since he stood out as an Asian, was a mainstay at the missions and soup kitchens, and engaged in entrepreneurial activities such as selling cartons of cigarettes to people who would then sell them as singles on the street. Also, he would generously loan money to other Skid Row residents, but he stopped when he estimated that the 30 percent or so of people who would not pay him back had cost him about $1,000. When we walked the streets of Skid Row together, passersby would greet him by calling "Go-Go," a nickname Kobo joked he probably received from a "crack head" who could not pronounce his name. He made a few trusted friends but was generally suspicious of the fluid street population, especially of substance abusers. Since he limited his social contacts and communication, he did not know there were transitional housing programs in the neighborhood that would give him regular access to a bed and help him save money. Finally, in January 2003, when he consulted with a staff person at a drop-in center who befriended him, he was told about the transitional housing program.

Robert, Kobo's case manager, helped him set up a plan to save money, a plan that Kobo felt would also keep him from gambling, help him set up a business, exit homelessness, and have some stability as he aged.[1]

> They ask me many questions [at intake], about a hundred questions, but easy questions. My case manager, his name is Robert, very, very nice guy. He ask me, "How can I help you?" I just want to save money, because I can't save money just myself. This building's rule is 75 percent of income you have to save. I say, "Okay, I have $100 income, so I want to save $80 a week." Every Monday I do. Next Monday, I'll have $2,000. Before I never save money because I told you I like to play gamble. But here, I have to make money order, give money order to my case manager. That is why I could save. If I leave here, maybe I get trouble again. But this time I want to save money because I am not young anymore. I want to be driver [for] this job [distributing flyers]. Me and my friend, I want to buy my car. My friend has no money. But if I buy car, he is American, okay. He is my partner. He can go to company and get contacts, and then we share the profits. I want to do it, but it will take one more year. Because at least I need $5,000.

For the first few weeks it was hard for Kobo to resist the urge to go gambling, but after that it became much easier. His goal was to save money with which he could purchase a car and start his own flyer delivery business with the help of an African American fellow day laborer and former crack addict whom he came to trust over seven years of working together. Since Kobo was working, his case manager did not enforce the program's requirements for job preparedness courses. He did require him to take an English class and to attend Alcoholic Anonymous meetings, even though he had no history of substance abuse, in order to meet the program's requirement of participating in a community activity.

Although Kobo was only able to earn about $400 per month in the day labor economy, he benefited greatly from the relationships he developed with case managers and staff of community organizations in Skid Row. In addition to being rewarded with a private room after three months of steady savings, with the help of a few case managers he was able to get eyeglasses. Given his long tenure in Skid Row, he was a victim of the high level of jaywalking ticketing there, a tactic critics claim is used to control and further burden the extremely poor. But with his case manager's referral, he had three jaywalking tickets and associated fines costing a total of $1,500 dismissed in Los Angeles's "homeless court." Also, he was able to see a doctor in the medical clinic on the first floor of the building to address his high cholesterol and a stomach ulcer. His friend who worked at a local nonprofit and helped him get into transitional housing was also helping Kobo get dental care, since many of his teeth had rotted and fallen out when he was living in the missions and the drop-in center.

Kobo got sick a few times, his employers would take a few weeks off, and the transitional housing program cut their free meal program to one meal per day, so he fell behind his savings schedule. However, he still had saved about $4,600 by the end of his stay in the transitional housing program. After getting a three-month extension on his two-year stay, he was transferred to a newly employed case manager who mistakenly and abruptly told Kobo that he had to leave the program. Kobo had applied for a room in a subsidized single room occupancy hotel several months before but had yet to be accepted. So he began staying in pay-by-the-day unsubsidized SRO hotels in Skid Row. He was extremely appreciative of the program's help but very upset at how his stay ended.

He followed up on his application for a subsidized SRO room and was luckily helped by a staff person who held a room for him for one month while he met paperwork requirements. It also did not hurt that a few of Kobo's friends already living in or employed by subsidized SROs stopped by the organization's office to put in a good word for him. The first criterion he had to meet was to have a disability, a requirement of most subsidized SRO housing. The staff person of the nonprofit that operates the subsidized SRO referred him to a local medical clinic. Initially Kobo did not want to lie, but he received some cues from the doctor that he should say that he had a drinking problem. Eventually Kobo did say that, and the doctor gave him paperwork stating that he has been diagnosed with alcoholism and that he should go to AA meetings for six months. Next, he had to show that he was "low income"—demonstrating that he was poor enough to deserve aid but still able to contribute to rent. He had his driver handwrite a receipt for his week's salary, but it was not acceptable. A staff person for the nonprofit operating the SRO told Kobo that he should apply for General Relief. Some people he knew on Skid Row told him that when asked where he was born, just to say, "Here in California." He did as advised, showed the county welfare office worker his California ID and Social Security number acquired when he first arrived in the United States, and was awarded GR benefits.

He took the appropriate paperwork back to the nonprofit and, finding it hard to lie again, told the staff person that he was really born in Tokyo. The staff person wrote this on his application, which he then took to the local housing authority, the agency responsible for final approval of his move into the federally subsidized SRO. At the housing authority, the worker looked over the notes indicating his birth in Tokyo and rather than questioning him about his citizenship, simply said, "Well, you look American to me and you have been issued GR," and approved his application. He moved into the SRO a month later where he paid $54 per month in rent. He liked his living arrangement because it allowed him more freedom and privacy and he could cook his own Japanese food. A few months after he had moved into the SRO, he attended a Hawaiian-themed graduation party for the transitional housing program. Wearing black slacks, a maroon buttoned-down shirt, and a green lei around his neck, Kobo took the opportunity to publicly thank Robert (also a case manager for Venetia and others)—who was dressed in a white and gold traditional African ceremonial gown and hat—and the SRO staff person who helped him and was seated in the front row:

> Before I came [to the program], more than ten years I was homeless. And then [the program] gave me single room, three meals every day. I can take shower *every* day, *any* time. [Kobo nods, crowd laughs and claps.] I was very, very happy. While I stay here, I try SRO hotel and I got in. Manager, right here. Thank you, Tanya. [Tanya waves, crowd claps.] So I'm very, very lucky. I could save a little, *little* bit of money. [Crowd laughs] I could look for next step. [Kobo chuckles, turns, and bows deeply to Robert, pausing to show respect.] Thank you very much. [Crowd applauds.]

He kept working and saving, but his plans with his American friend to start a flyer distribution business turned tragic. Despite being very cautious about whom he associated with and trusting this "best friend" because he looked after Kobo during his early years on Skid Row, he was betrayed. Kobo gave his friend

Kobo in his subsidized SRO room, soon after moving from transitional housing

money to buy a vehicle and had the friend register it in his name. He also had the friend hold the remainder of his savings, because having it in his bank account would make him ineligible for GR, and he heard that his room might be searched if he tried to hide it under a mattress. But eventually the friend disappeared with the car and the money. Kobo was crushed that he had lost the savings he had acquired over a few years of poorly paid work walking the neighborhoods of suburban Southern California, and his long-term plans for stability were put in jeopardy. But it was not the first time he had been misled since coming to Skid Row, and he was thankful for the aid from the state, especially his subsidized SRO room. Also, this safety net not only allowed him to exit homelessness but also to avoid a return despite having his savings stolen. His GR was eventually terminated because of his undocumented status, but his case manager at the Housing Authority accepted proof of employment from a driver who had company letterhead. Regarding his immigration status, the case manager simply told him that he needed to get a temporary passport from the Japanese embassy and begin working on applying for citizenship. He was still living in his subsidized room and distributing flyers as a day laborer when we last met just after New Year's Day, 2014.

THE MULTILEVEL CONTEXTS OF EXITING HOMELESSNESS

Kobo is the only Japanese person experiencing homelessness I have met in Los Angeles's Skid Row during over twenty years of intermittent fieldwork. Another transitional housing user in Los Angeles, David, the thirty-five-year-old American with an Italian Mexican mother and Italian American father and a bachelor's degree in economics, introduced himself to me by saying apologetically, "I'm an outlier."[1] However, despite an at least equally unusual situation, Kobo is best viewed not as an outlier, I think, but as an "actually existing counterfactual." Counterfactuals are generally used in thought experiments in which scholars analyze theoretically interesting but hypothetical cases to better understand the validity of postulated causal mechanisms. So Kobo, a postwar Tokyoite with a background similar to many of my Tokyo interviewees, but who fell into homelessness in Los Angeles, provides an actually existing counterfactual that demonstrates how *contextual awareness* (Maloutas 2007) matters in understanding individual efforts to exit homelessness in global cities.

Had Kobo continued on the path of many of my Tokyo interviewees his age, he might have fled his threatening debtors to anonymity in San'ya, Tokyo's day labor ghetto, in 1984. There, he could have worked low-skill day labor and lived in pay-by-the-day flophouses through the bubble years. But as he had aged and the construction industry contracted during the recessions and stagnation of the "lost decade" of the 1990s, he would have been vulnerable to literal homelessness. Should he have ended up on the streets, he may have attempted to escape his predicament by entering a self-sufficiency support center. If fortunate enough to follow the path of my successful Tokyo interviewees, Kobo would have exited homelessness largely without social ties but through fighting barriers such as age discrimination for a spot in the precarious low-wage service sector. Instead, he fled to Los Angeles where, amid a crackdown on hiring of undocumented immigrants, he ended up cycling between the streets, missions, and twenty-four-hour drop-in centers. In the context of Los Angeles's more globalized and competitive labor and housing markets, he lacked legal status to work so he toiled at day labor, unable to earn enough to rent an apartment. When he finally made his way into transitional housing, like other Los Angeles interviewees who exited homelessness, he developed bonds with program staff amid a more holistic, flexible, and homophilous organizational setting, and he was linked with a variety of resources, perhaps most importantly a subsidized SRO room. However, Kobo's familial context remained Japanese, and he terminated contact with his wife and children a few years after arriving in Los Angeles without reaching out to them for help, following the cultural script of complete severance of ties (*zetsuen*). Although he was betrayed by an American friend and lost all of his savings, his subsidized room in Skid Row allowed him to avoid a return to homelessness. Kobo's experience shows that contrary to depictions of homelessness as resulting solely from individual failure or insurmountable structural conditions, the condition and how it is overcome are profoundly shaped by contexts at multiple social levels. This contextual importance made visible by Kobo's unique case, alongside my broader comparisons, enables elaboration of scholarly theories of homelessness and urban marginality amid globalization.

More practically, my comparative analysis of the multiple contexts that shape exits from homelessness highlights various *forgiving contexts* that show potential to effectively ameliorate homelessness at individual and societal levels. Like other "key nodes of the global economy" (Sassen 2001), Los Angeles and Tokyo have seen surges of homelessness in the last decades of the twentieth century and into the new millennium, the time span that corresponds to an era of heightened economic, demographic, and ideological globalization. Even though there have been recent decreases in street homelessness, sizeable populations experiencing homelessness have persisted despite periods of economic growth and the development of various housing programs to aid them. Thus, although there has been a shift from the streets to shelters and programs, the problem of homelessness appears to have become an entrenched feature of the global urban social landscape. Nevertheless, in recent years, in both Los Angeles and Tokyo, coalitions of nonprofit organizations, volunteer groups, religious organizations, advocacy groups, and various government bodies and their representatives have adopted the ambitious rhetoric of "ending homelessness" and have implemented plans to achieve this goal. Social science research has provided valuable insights into one side of the puzzle to ending homelessness, how to stop the flow of people into the condition, namely by pointing out the need to address the structural roots of the problem by increasing the stock of stable, living-wage employment; affordable housing; and adequate social safety net provisions (Burt et al. 2001; Hopper 2003; Rossi 1989; Snow and Anderson 1993; Wagner 1993). I try to also shed light on the other side of the puzzle to end mass homelessness: how to help individuals exit the condition. After outlining the major theoretical contributions of my analysis in preceding chapters, I make recommendations derived from my research on exits that I hope can contribute to broader efforts to end homelessness in contemporary cities seeing trends associated with globalization.

Contextually Aware Theories of Homelessness and Marginality in Global Cities

The main broad theoretical contribution of this book is that it shows how contexts at multiple social levels shape the process of exiting homelessness in important ways. I begin with an argument for a reconceptualization of homelessness as not an individual attribute or identity, nor as a way of life or culture, but primarily as a socially generated, tragic predicament that people do their best to avoid. Some ethnographic research on homelessness focuses on how people in the condition creatively adapt to structural deprivation and create a "homeless (sub)culture" and a "homeless community" to meet their material and psychological needs, in a sense creating a "home on the streets" (Wasserman and Clair 2010, 2011). By highlighting the structural constraints that people experiencing homelessness battle, as well as the creative strategies people construct to survive, this research can improve public awareness as well as policy. For example, by showing how dismal conditions in emergency shelters can make sleeping in public spaces a rational decision, I challenge the claims of "service resistance" used by those who are primarily concerned with clearing commercial spaces of visible forms of poverty through punitive approaches. However, I argue that the struggle to transcend homelessness is more central to the experience of the predicament than is adaptation to a homeless identity, culture, or community. I encourage future studies of homelessness not to treat homelessness primarily as an endpoint.

By also looking at how people are often able to get out of the predicament, social science research can move public understanding of homelessness even further away from entrenched stereotypes. A disheveled, distressed, and disabled person in public space is the most visible form of homelessness and often inhabits the public imagination. However, although chronic street homelessness is still a cause for substantial concern and adequate aid, due to the success of housing first, supportive-housing programs, it is a form of homelessness that seems to be on the decline. Persons with disabilities experiencing homelessness over the long term or chronically make up a small and decreasing fraction of the population that experiences homelessness in the United States (16 percent at a point-in-time in 2012, declining by 19.3 percent since 2007), whereas the population in shelters and housing programs remains stable and larger (HUD 2013). This is also true in Japan, as I showed in Chapter 1, with street populations declining considerably and shelter populations remaining stable (Kitagawa 2011; MHLW 2011). Therefore, by looking at homelessness as a form of liminality (Hopper 2003) and analyzing how it is transcended, rather than looking at it as an entrenched state, identity, or culture, we see it as a structurally driven phenomenon that very negatively impacts people, but one that can be conquered. This not only dilutes the stereotypical images but also opens up more room for the social imagination to explore measures that could lead to ending homelessness.

In that sense, I challenge depictions of "homeless culture" or a "homeless life-style" as a magnetic force that is both attractive and sticky, drawing people in and preventing them from escaping (Ravenhill 2008). In these depictions, amid the loss of housing, an individual moves through a process of becoming a "homeless person," obtaining a "homeless identity," and becoming embedded in social networks made up of other "homeless people." Getting out of homelessness thus involves shedding that identity, severing ties, and disembedding from a culture of homelessness that is always luring the person. For some, a homeless identity was the only one they had, so shedding it, or separating from a "homeless self," can bring on feelings of insecurity, in a sense trapping them in the homeless identity (McNaughton 2008). In this research, even those who exited homelessness are described as largely experiencing the transition as social isolation, a loss of identity and social networks, and intense vulnerability to a return to homelessness. However, for the few of my interviewees who did not exit, or who returned to homelessness, like Venetia, Andō-san, and others, it was violence, addiction, and the inability to secure employment that pushed them back, rather than the attraction of street life.

Indeed, distancing from a homeless identity and others that embody stereotypes of homelessness is a commonly deployed strategy to "salvage the self" amid the many indignities of the predicament (Snow and Anderson 1993). For example, at the beginning of our first interview, Raymond, the fifty-year-old African American/Native American former postal worker, said, "Really, I'm not homeless. You know, I look at it like this. What I describe as homeless is people that are out there in the streets, sleeping on the street that have nowhere to go. I'm just [in transitional housing] taking care of what I need to take care of and I need a place to live." Takagi-san, the thirty-eight-year-old from Ibaraki Prefecture, like other interviewees in Tokyo, expressed a strong distaste for transitional housing users who had not found work, the "real homeless" (hontō no hōmuresu) whom he described as lazy, dependent on aid from the state, and morally bankrupt. Claims that others embodied such popular stereotypes of homelessness as laziness, lack of morals, and a poor work ethic abounded in my interviews among transitional housing users. But even in my broader fieldwork outside these programs, people who exhibited or verbally embraced these attributes or attitudes were very hard to find, and even these rare cases often had an exit plan that they had not yet been able to implement.

Although not all transitional housing users were able to exit homelessness while I followed them, the preceding chapters have shown that their cognition and behavior were oriented toward overcoming homelessness by securing stable income and housing. My interviewees did not embrace an identity as homeless or see themselves as settled into a homeless community. A few, like Venetia and Jill, who had been without stable conventional housing for extended periods of time (around twenty years), described a time in the past when they were entrenched in their addictions, but at the same time they had made considerable attempts to attain the most secure housing available to them. Ishimura-san, a thirty-seven-year-old former bartender from Hokkaidō, had lived for seven years on the streets of Tokyo and Osaka, sometimes sleeping in a pull-cart that he used to collect recyclables. However, he described that situation as something he had to do to survive rather than a lifestyle he preferred to the stresses of conventional work that are required to maintain an apartment. Thus, rather than trying to define a homeless identity or culture and defend it as something in opposition to or even consistent with mainstream cultural frameworks, I argue that ethnographic researchers of homelessness should shift their focus to how the multiple resources—economic, social, emotional, and informational—necessary to exit homelessness are procured. This calls for a shift in ethnographic studies of homelessness to investigate how cultural frames are reinforced, and mitigated, by social structures that shape the decisions people make to help them access resources.

For example, I have shown that Japan's work-centered welfare regime promotes cultural frames of distaste toward and disentitlement to welfare benefits, and thus the vast majority of my Tokyo interviewees often did not even pursue them. A work-centered welfare regime also promotes a cultural frame of complete severance of ties (zetsuen) since unemployed and underemployed men feel they have no place in the family. Instead, mainstream labor and housing markets are framed as providing the sole pathway out of homelessness and the only focus of individuals' efforts. In Los Angeles, near total exclusion from living-wage employment and affordable housing drives many transitional housing users to frame mainstream labor and housing markets as impenetrable, so many disengage and instead seek subsidized housing in Skid Row. For some, American myths of rags-to-riches social mobility promote fruitless entrepreneurial pursuits. In the transitional housing program in Los Angeles operated by a private nonprofit organization, staff frames of clients and appropriate practices reflect holism, flexibility, and homophily. As a result, program users there generally trusted staff and saw ties with them as helpful to their efforts to exit homelessness. Without a strong male breadwinner model, many transitional housing users in Los Angeles saw mutual aid from family members as an appropriate resource to tap to exit homelessness, but this was often obstructed by poverty throughout the family and restrictions imposed by the penal state.

My conceptualization of homelessness as a tragic but surmountable predicament and my focus on the process of exiting homelessness thus call for updates of theories of cognitive and behavioral acculturation to homelessness (Snow and Anderson 1993). These theories were developed primarily through observation of street homelessness at a time when relief efforts in the United States were predominantly emergency shelters. With less aid to find employment and housing, it is possible that people experiencing homelessness were more likely to seek out respite in communities of other people in the same predicament. But as I have shown, the landscape of homelessness relief has changed dramatically, calling for an adjustment to theories about how people adapt to, resist, and transcend the condition of homelessness. Accommodation theory posits that, over time, people experiencing homelessness move from trying to procure mainstream employment and housing to securing resources to survive amid homelessness. Complete entrenchment in homelessness is estimated to take about two years. I found very little empirical support for such a process, especially one that takes a linear form or has a clear tipping point. A number of interviewees in both Los Angeles and Tokyo who had been homeless for many years successfully exited the condition in a durable fashion.

Even though this is not a wholesale rejection of the accommodation hypothesis, it shows that long-term homelessness does not prevent exiting in a deterministic or linear fashion through acculturation. Indeed, quantitative studies have found that length of homelessness and identification with other people experiencing homelessness have negative net effects on the likelihood of exiting (Piliavin et al. 1993, 1996; Sosin, Piliavin, and Westerfelt 1990; Wong, Culhane, and Kuhn 1997; Wong and Piliavin 1997). Ethnographic studies have presented examples of persons who live on the street for a long time as cognitively, socially, and behaviorally oriented to street life (Snow and Anderson 1993). But the complete absence of descriptions of cognitive and behavioral accommodation to homelessness in my interviews and observations of transitional housing users suggests that any negative effects of long-term homelessness on exits from homelessness may be merely correlated with barriers to the resources that facilitate exits. Thus, my findings suggest at least three revisions to acculturation theory: (1) acculturation to homelessness does not occur linearly over time, but fluctuates in relation to opportunities for economic, social, and emotional resources (importantly, trust); (2) it likely occurs only among a small portion of the population that experiences homelessness; and (3) to the extent that acculturation occurs, program entry or access to aid can be a critical step away from it. Moving away from a narrow focus on acculturation, either due to individual flaws or oppressive structural constraints, I now outline a multilevel theory to better understand how multiple contexts, from global to local levels, affect access to the various resources needed to exit homelessness.

A Multilevel Contextual Theory of Exiting Homelessness

Many analyses of exits from homelessness, especially those using conventional quantitative techniques (Piliavin et al. 1993, 1996; Sosin, Piliavin, and Westerfelt 1990; Wong, Culhane, and Kuhn 1997; Wong and Piliavin 1997), have placed various theoretical perspectives in competition against one another, usually using multivariate regression analysis to assess which perspective is *the* most powerful predictor of exiting homelessness. Qualitative analyses of exits from homelessness generally emphasize a specific perspective or causal process such as social capital (Iwama 2003) or governmental programs (Conley 1996; von Mahs 2005) as driving success or failure in efforts to exit homelessness. The strategy of focusing on single perspectives, variables, or processes can be improved upon. I prefer approaches that combine perspectives and focus on various causal conditions, variables, and processes operating at multiple levels, yet that also strive for parsimony. The qualitative studies of exits from homelessness that have considered more than a single perspective, variable, or process often provide "laundry lists" of primarily individual-level factors affecting exits (MacKnee and Mervyn 2002; McNaughton 2008; Ravenhill 2008: Snow and Anderson 1993). I move beyond these studies by advancing a multilevel theory of the process of exiting homelessness, integrating various perspectives and showing how various conditions *combine* and *interact* to shape exits from homelessness (Marr 2012). Key to this strategy has been my comparative approach that provides variation in contexts at multiple levels in Los Angeles and Tokyo.

I have demonstrated that processes of neoliberal globalization constrain exits from homelessness in the world's leading urban areas, but more local contexts, especially at national, local (city-region), organizational, and microsocial (network) levels also interact to hinder or facilitate the process of entering and exiting homelessness. In Chapter 1, I combined local-level secondary data on labor and housing markets, welfare protections, and social services, and ethnographic data from individual experiences of becoming homeless, and showed that national- and local-level trends fueled by neoliberal globalization—such as increased income inequality, a decrease of living-wage jobs, immigrant competition for employment, welfare retrenchment, real estate speculation, and a lack of affordable housing—produce more homelessness in Los Angeles than in Tokyo. In Chapters 2 and 3, I showed that since many of these trends are more advanced in Los Angeles, where it is more difficult to exit homelessness through conventional welfare systems and labor and housing markets. This increased difficulty in exiting was evident in the nearly complete inability of Los Angeles interviewees to earn a monthly income equivalent to what would be acquired at the minimum wage working at least forty hours per week. The inability of Los Angeles interviewees to exit homelessness through mainstream labor and housing markets was due to transformed labor market conditions, possession of debilitating vulnerabilities reflecting thoroughly incapacitated social safety nets, and the much higher rents they faced due to greater inequality, population growth, real estate speculation, and gentrification. But Chapters 1, 2, and 3 also show how trends associated with globalization interact with national and local contexts, with macroeconomic policy, welfare regime, and social services systems, and with cultural patterns of racial exclusion, to increase or minimize the risks of economic vulnerability in the processes of entering and trying to exit homelessness.

There is also interaction between trends associated with globalization and conditions at lower social levels in the process of exiting homelessness. In Chapter 4, I showed that at the organizational level, housing programs with holistic, flexible, and homophilous organizational cultures foster the development of facilitative relationships between staff and clients that can aid exits out of homelessness. Thus it is not just whether or not one has access to an aid program; the program's organizational culture can also affect the role that staff does or does not play in facilitating exits. Also, in Chapter 5, I showed that at the network or microsocial level, a stronger, more heavily gendered cultural stigma attached to the condition of homelessness, as well as generational factors, can impede exits by obstructing ties between people who become homeless and their housed family. But these contextual effects are also shaped by social structures at large scales, namely national and urban welfare regimes. Thus, the trust-stifling organizational culture of Tokyo's transitional housing programs is influenced by national and municipal guidelines that imposed a short time limit, narrow definitions of acceptable work conditions, and limited connections with nongovernmental support organizations. Also, Japan's welfare regime places a heavy burden on male breadwinners, and when men fail to meet that expectation, the cultural frame of complete separation becomes viable to follow; many halt all contact with family in order to avoid becoming a burden on them. Although a heavy gendered stigma was not as evident in my Los Angeles interviews, many relationships with family were affected by the extensive and invasive U.S. penal state.

Another point of my multilevel theory emerging from Chapters 4 and 5 is that factors and processes at lower levels become more important in exits from homelessness when conditions at the local and national levels are more constrained. For example, in Los Angeles, the pressures of neoliberal globalization interacted with more dismal national and local conditions to make it very difficult to exit homelessness through mainstream labor and housing markets. In this context, conditions at the organizational and microsocial (network) levels became very important, and when favorable, were largely responsible for exits out of homelessness. In Tokyo, largely due to a more interventionist developmental state at national and urban levels, labor and housing market conditions were more favorable, and thus organizational and social capital contexts were not as important in exits from homelessness. This does not imply that should market conditions worsen in Tokyo, beneficial relationships between staff and program participants or ties with housed friends and family would naturally flourish, but rather the opposite. If labor and housing market conditions worsened considerably but other contexts remained static, exits from homelessness would become more difficult, and transitional housing users would be more desperate because organizational and microsocial (network) level contexts would remain unfavorable. However, it would become more important (while still difficult) for individuals in Tokyo to develop beneficial relationships with program staff and reach out to any housed family if they were not to persist in their homeless condition. My multilevel theory maintains that conditions at various scales are not static but in flux and can change to become more forgiving and promoting of exits from homelessness. This is particularly important at the organizational level. As I noted in Chapter 5, Tokyo's transitional housing programs were in their early years of implementation during my fieldwork and subsequently have made program changes to become more flexible. This has occurred perhaps most notably through allowing some clients who are unable to find full-time work to combine part-time work and welfare benefits in a half-work/half-welfare (*han-shūrō/ han-fukushi*) arrangement.

Since my multilevel framework of exiting homelessness allows for change in contexts at various levels, it challenges strong forms of critical urban studies that depict the spread of American-style neoliberal globalization in potentially monolithic form (Mitchell 2003; Vitale 2009; Wacquant 2009). My findings are consistent with and thus add further support to theories of social polarization and advanced urban marginality that attribute the rise of mass homelessness and other manifestations of marginality to the shift to neoliberal post-Fordism and global city status (Sassen 2001; Wacquant 2008). Indeed, many of my inter-viewees who exited homelessness in both cities worked in low-wage, precarious employment, rendering them vulnerable to returns to homelessness. Also, some in Los Angeles remained under surveillance or indirectly affected by the penal system, as predicted by theories of expansive neoliberal punitive and disciplin-ary approaches to managing social insecurity and marginal populations. But my analysis highlights greater complexity and potential for *agency at various social levels* to resist and challenge the marginalizing forces of neoliberal globalization. Although at the macro level such strong depictions of American-style neoliberal-ization shed light on the harsh structural conditions that have driven the growth and apparent entrenchment of homelessness across global cities, they neglect "path dependence" in different urban areas and can obscure variation at more local levels (Brenner and Theodore 2002; Peck and Tickell 2002), overlooking alternatives that can possibly ameliorate and eventually end mass homelessness. Thus my findings demonstrate that neoliberal globalization is not a uniform pro-cess; global, national, and local contexts are embedded in intertwined processes of "glocalization."

More light needs to be shed on alternatives to the polarizing tendencies of neoliberal globalization, including societal responses to homelessness. Recently urban scholars have begun to identify and explore a greater diversity of responses beyond the punishment of "quality of life" crime policing and the discipline of workfare, including abeyance (containment), sustenance, and care (Cloke, May, and Johnson 2010; DeVerteuil 2013; DeVerteuil, May, and von Mahs 2009; John-sen and Fitzpatrick 2010; May and Cloke 2013). Chapter 4, in particular, ad-vances this movement by demonstrating how variation at the ground level of social service programs is shaped by urban- and national-level welfare regimes. Transitional housing programs did serve a disciplinary function by emphasiz-ing individual responsibility for homelessness and pressuring my interviewees to reenter the low-wage labor market. Also, they served an abeyance function by simply warehousing some interviewees before they were churned back to the streets or to other programs or shelters without exiting homelessness. But these functions interacted differently with more caring functions promoting exits from homelessness in the two cities. The Los Angeles transitional housing program was more holistic, flexible, and homophilous and thus served a greater caring function than its Tokyo counterparts. Interestingly, the trust-promoting context of the Los Angeles program was at least in part promoted by neoliberal welfare restructuring. Specifically, the subcontracted, competitive neoliberal model re-quires mobilization of private resources by NPO service providers, but it also al-lows freedom to develop more flexible, holistic, and homophilous programs. The developmental welfare approach in Tokyo transitional housing took the form of direct subcontracting to semigovernmental agencies and conservative restrictions on acceptable forms of aid. These contrasts show the complex mixing of disciplinary and caring functions in transitional housing programs, but also that some aspects of neoliberal approaches can actually enable caring functions.

By examining the interactive relationships of causal contexts operating at multiple social levels, I draw on movements in sociology and geography that challenge reductionist explanations of social problems and phenomena such as homelessness that place causality with the individual (Duster 2006), and that challenge deterministic depictions of globalization that neglect the interaction and generative roles of more local contexts (Burawoy et al. 2000; Gille and O'Riain 2002; Massey 1997; Wolch 1996; Wolch and DeVerteuil 2001). The main point of my multilevel contextual theory is that studies of exits from homelessness and other forms of social exclusion and mobility at the margins of global cities need to explore the complex interactions of these contexts at various social levels to understand individual experiences of marginality and efforts to attain social mobility. This multilevel approach could be applied to studies of transition out of stigmatized roles, many of them overlapping with being homeless, such as mental patient, prisoner, substance abuser, ward of foster care, and the like. Practically, more contextual awareness is necessary to highlight the various forgiving contexts at multiple levels that can contribute to alleviating social marginality in global cities.

Forgiving Contexts

My findings challenge neoliberal, "individual deficits" and "medical model" approaches to addressing homelessness, such as transitional housing. These approaches focus on providing short-term housing and fixing an individual's problems so he or she can compete in mainstream labor and housing markets. But such approaches are criticized for overemphasizing discipline and internalization of responsibility for homelessness while not addressing structural conditions in labor markets, housing markets, and welfare and social services that produce homelessness (Lyon-Callo 2004; Tamaki 2002). People who exit homelessness remain vulnerable to a return and are simply replaced by others pushed into the condition by persistent structural arrangements. My findings show that these broader conditions need to be addressed not only to prevent people from falling into homelessness but also to facilitate enduring exits. For example, more extensive structural inequalities in labor markets, housing markets, and welfare systems contribute to a substantially larger population experiencing homelessness in Los Angeles than in Tokyo. Also, transitional housing users in Los Angeles are largely unable to exit homelessness through mainstream labor and housing markets. In Tokyo, many transitional housing users were able to exit homelessness through mainstream labor and housing markets since opportunities were less constrained there, but low wages and unstable employment arrangements rendered them vulnerable to returns to homelessness.

Therefore, truly ending mass homelessness in global cities cannot be achieved by merely developing better programs to aid persons who fall into homelessness, but must involve broad structural changes in how opportunity, risk, and reward are distributed in society. These changes must also extend beyond recent "rapid rehousing" and other preventative measures and must focus on reducing the larger population that is vulnerable to homelessness. Efforts to improve labor market conditions, such as living-wage movements; to improve housing market conditions, such as affordable housing movements; and to improve welfare and social services, such as advocacy for welfare recipients and elimination of "dumping" practices, are fundamental to ending homelessness. Creating more forgiving contexts will require collaborative coalitions to pressure local and national governments to promote employment at a living wage, affordable housing, and adequate welfare supports. The Occupy movement in the United States in 2011 and antipoverty movements in Japan such as the "dispatch village" (*haken mura*) movement of 2008 show promise for their broad-based concern about rising structural inequality and for burgeoning collaborative efforts to address it. However, there is ample reason for tempering optimism since both movements were short lived and produced less than satisfactory results for many participants who were experiencing homelessness. For example, although participation in the Occupy movement helped some exit homelessness (Smith, Casteñeda, and Heyman 2012), when protest encampments in places like Zuccotti Park were cleared many of these participants likely remained homeless. In Tokyo, temporary shelters that were created to help dislocated workers survive the winter were abruptly closed, forcing many to return to the streets.

These limited gains point to the need for even deeper structural change. Movements that aim to change structural conditions are necessary because inequality and poverty have not improved substantially even with economic growth, as seen in the late 1990s United States, but have only become further entrenched. Since economic growth has been predicated on low-wage labor and on governments' promoting corporate expansion rather than social redistribution, under post-Fordist neoliberalism urban marginality has increased in times of both economic growth and stagnation (Wacquant 2008). Therefore, concerned citizens in globalizing cities cannot simply wait for economic growth and instead must actively forge broad-based collaborative movements that challenge structural inequality. Perhaps limited understanding of the societal arrangements that buffer against wide inequality, poverty, and homelessness prevents the development of broad social movements to attack the structural conditions that perpetuate these conditions. One route toward better understanding could be to break away from American and Japanese parochialism and explore countries where there is more equality and less poverty and homelessness. Thus, a forgiving context at the global level would be one in which dialogue about various forms of capitalism and welfare regimes and their strengths and weaknesses is encouraged and used as a springboard for action and policy change.

Sociologist Lane Kenworthy (2014) suggests that "modern social democracy," like that found in Nordic countries such as Denmark and Sweden, is a likely future if advanced capitalist countries such as the United States are to better help citizens cope with the heightened risks of global capitalist society. Social democracy does not simply mean that government provides a large public safety net as an alternative to private sector employment, but also that government provides aid and services aimed at buffering risks and enhancing economic productivity and growth. Examples include universal access to early education and health care, robust labor market programs, investment in public infrastructure, and support for research and development. Regulations are needed to protect workers, consumers, and the environment, but the broader institutional context still encourages flexibility in the business sector, making it easier for entrepreneurs to start or close businesses, access human capital, hire and fire, adjust work hours, and contain labor costs. This private-sector flexibility is enabled through expanded unemployment insurance and earned income tax credits as well as insurance to compensate for loss of wages when skills become redundant and workers have to move into lower paying occupations. Although the minimum wage needs to be raised to the level of a living wage and indexed to inflation, these other measures can limit labor costs for employers. For those displaced from the labor market, welfare benefits should be set to rise with GDP growth and inflation, and social services, especially those to promote employment, should be enhanced. As a last resort, government-sponsored employment can be used.

Together these programs would greatly limit the economic insecurity my interviewees in Los Angeles and Tokyo experienced, providing a better buffer against traumatic life experiences that were often the final push into homelessness. Universal access to early education and health care, child tax credits, expanded access to higher education, and treatment rather than punishment for substance abusers can improve the supply of human capital, further contributing to the economic strength of a nation. Such programs would also considerably limit inequality in early life, which greatly impacts longer-term life outcomes such as experiences of homelessness. This is extremely important considering that most interviewees in both cities came from lower than middle class, if not extremely poor, backgrounds. To skeptics, Kenworthy points out that the social safety net has already been expanding in the United States for decades since the New Deal, providing a base of programs and a track record on which to build. Also, social democratic countries with broad and dense social safety nets supported by the public sector have managed to maintain economic growth through programs designed to facilitate private-sector flexibility and vitality. Kenworthy argues that although funding an expansion of social insurance will require sacrifices, the increasingly tangible social costs of gaping inequality and the heightened risks of global society will continue to push Americans (and by implication, citizens of other wealthy capitalist countries like Japan) to be willing to accept greater burdens such as a national consumption tax (or a higher one in Japan).

Although broad solutions to limiting risk amid global neoliberalism may be found elsewhere, my comparison of exiting homelessness in Los Angeles and Tokyo reveals a number of ways that policymakers and citizens in the two places can learn from each other to better develop forgiving contexts that can limit homelessness. Lower overall levels of homelessness in Tokyo, and a greater role for employment in exits out of homelessness compared to Los Angeles, reflect the strengths of a developmental state that is more interventionist in the labor market and economy. Support from the federal state to cities, focusing on bolstering employment, can provide resources and alternative models to more entrepreneurial, neoliberal regimes that emphasize attracting global capital but erode efforts to improve equality. However, various approaches in Japan that combine to keep unemployment, inequality, and poverty at bay, such as legal barriers to mass layoffs and "convoy capitalism" in which less competitive firms in targeted sectors are prevented from going under, are often criticized for running up government debt and for being incompatible with economic globalization and demographic changes such as aging. Also, it would be impossible to simply transfer an entire social system or even specific aspects of it to the United States. Similarly, aspects of America's social structure that contribute to higher levels of homelessness, such as institutionalized racial inequality, far higher levels of single parenting, rampant substance abuse, mass imprisonment, and higher population growth, cannot easily be eradicated. Nevertheless, even though each approach must be adapted to the local context, my comparison suggests that a greater role for national and local government programs in the management of risk in increasingly turbulent labor markets is necessary for global cities to move toward ending homelessness. Indeed, recently there has been considerable pressure on Japan to liberalize its economy and labor force, including encouraging more foreign direct investment and the loosening of labor protections. My findings suggest that such a pathway without an ample social safety net would be disastrous to Tokyo's efforts to end homelessness in a broad sense. Instead, the apparent effectiveness of a more interventionist state on employment, which plays a greater buffering role to homelessness in Tokyo, provides support for the expansion of the social democratic programs outlined above.

Addressing affordable housing deficits is also crucial in eliminating mass homelessness; the high cost of rental housing is a robust predictor of high rates of homelessness in U.S. cities (Byrne et al. 2013). Very broadly, housing needs to be viewed more as a right than as an instrument of financial speculation (Pattillo 2013). The fact that nearly all of my Tokyo interviewees who had moved into rental housing lived in small and austere apartments, but not downgraded "slum" housing like Michelle's studio, suggests that simple, low-rent housing is a crucial resource to be preserved rather than an opportunity for private-sector specula- tion and gentrification. Certainly such housing needs to meet basic standards, but it should not simply be torn down and developed into housing that is out of reach for low-income earners. The widespread demolition of single room oc- cupancy hotels has long been demonstrated to be a contributing factor to rising homelessness in American cities such as Los Angeles (Hoch and Slayton 1989; Wolch and Dear 1993). Additionally, the affordable housing stock could be bol- stered through awarding more low-income housing tax credits for developments targeted to people at risk of homelessness as well as expanding the supply of rental subsidies such as those available through the Section 8 program in the United States. In highly polarized housing markets, targeted subsidies and a tax credit for renters could ease the burden of extremely high rents. In Tokyo, the re- source of simple, inexpensive housing that was crucial for many of my interview- ees' exits is currently under threat. The national government has changed zoning laws on building height and created special zones as a means to bolster economic growth from real estate development, causing a substantial increase in high-rise condominiums, especially visible in Tokyo's working-class east side (Sorensen, Okata, and Fujii 2010). Such development should be tempered so that it meets the needs of young families working in central Tokyo as well as aging workers, especially those with low incomes and limited familial support.

Under neoliberal globalization, national and urban regimes emphasize cor- porate expansion over social redistribution, depleting the institutional infra- structure available to aid vulnerable populations (Wacquant 2008). Thus, social service systems need to be bolstered to ensure that wards of public institutions are not dumped into homelessness but instead that accessing such bodies results in exit from or prevention of homelessness. A study of usage of public services such as hospitals, mental health treatment, and substance abuse programs, as well as involuntary incarceration in punitive facilities such as jails and prisons in Los Angeles, has shown that contact with these facilities increases just prior to the onset of homelessness (Economic Roundtable 2009). This suggests that these institutions fail as preventative or ameliorative mechanisms, and that they can actually exacerbate vulnerability to homelessness. As demonstrated in the cases of Sinee, who moved from a short-term board-and-care facility to emergency shelter after being discharged from a psychiatric ward, and Vernon, who left the Los Angeles County Jail for the streets of Skid Row, discharge planning from such institutions such as hospitals, psychiatric facilities, jails, and prisons needs to be improved dramatically. These institutions need to be able to identify and target people vulnerable to homelessness. Such an approach in Veterans Affairs hospitals across the United States has proven effective in recent reductions of homelessness among veterans (United States Interagency Council on Homelessness [USICH] 2012) and thus should be expanded to institutions serving the general population. In Japanese cities such as Tokyo, these systems also need to be more effective in aiding the transition back into conventional housing and employment, given that a number of my interviewees had been discharged from hospitals to the streets or emergency housing and there has been an increase in persons with disabilities turning up in emergency housing programs (Kitagawa 2011). Adequate transitional support out of such social services and public institutions could lessen use of shelters, which tend to be very costly. But to bolster these systems, there must be a reversal of the decline in government financial support that is emblematic of the neoliberal tendency.

Although cash benefit welfare programs have been under threat in both countries, they should instead be supported in order to provide holistic prevention of homelessness. The United States lacks a broad safety net program that guarantees a minimum standard of living like Japan's livelihood protection (*seikatsu hogo*). Also, the Temporary Aid to Needy Families program implemented in welfare reform during the mid-1990s dramatically reduced use of welfare benefits for adults with dependent children. In the fall of 2013, food stamp benefit amounts were reduced nationally. More locally, Los Angeles's General Relief program periodically faces threats in terms of reductions in the length of time an eligible person can receive the benefit and increased workfare requirements. Amid rising welfare rolls in Japan due to increased inequality, unemployment, and the aging of the population, livelihood protection has recently seen cuts to the benefit amount. Also, there is discussion of further restrictions, such as on cutting the length of time one can receive benefits over a lifetime and increasing the authority of welfare offices to investigate the resources of family members who may be able to contribute financially to applicants.

Although welfare reform in the United States succeeded in moving many families off the rolls and into employment, this occurred during a rare period of extended economic growth in the late 1990s, and it failed to move them out of poverty (Danzinger 2010). Even though an empirical link is difficult to demonstrate, it is likely that erosion of these welfare benefits has contributed to increases in the poverty rate and in families as a growing subpopulation experiencing homelessness in the United States (USICH 2010). Thus, rather than further eroding coverage of welfare benefits, in both countries barriers to access should be removed, benefits should be indexed to price increases, and support for increasing income through employment should be implemented in a flexible and holistic manner. In the United States, the SSI/SSDI Outreach, Access and Recovery Initiative (SOAR) and Homeless Outreach Projects and Evaluation Initiative (HOPE) have made strides in improving access to benefits for persons with disabilities. The United States Interagency Council on Homelessness (USICH 2010) has recommended that the long-term effects of addiction be recognized as a disabling condition and that access to acceptable forms of proof of identification needed to access benefits be expanded. In Japan, expanded access to welfare benefits has contributed to the countercyclical decline in street homelessness amid rising unemployment and poverty, a fact that seems lost on recent attacks on the livelihood protection program in the Japanese media and national legislature.

In terms of specific programs to address the predicament of those who have found themselves homeless, my findings support movement away from the transitional housing model. Transitional and emergency housing have been criticized because of their high cost and limited success in moving people out of homelessness (Burt et al. 2001; Culhane 1992; Lyon-Callo 2004; Yamada 2009). Major policy alternatives to transitional housing have been "housing first" and "rapid rehousing" approaches, which emphasize early subsidy of housing and supportive services to promote long-term stability, including assistance in securing employment. For those with disabilities, permanent supportive housing has demonstrated greater success in producing long-term exits from homelessness than emergency and transitional housing, at a cost lower than that incurred by use of public services by persons left to subsist amid homelessness on the streets or in shelters (Culhane 2008; Culhane, Metreaux, and Hadley 2002; Tsemberis and Asmussen 1999; Tsemberis and Eisenberg 2000; Tsemberis, Gulcur, and Nakae 2004). These studies have generally shown that retention in permanent supportive housing is around 80 percent whereas transitional housing generally helps move no more than 50 percent of clients into conventional housing, even for a single night. As explained in the introduction, this discrepancy in success rate is also found in housing-first versus transitional housing programs in Tokyo. Once in permanent supportive housing, persons with disabilities tend to stabilize, and substance abuse and mental health outcomes improve (Padgett et al. 2011). The housing-first approach has demonstrated more success in keeping individuals housed since there is no time limit on tenure and thus residents do not face the possibility of timing out of programs, which can result in sudden loss of housing and possibly a return to homelessness. Also, there are fewer rules and requirements governing the lives of individuals in housing-first programs compared to transitional housing, meaning that there are fewer opportunities for program infractions, which can lead to immediate loss of housing.

Permanent supportive housing in Los Angeles for people with low incomes but without disabilities such as mental illness has been shown to stabilize housing through high retention rates, but may not have the high savings to broader public costs of housing targeted to people with disabilities (Economic Roundtable 2009). Instead, preventative measures and rapid rehousing approaches implemented in the United States as part of the American Recovery and Reinvestment Act of 2009 show promise in replacing transitional housing for persons without disabilities. Preventative measures provide short-term subsidies to persons at risk of homelessness, defined as having very low income and being in a crisis situation such as being unable to pay rent or utility bills. Rapid rehousing aims to avoid stays in emergency or transitional housing and instead to place persons experiencing homelessness in housing that can be subsidized short-term with an eventual transition off of subsidies. Recipients of such aid are allowed to "transition in place" (USICH 2010), receiving job search assistance and other forms of aid such as case management and counseling while living in rental housing. Both preventative measures and rapid rehousing have been effective in keeping a surge of homelessness at bay in the United States amid the global economic crisis (USICH 2012). If such measures were available to some of my transitional housing users in Los Angeles when they first lost employment, such as Rita, they could have avoided a drift into Skid Row from where it took them years to return to conventional employment and housing. Although preventative and rapid rehousing measures have shown promise, problems identifying persons in need as they fall into homelessness as well as meeting massive need are great challenges. Such measures will not be successful without broader remedies for structural inequality.

In Japan, livelihood protection (*seikatsu hogo*) welfare benefits can serve a similar preventative and rapid rehousing function. By alleviating the stigma of benefit receipt through the reduction of street-level bureaucratic practices, people vulnerable to homelessness due to insufficient employment and debt could avoid the predicament. Private NPOs that provide housing in a more flexible way than existing transitional housing programs could also use the welfare system in a rapid rehousing fashion. Much concern has been raised that "poverty businesses" are warehousing persons experiencing homelessness, putting them on benefits, and providing substandard housing and aid while profiting from the cash benefit. However, with improved oversight of organizations using this model, it could be expanded to promote more durable exits from homelessness than the transitional housing model that simply pushes people back into the precarious low-wage service sector. A few of my Tokyo interviewees, such as Tsukada-san, the fifty-five-year-old former computer programmer from Saitama, and Takahashi-san, the fifty-five-year-old Tokyoite and former day laborer, used both publicly subcontracted transitional housing and privately operated housing funded through welfare benefits. Both believed the programs were similar in terms of having to search for work by oneself, but felt that they benefited from more time to search for work and looser constraints on the types of work deemed acceptable in the welfare-funded facilities. This approach could move closer to the rapid rehousing model by providing transitional support services to people in simple apartments paid for by welfare benefits, rather than warehousing them in small and dismal shelters like the one endured by Pak-san that was described in Chapter 1.

Although I argue for new measures that avoid the time-limited, facility-based approach of transitional housing, the strong positive role that relationships with program staff played in exits from homelessness in Los Angeles suggests that alternative programs should be structured to ensure resident access to potentially helpful organizational ties. This suggests a need for various forms of service-enriched housing. Supportive housing measures can be provided through either pairing rent subsidies with services, creating new units with supportive services at a single site, or creating set-aside subsidized units within an affordable housing community (USICH 2010). Thus staff should either be on-site or make regular visits to subsidized housing facilities or apartments in a manner that promotes client trust, so substance abuse relapses, problems at the workplace, and other crises may be avoided, and necessary material resources provided. An approach combining subsidized housing and accessible supportive services in various ways can help address the risk of return to homelessness after exit. This risk loomed for my Tokyo interviewees due to their precarious employment conditions, but seemed less of a concern to my Los Angeles interviewees in subsidized housing. In subsidized housing, a sudden loss or decline of income from employment would not dramatically increase the risk of return to homelessness since income loss would be made up by an increased housing subsidy. Also, staff would be accessible to help people through times of crisis in a holistic fashion. Oftentimes, the crucial assistance provided by caseworkers and other staff requires considerable effort and work hours beyond specified job requirements. Thus, supportive services should be sufficiently funded and caseworkers adequately compensated. Also, while private nonprofit organizations in both Los Angeles and Tokyo demonstrate the innovation and flexibility necessary to foster the trust and social capital of persons experiencing or at risk of homelessness, their efforts should not be co-opted into neoliberal retreat from government support of social safety nets. Thus, the reliance on private nonprofit service providers should be embedded in the broader expansion of public-sector safety nets described above.

Expanding supportive housing, prevention, and rapid rehousing over transitional housing is consistent with the USICH's (2010) Opening Doors plan to transform the American homeless services system to a crisis response system directed toward quickly moving people into stable housing. A similar view of changes in homelessness support services in Japan has also been expressed to me in interviews at Japan's Ministry of Health, Labor, and Welfare and with administrators of Tokyo's self-reliance support centers. However, as early interventions in the United States in the 1980s and in Japan in the 1990s have shown, crisis systems that do not address the structural forces driving increases in homelessness will face limitations in ending the problem. The USICH (2010, 2012) says that emergency and transitional housing are crucial parts of this system, but that they should be focused on rapidly moving users into stable, long-term housing. Rapid rehousing measures have been shown to most often require only short-term subsidies of a few months' time to allow people to avoid homelessness. However, the problems created by Tokyo's short time limit on use of its self-reliance support centers suggest that aid programs should not have short or rigid time limits. Additionally, the high cost of transitional housing and its limited effectiveness in promoting exits supports movement away from this model. Indeed, many of my Los Angeles interviewees merely moved from transitional housing into subsidized SRO hotels, where they eventually stabilized. Also, they felt their lives had improved over transitional housing where they often had to live in shared quarters and faced constant stress from the possibility of being terminated for rule violations. Like Kobo in the vignette that preceded this chapter, they greatly appreciated the privacy and independence afforded by supportive housing, but they also appreciated the aid that they received from on-site staff and the staff of other programs in Skid Row. These cases call into question the requirement to first stay in transitional housing for up to two years before earning the right to subsidized housing. Since the use of public services declines over time while in subsidized housing (Economic Roundtable 2009), earlier placement should be seen as a cost-effective investment that prevents the financial and human costs of time-limited transitional housing.

Also, all interventions should have adequate employment services to discourage overreliance on state welfare. This is not simply because policy measures should be implemented solely on the basis of cost effectiveness, but also because of the sense of meaning and worth provided by work, as expressed by my interviewees. But these employment services need to be more than simply the job-preparedness assistance provided in the transitional housing programs I studied. As shown in Chapter 3, job developers need to provide actual job leads to which program participants do not already have access through public employment agencies. Job developers need to cultivate relationships with local employers who provide living-wage employment. Also, persons experiencing or at risk of homelessness need access to educational and job skills training that improves their employability. Many of the transitional housing users that I followed had worked extensively in the past, but their skills and experience had become outdated. They should be given the time and support needed to update or acquire new skills that would allow them to avoid low-paying precarious jobs and thus decrease their risk of returning to homelessness. Targeted programs for veterans and persons with disabilities, such as vocational rehabilitation and incentives for hiring veterans, have likely contributed to the decrease in homelessness among these groups (USICH 2012). Access to such programs should be expanded. Although the broader value of work is extremely important, given low wages in expanding sectors such as services, many in global cities like Los Angeles and Tokyo who do find work will still need aid to avoid homelessness. The use of half-work/half-welfare (*han-shūrō/han-fukushi*) in Tokyo to augment low wages and encourage employment is a promising approach.

The last forgiving context to ameliorate homelessness is that of the aid provided by family in exits from homelessness, explored directly in Chapter 5. Family ties were used considerably more widely in Los Angeles compared to Tokyo, due to a mix of generational factors and an institutionalized gendered stigma of failure, which caused men in Tokyo who were unable to live up to the responsibility of being a breadwinner to completely sever ties with their families. Since this stigma is culturally rooted in Japan's welfare regime, this context is likely to be difficult to change quickly. Also, it is important to note that shared familial responsibility to provide mutual aid to members so that they avoid the most extreme forms of poverty likely contributes to Japan's overall low level of homelessness compared to the United States (Aoki 2006). However, as inequality and insecurity affect a broader segment of Japan's population, it is possible that conditions such as homelessness may unfortunately get normalized. This could have the ironically positive effect of diluting the stigma of unemployment and homelessness, which is particularly acute among men. A benevolent trajectory would be that traditional familial practices of mutual aid in Japan continue to buffer against homelessness, but the stigma of unemployment among men recedes in pushing them out of homes and preventing them from reunifying. Since the strong stigma of unemployment and failure is rooted in the Japanese welfare regime's strong reliance on male breadwinners, changes in this system may be the key to reducing stigma. Here we can see that addressing high gender inequality in Japan in labor markets and households can serve the interests of men as well, by liberating them from the narrow and burdensome role of primary breadwinner.

However, as with improving the ameliorative role of social service organization staff, caution must be taken to avoid a neoliberal downloading of state responsibility for safety nets onto increasingly fragile families. As household size becomes smaller in both countries, the risk-buffering role of the family as a social institution can erode. Thus it is important that broader social safety nets be bolstered, rather than dumping greater social responsibility on a weakening institution.

In order to end homelessness in global cities, localities must extend dialogue and efforts beyond those focused on persons on the streets over the long term and promote forgiving contexts at multiple levels that can make even short-term homelessness a rarity. Although broad social mechanisms and public policies that contribute to the end of homelessness cannot be simply transplanted from one global city to another, awareness of alternative and more forgiving contexts increases the possibilities for meaningful change. Global cities have succeeded in accumulating unprecedented wealth. However, at the same time, they exemplify a global trend of widening inequality and marginality. It is thus imperative that these cities expand beyond a narrow focus on macroeconomic indicators and do the hard work necessary to include the most vulnerable citizens as beneficiaries of economic growth. Only then will the title of "global city" no longer be grandiose, but reflect true leadership in both the economic and civil sectors of global urban society.

Notes

EXIT STORIES: CARLOS AND TAKAGI-SAN

1. All names of interviewees used in this book are pseudonyms unless otherwise noted. Also, I try to use the exact labels that my interviewees used to describe their ethnicity or racial background, resulting in alternation of some labels (e.g., African American for some, black for others). As is common in a multiethnic city like Los Angeles, many had complicated descriptions of their ethnic background. In such cases I used the most parsimonious descriptor I could come up with. For example, see David's ethnic background in chapter 2.

2. All quotations presented in this book from interviewees were tape recorded, transcribed by a professional, and then checked for accuracy by me.

3. General Relief is Los Angeles County's assistance program that provides cash benefits and job readiness services to extremely poor households. See chapter 1 for an explanation of its requirements and obligations.

4. Pseudonyms for Tokyo interviewees are surnames and the honorific "-san," following the common practice in Japan among adults who are not relatives or very close friends. This is the manner in which I addressed interviewees in our interactions.

5. When converting yen amounts to U.S. dollars in this book, I use the exchange rate for the approximate midpoint of my data collection August 1, 2004 (1¥ = $0.00897).

6. The minimum wage in Tokyo in 2004 was 710 yen (about $6.37 per hour). For comparison, the minimum wage in Los Angeles in 2004 was $6.75 per hour. The rate for Tokyo was accessed from the website of the Japanese Ministry of Health, Labor, and Welfare at http://tokyo-roudoukyoku.jsite.mhlw.go.jp/jirei_toukei/chingin_kanairoudou/toukei/saitei_chingin/20081022-chingin.html. The rate for Los Angeles was accessed from the website of the State of California Department of Industrial Relations at http://www.dir.ca.gov/iwc/minimumwagehistory.htm.

INTRODUCTION

1. Living wages are generally substantially higher than minimum wages because they include the various local costs to sustain households of different sizes over the long term, divided by full-time hours (Luce 2004). The U.S. Department of Housing and Urban Development (HUD) considers housing to be affordable if it costs no more than one-third of a household's income. See HUD's website at http://www.hud.gov/offices/cpd/affordablehousing/.

2. *Yoseba* or *doyagai* are areas in Japanese cities where simple, pay-by-the day lodgings called *doya* are clustered. In recent history, these were used by day laborers in construction, manufacturing, and shipping, supporting economic growth in the miracle and bubble economies of postwar Japan. With economic stagnation, the decline of the construction industry, and the aging of residents, these districts have become areas where homelessness, welfare recipients, and support organizations are clustered, following a trajectory analogous to American skid rows (see Fowler 1998; Gill 2001; Marr 1997).

3. SRO hotels are residency hotels with small and simple rooms historically used by single, low-income, and often mobile people. They are often clustered in skid row districts in U.S. cities and are similar to Japanese *doya* described in the preceding note.

In many cities in both countries, nonprofit organizations have renovated SROs and used government subsidies to provide housing and supportive services to people who have experienced or are at risk of homelessness.

4. Ed, a fifty-one-year-old African American chef from Baltimore, shows the other side of these dynamics. Ed ended up homeless in 2002 after moving to Los Angeles and being robbed of his belongings outside a Skid Row hotel. I interviewed him a few months later in a short-term temporary housing program in Hollywood from which he was soon to move into permanent subsidized housing. Here is his description of how what he thought to be a major vulnerability turned out to be an asset: "Being HIV positive in certain aspects is like a blessing. I would have never got into the Shelter Plus Care [permanent supportive housing] program. I would have had to apply for Section 8 [federal subsidized housing for low-income households] but I understand that it takes two to three years to get Section 8. I wouldn't have been able to come into [this housing program]. Yeah, it's sort of like a plus, but me personally I see no downside to it right now other than health issues but yet, like I said, I'm not going to go out with a banner and say, 'Hey, I'm HIV!'"

5. From the website of Kroll, the consulting firm led by Chairman William Bratton, at http://www.altegrity.com/Kroll.aspx.

6. According to HUD (2011, 3), "A chronically homeless person is defined as an unaccompanied homeless individual with a disabling condition who has either been continually homeless for a year or more or who has had at least four episodes of homelessness in the past 3 years. To be considered chronically homeless, a person must have been on the streets or in emergency shelter (e.g. not in transitional or permanent housing) during these stays."

7. This was expressed in an interview with the TMG Welfare Division representative who visited New York on this trip and was responsible for designing the housing first program.

8. According to HUD (2011, 3), unsheltered refers to a "homeless person who is living in a place not meant for human habitation, such as the streets, abandoned buildings, vehicles, parks, and train stations."

9. From unpublished documents of the MHLW provided in interviews in July 2011.

CHAPTER 1

1. For example, see Aoki 2006; Dordick 1997; Fukuhara 2000; Helvie and Kuntsmann 1999; Marpsat and Fiordion 1998; Santos 1996; Toro et al. 2007; von Mahs 2005; Wolch and Dear 1993.

2. Numbers from the Tokyo Metropolitan Government's Bureau of Welfare and Public Health, http://www.fukushihoken.metro.tokyo.jp/seikatsu/rojo/homelesstaisaku.files/homeless2511.pdf.

3. These figures exclude cities such as Glendale, Long Beach, and Pasadena that conducted independent counts. Between 2011 and 2013, this area did see a 21 percent increase in street homelessness, possibly influenced by changes in the sampling of census tracts for the street count, and a 22 percent decrease in the shelter population attributed to expiring funding for shelters and increased use of motel vouchers (LAHSA 2013).

4. County population estimates are from the American Community Survey, viewed on the American FactFinder website, http://factfinder2.census.gov/faces/nav/jsf/pages/index.xhtml.

5. From a report of the MHLW, www.mhlw.go.jp/shingi/2010/05/dl/s0531–14c_1.pdf—2010–07–21.

6. Data on the Los Angeles unsheltered population from LAHSA (2012), Los Angeles's total population from AmericanFactfinder (factfinder2.census.gov), and Tokyo's total

population from the TMG website, http://www.metro.tokyo.jp/ENGLISH/PROFILE/overview03.htm.

7. Unless otherwise indicated, county-level data presented in this section are from the AmericanFactfinder website of the U.S. Census Bureau (factfinder2.census.gov).

8. Gini ratios measure income disparity, with 1.0 indicating completely equal receipt of income, and 0 indicating total monopoly of income by one person. Ratios for 1970–2000 were calculated by Telles and Ortiz (2009) with U.S. Census data.

9. From "Tokyo Metropolis Indicators and Basic Data," published by the Tokyo Metropolitan Government on its website, www.tokei.metro.tokyo.jp/ssihyou/ss-etosi.htm#1.

10. Analysis of Japanese census data (*zenkoku shohizei jittai chōsa*) by Ashida (2005) found a Gini coefficient for Tokyo of 0.31 in 1999. A separate analysis of Japanese census data by a private researcher found a Gini coefficient for Tokyo of 0.31 in 2004 and 0.315 in 2009 (http://www2.ttcn.ne.jp/honkawa/7357.html).

11. From the Tokyo Statistical Yearbook maintained by the Tokyo Metropolitan Government at http://www.toukei.metro.tokyo.jp/tnenkan/tn-eindex.htm.

12. From historical Fair Market Rent data published by HUD at http://www.huduser.org/portal/datasets/fmr.html.

13. Figures calculated using the National Low Income Housing Coalition's Housing Wage Calculator at http://nlihc.org/library/wagecalc.

14. From "Tokyo Metropolis Indicators and Basic Data," a report of the Tokyo Metropolitan Government, www.tokei.metro.tokyo.jp/ssihyou/ss-etosi.htm#1.

EXIT STORIES: MICHELLE AND TSUKADA-SAN

1. The "twenty-eight day shuffle" is a practice by unsubsidized SROs of moving guests out of rooms after twenty-eight days, preventing them from establishing residency and earning renter's rights.

CHAPTER 2

1. As reported in January 28, 2013, article on the *Japan Times* website, http://www.japantimes.co.jp/news/2013/01/28/business/welfare-payments-to-be-slashed-¥74-billion-to-root-out-the-comfortably-poor/#.USEelY5OHBE.

2. Both SSI and SSDI are federal aid programs for persons with disabilities. Persons that have paid a sufficient amount of Social Security taxes are eligible for SSDI whereas those who do not meet this requirement can apply for SSI. Since my interviewees generally did not make distinctions between the two programs, in this chapter I generally refer to both programs as SSI, following their practice.

3. On the SSA's website, http://www.ssa.gov/dibplan/dqualify4.htm.

4. The transitional housing program's savings requirement was in conflict with the income requirements of GR. The program helped conceal participants' savings by having them purchase postal money orders and hand them over to case managers who kept them under lock and key. Program participants were told to not report this savings to DPSS in their quarterly reports since this would disqualify them from benefits, causing them to be terminated.

5. From Japanese Law Translation, a website managed by Japan's Ministry of Justice that provides English translations of Japanese laws and regulations alongside the Japanese original: http://www.japaneselawtranslation.go.jp/law/detail/?ft=2&re=02&dn=1&yo=%E7%94%9F%E6%B4%BB%E4%BF%9D%E8%AD%B7&x=0&y=0&ky=&page=1.

6. Translated from the Ministry of Health, Labor, and Welfare website, http://www.mhlw.go.jp/seisakunitsuite/bunya/hukushi_kaigo/seikatsuhogo/seikatuhogo/index.html.

7. Venetia was one of a few interviewees who preferred that their real names be used in this book.

CHAPTER 3

1. This is a practice common in postwar Japan in which urban employers, often in manufacturing, hire groups of students, often from the countryside, directly from schools and usually for live-in employment.

2. *Gādoman* are stationed at construction sites in Japan to guide traffic and pedestrians by the site to ensure their safety. This is often translated as "security guard," which is not quite accurate since that term conjures up images for Americans of security work at special events, the type of work that Michelle did in Los Angeles, or to protect property.

3. This is likely influenced by the difficulty of detecting contemporary, "aversive" racial prejudice rather than simply an indicator of a lack of racial prejudice against my interviewees. Employers are unlikely to make racial prejudice in hiring practices apparent to job applicants, given the illegality and political incorrectness of prejudice. Also, it is possible that some interviewees were uncomfortable discussing racial prejudice with a white, male interviewer. But as I argue in chapters 1 and 2, the racial aspect of homelessness in Los Angeles and across the United States, namely the gross overrepresentation of African Americans, is perhaps one of the starkest contrasts with homelessness in Tokyo and Japan.

4. One transitional housing user, Hirota-san, a forty-three-year-old Tokyoite, was resident Korean. This means that his parents came to Japan prior to the end of World War Two, and he is not a Japanese citizen, despite being born and raised in Japan and culturally Japanese. When he first entered the program, he needed to register as a foreigner with the local ward office, and a staff person gave him special attention in this process. Although his non-Japanese status was visible to employers because he had to submit his foreign registration rather than a proof of residence (*jūminhyō*) as identification, he did not say that this was a problem in his job search. Of course, employers simply could have concealed their aversion to hiring a resident Korean. He had ten interviews before he was offered a job at a small printing company, but this was not unusual in Tokyo, and he felt it was because he lacked experience in the fields he was applying for (jobs in semiskilled manufacturing and warehousing that required use of computers) and because he is shy in interviews.

5. Nakamura-san, a thirty-five-year-old former gangster who had served time for murdering a rival, was able to quickly secure a low-paying but full-time cleaning job. He had completely falsified his work history on his application and felt that he was hired because he was relatively young. Questions about felonies and convictions are rare in job applications and interviews in Japan. None of my interviewees in Tokyo reported being asked about their criminal records when applying for jobs.

6. This is Southern California slang meaning "many." Here she is not saying that they were gang members.

7. This was the formal title for staff in Los Angeles assigned to help transitional housing users with issues related to employment. However, since the content of their work generally consists of "developing" jobs by seeking out employers and developing hiring relationships with the program, I put the title in quotes. As shown in this section, this reflects the views of my interviewees.

EXIT STORIES: VENETIA AND SAWA-SAN

1. In addition to teachers and doctors, licensed professionals such as lawyers, paralegals, and accountants are also commonly referred to as "*sensei*" in Japanese.

CHAPTER 4

1. For demonstrations of a more facilitative role, see MacKnee and Mervyn (2002), Marr (2005a), McNaughton (2008), Ravenhill (2008), and Rowe (1999). For examples of the latter perspective, see Dordick (1997), Joniak (2005), and Marr (2005b).

2. Dordick (1997) compared large warehouse-style shelters and smaller church-based shelters in New York City, but describes relationships between staff and shelter users as similarly conflictive in both settings. Since the time that Dordick's data were collected, programs addressing homelessness have increased in number and diversified in approach.

3. I interviewed more staff persons in Tokyo because I covered five programs there, whereas I covered only one program in Los Angeles. Also, I conducted staff interviews in Tokyo as part of a collaborative research project (Kitagawa 2005), facilitating collection of a larger sample.

4. This refers to a clan in the southern regions of Japan that is believed to serve as the founding people of premodern Japan.

5. Hirota-san, a forty-three-year-old former print factory worker, was the only person of the seventeen transitional housing program participants I followed who disclosed minority status. He was a resident Korean, born and raised in Tokyo. His case manager (ethnic status unknown) helped him renew his foreign registration card so he could look for work. Resident Koreans, despite most often being born and raised in Japan, are not Japanese citizens, but can naturalize.

6. From http://www.lahsa.org/who_we_fund/metro_los_angeles_spa4.asp.

7. The social distance between the *shakai fukushi hōjin* that ran the transitional housing programs and the NPO that provided consultation and guarantors was particularly palpable when I would accompany NPO staff on biweekly visits to the programs. NPO staff were not allowed to set foot in the program beyond the entryway and were not provided any space to meet with clients. Transitional program staff would announce that we had arrived and anyone interested in talking with NPO staff could go outside. Consultations would generally be conducted in a nearby park, which was pleasant when the weather was good, but hardly practical in the rain and cold.

8. Well aware of the importance of developing connections with other community organizations, the Los Angeles program required participants to attend two "outside meetings" per week. This requirement was flexibly applied, with any outside social activity, including attending church, for example, being acceptable.

CHAPTER 5

1. Like Venetia, Raymond was an interviewee who wanted his real name used.

EXIT STORY: KOBO

1. Although in our first interview Kobo spoke in Japanese, in later interviews he spoke in English.

CONCLUSION

1. David may have been correct about his uniqueness in terms of his ethnicity, college education, and limited social ties with coethnic immigrants, but his difficulty in securing income in Los Angeles's low-skill labor market was hardly unique.

References

Abe, Aya. 2010. "*Dare ga Rojō ni Nokotta ka?*" [Who is left on the streets?]. *Hōmuresu to Shakai* [Homelessness and Society] 3:18–25.

Abu-Lughod, Janet. 1999. *New York, Chicago, Los Angeles: America's Global Cities.* Minneapolis: University of Minnesota Press.

———. 2007. "The Challenge of Comparative Case Studies." *City* 11 (3): 399–404.

Aoki, Hideo. 2000. *Gendai Nihon no Toshi Kaso: Yoseba to Nojukusha to Gaikokujin Roudousha* [The urban underclass in contemporary Japan: *Yoseba*, the homeless, and foreign laborers]. Tokyo: Akashi Shoten.

———. 2003. "Homelessness in Osaka: Globalization, *Yoseba*, and Disemployment." *Urban Studies* 40 (2): 361–79.

———. 2006. *Japan's Underclass: Day Laborers and the Homeless.* Melbourne, Australia: Trans Pacific Press.

Aoki, Hideo, Mitsutoshi Nakane, Ayumi Kariya, Akihiko Nishizawa, and Keiko Yamaguchi. 1999. *Basho wo Akero! Yoseba/Hōmuresu no Shakaigaku* [Open a place! Sociology of *yoseba*/homelessness]. Tokyo: Shoraisha.

Aoki, Osamu, and Deborah McDowell Aoki. 2005. "Invisible Poverty in Japan: Case Studies and Realities of Single Mothers." *Journal of Poverty* 9 (1): 1–21.

Ashida, Takuma. 2005. "*Shotoku to Shitsugyōritsu kara miru Tōkyō no Bunkyoku no Yukue*" [The status of Tokyo's polarization as seen from income and unemployment]. In *Posuto Seichōki ni okeru Shizokukano na Chīki Hatten no Kōsō to Genjitsu: Kaihatsushugi no Monogatari wo Koete* [The design and reality of possibly enduring community development in the postgrowth period—beyond the tale of developmentalism], edited by Takashi Machimura, 68–77. Tokyo: Hitotsubashi University Graduate School of Social Sciences.

Auyero, Javier. 2011. "Researching the Urban Margins: What Can the United States Learn from Latin America and Vice Versa?" *City & Community* 10 (4): 431–36.

———. 2012. *Patients of the State: The Politics of Waiting in Argentina.* Durham, NC: Duke University Press.

Befu, Harumi. 2001. *Hegemony of Homogeneity: An Anthropological Analysis of Nihonjinron.* Melbourne, Australia: Trans Pacific Press.

Benedict, Ruth. 1948. *The Chrysanthemum and the Sword: Patterns of Japanese Culture.* Rutland, VT: Tuttle.

Benford, Robert D., and David A. Snow. 2000. "Framing Processes and Social Movements: An Overview and Assessment." *Annual Review of Sociology* 26:611–39.

Berk, Richard, and John MacDonald. 2010. "Policing the Homeless: An Evaluation of Efforts to Reduce Homeless-Related Crime." *Criminology & Public Policy* 9 (4): 813–40.

Blasi, Gary, and the UCLA School of Law Fact Investigation Clinic. 2007. "Policing Our Way out of Homelessness? The First Year of the Safer Cities Initiative on Skid Row." http://www.worldcat.org/title/policing-our-way-out-of-homelessness-the-first-year-of-the-safer-cities-initiative-on-skid-row/oclc/187332352.

Bourgois, Phillipe, and Jeff Schonberg. 2009. *Righteous Dopefiend.* Los Angeles: University of California Press.

Brenner, Neil, and Nik Theodore. 2002. "Cities and the Geographies of 'Actually Existing Neoliberalism.'" *Antipode* 34 (3): 349–79.

Brinton, Mary. 2010. *Lost in Transition: Youth, Work, and Instability in Postindustrial Japan*. Cambridge: Cambridge University Press.

Burawoy, Michael, ed. 1991. *Ethnography Unbound: Power and Resistance in the Modern Metropolis*. Los Angeles: University of California Press.

———. 2009. *The Extended Case Method: Four Countries, Four Great Transformations, and One Theoretical Tradition*. Los Angeles: University of California Press.

Burawoy, Michael, Joseph A. Blum, Sheba Miriam George, Zsuzsa Gille, Millie Thayer, Teresa Gowan, Lynne Haney, Maren Klawiter, Steve H. Lopez, and Sean O'Riain. 2000. *Global Ethnography: Forces, Connections, and Imaginations in a Postmodern World*. Los Angeles: University of California Press.

Burt, Martha, Laudan Y. Aron, and Edgar Lee, with Jesse Valente. 2001. *Helping America's Homeless: Emergency Shelter or Affordable Housing*. Washington, DC: Urban Institute Press.

Byrne, Thomas, Ellen A. Munley, Jamison D. Fargo, Anne E. Montgomery, and Dennis P. Culhane. 2013. "New Perspectives on Community-Level Determinants of Homelessness." *Journal of Urban Affairs* 35 (5): 607–25.

Cave, Peter. 2011. "Explaining the Impact of Japan's Educational Reform: Or, Why Are Junior High Schools So Different from Elementary Schools?" *Social Science Japan Journal* 14 (2): 145–63.

Chi'iki Seikatsu Ikō Shien Jigyō Kōka Kentō Iinkai (Transition to Community Living Support Project Research Group). 2011. *Hōmeresu Chiiki Seikatsu Ikō Shien Jigyō Hōkokusho* [Homeless transition to community living support project report]. Unpublished report. Tokyo: Chi'iki Seikatsu Ikō Shien Jigyō Kōka Kentō Iinkai.

Cloke, Paul, Jon May, and Sarah Johnsen. 2010. *Swept Up Lives? Re-envisioning the Homeless City*. Malden, MA: Wiley-Blackwell.

Conley, Dalton Clark. 1996. "Getting It Together: Social and Institutional Obstacles to Getting off the Streets." *Sociological Forum* 11 (1): 25–40.

Culhane, Dennis P. 1992. "The Quandaries of Shelter Reform: An Appraisal of Efforts to Manage Homelessness." *Social Service Review* 66 (3): 428–40.

———. 2008. "The Costs of Homelessness: A Perspective from the United States." *European Journal of Homelessness* 2:99–114.

———. 2010a. "Tackling Homelessness in Los Angeles' Skid Row: The Role of Policing Strategies and the Spatial Deconcentration of Homelessness." *Criminology & Public Policy* 9 (4): 851–57.

———. 2010b. "To Fight Homelessness, Turn Project 50 into Project 10,000." *Los Angeles Times*, August 13. http://articles.latimes.com/2010/aug/13/opinion/la-oew-culhane-project50–20100813.

Culhane, Dennis P., Stephen Metraux, and Trevor Hadley. 2002. "Public Service Reductions Associated with Placement of Homeless Persons with Severe Mental Illness in Supportive Housing." *Housing Policy Debate* 13 (1): 107–63.

Cybriwsky, Roman A. 1998. *Tokyo: The Shogun's City at the Twenty-First Century*. New York: John Wiley and Sons.

Danziger, Sandra K. 2010. "The Decline of Cash Welfare and Implications for Social Policy and Poverty." *Annual Review of Sociology* 36:533–45.

Davis, Mike. 1990. *City of Quartz*. New York: Vintage Books.

Dear, Michael. 2002. "Los Angeles and the Chicago School: Invitation to a Debate." *City & Community* 1 (1): 5–32.

Dennis, Deborah, Margaret Lassiter, William H. Connelly, and Kristin S. Lupfer. 2011. "Helping Adults Who Are Homeless Gain Disability Benefits: The SSI/SSDI

Outreach, Access, and Recovery (SOAR) Program." *Psychiatric Services* 62 (11): 1373–76.

DeVerteuil, Geoff. 2006. "The Local State and Homeless Shelters: Beyond Revanchism?" *Cities* 23 (2): 109–20.

———. 2013. "Does the Punitive Need the Supportive? A Sympathetic Critique of Current Grammars of Urban Injustice." *Antipode* (early online view). http://online library.wiley.com.ezproxy.fiu.edu/doi/10.1111/anti.12001/full.

DeVerteuil, Geoff, Jon May, and Jurgen von Mahs. 2009. "Complexity Not Collapse: Recasting the Geographies of Homelessness in a 'Punitive Age.'" *Progress in Human Geography* 33 (5): 646–66.

DiMaggio, Paul. 1997. "Culture and Cognition." *Annual Review of Sociology* 23:263–87.

DiMassa, Cara Mia. 2006. "Alleged Skid Row Dumping Is Captured on Video Tape." *Los Angeles Times,* March 23. http://articles.latimes.com/2006/mar/23/local/me-dumping23.

Dordick, Gwendolyn A. 1997. *Something Left to Lose: Personal Relations and Survival Among New York's Homeless.* Philadelphia: Temple University Press.

Dreier, Peter, John Mollenkopf, and Todd Swanstrom. 2004. *Place Matters: Metropolitics for the Twenty-First Century.* Lawrence: University Press of Kansas.

Duster, Troy. 2006. "Comparative Perspectives and Competing Explanations: Taking on the Newly Configured Reductionist Challenge to Sociology." *American Sociological Review* 71 (1): 1–15.

Economic Roundtable. 2009. *Economic Study of the Rent Stabilization Ordinance and the Los Angeles Housing Market.* Los Angeles: City of Los Angeles Housing Department.

Esping-Anderson, Gosta. 1999. *Social Foundations of Postindustrial Economies.* New York: Oxford University Press.

Estévez-Abe, Margarita. 2008. *Welfare and Capitalism in Postwar Japan.* New York: Cambridge University Press.

Fairbanks, Robert P., II. 2009. *How It Works: Recovering Citizens in Post-Welfare Philadelphia.* Chicago: University of Chicago Press.

Feuss, Harald. 2004. *Divorce in Japan: Family, Gender, and the State.* Stanford, CA: Stanford University Press.

Förster, Michael, and Marco d'Ercole. 2005. *Income Distribution and Poverty in OECD Countries in the Second Half of the 1990s.* Paris: OECD.

Fowler, Edward. 1998. *San'ya Blues: Laboring Life in Contemporary Tokyo.* Ithaca: Cornell University Press.

Fujita, Kuniko. 2003. "Neo-Industrial Tokyo: Urban Development and Globalization in Japan's State-Centered Developmental Capitalism." *Urban Studies* 40 (2): 249–81.

———. 2011. "Financial Crises, Japan's State Regime Shift, and Tokyo's Urban Policy." *Environment and Planning A* 43:307–27.

Fujita, Kuniko, and Richard Child Hill. 1995. "Global Toyotaism and Local Development." *International Journal of Urban and Regional Research* 19 (1): 7–22.

———. 2012. "Residential Income Inequality in Tokyo and Why It Does Not Translate into Class-Based Segregation." In *Residential Segregation around the World: Why Context Matters,* edited by Thomas Maloutas and Kuniko Fujita, 37–68. Burlington, VT: Ashgate.

Fukuhara, Hiroyuki. 2000. *Kankoku ni okeru Nojukusha Mondai no Genjō to Taiōsaku* [The current state of Korea's homeless problem and policy]. *Shelter-less* 8:8–20.

Gill, Tom. 2001. *Men of Uncertainty: The Social Organization of Day Laborers in Contemporary Japan.* New York: State University of New York Press.

———. 2012. "Failed Manhood on the Streets of Urban Japan: The Meanings of Self-Reliance for Homeless Men." *Asia-Pacific Journal* 10 (1). http://www.japanfocus.org/-Tom-Gill/3671.

Gille, Zsuzsa, and Sean O'Riain. 2002. "Global Ethnography." *Annual Review of Sociology* 28:271–95.

Goffard, Christopher. 2010. "Project 50: Four Walls and a Bed." *Los Angeles Times*, August 7. http://www.latimes.com/news/local/la-me-homeless-project50%2C0%2C4610742.htmlstory.

Gonzales-Baker, Susan. 1996. "Homelessness and the Latino Paradox." In *Homelessness in America*, edited by James Baumohl, 132–40. Phoenix, AZ: Oryx Press.

Gotō, Hiroshi. 2010. *"Daitoshi 'Hōmuresu' no Jittai to Shien Kadai: Seikatsu Hogo Seido wo Chūshin ni"* [Conditions and support issues for the homeless of major urban areas: A focus on the livelihood protection system]. *Hinkon Kenkyū* [Poverty Research] 4:108–17.

Gowan, Teresa. 2002. "The Nexus: Homelessness and Incarceration in Two American Cities." *Ethnography* 3 (4): 500–534.

———. 2010. *Hobos, Hustlers, and Backsliders: Homeless in San Francisco*. Minneapolis: University of Minnesota Press.

Grant, David M., Melvin L. Oliver, and Angela D. James. 1996. "African Americans: Social and Economic Bifurcation." In *Ethnic Los Angeles*, edited by Roger Waldinger and Mehdi Bozorgmehr, 379–412. New York: Russell Sage Foundation.

Hagiwara, Keisetsu. 2001. *"'Heisei Jūichi-nendo Rōjōseikatsusha Jittai Chōsa' Hōkokusho Kara."* [Report from the "Tokyo Metropolitan Government 1999 homeless survey"]. *Shelter-less* 10:107–28.

Hallett, Tim. 2003. "Symbolic Power and Organizational Culture." *Sociological Theory* 21 (2): 128–49.

Harding, David. 2010. *Living the Drama: Community, Conflict, and Culture among Inner-City Boys*. Chicago: University of Chicago Press.

Harvey, David. 1990. *The Condition of Postmodernity: An Enquiry into the Origins of Cultural Change*. Cambridge, MA: Blackwell.

———. 2005. *A Brief History of Neoliberalism*. New York: Oxford University Press.

———. 2006. "Neoliberalism as Creative Destruction." *Geografiska Annaler: Series B, Human Geography* 88 (2): 145–58.

Hasegawa, Miki. 2005. "Economic Globalization and Homelessness in Japan." *American Behavioral Scientist* 48 (8): 989–1012.

———. 2006. *We Are Not Garbage! The Homeless Movement in Tokyo, 1994–2002*. New York: Routledge.

Helvie, Carol O., and Wilfred Kuntsman, eds. 1999. *Homelessness in the United States, Europe, and Asia: A Comparative Perspective*. Westport, CT: Bergin and Garvey.

Hill, Richard Child, and Kuniko Fujita. 2000. "State Restructuring and Local Power in Japan." *Urban Studies* 37 (4): 673–90.

Hoch, Charles, and Robert A. Slayton. 1989. *New Homeless and Old: Community and the Skid Row Hotel*. Philadelphia: Temple University Press.

Hombs, Mary Ellen. 2011. *Modern Homelessness*. Santa Barbara, CA: ABC-CLIO.

Hopper, Kim. 2003. *Reckoning with Homelessness*. Ithaca: Cornell University Press.

Hopper, Kim, and Jim Baumohl. 1994. "Held in Abeyance: Rethinking Homelessness and Advocacy." *American Behavioral Scientist* 37 (4): 522–52.

Inaba Tsuyoshi. 2009. *"Sumai no Hinkon" to Mukiau* [The housing poor: Understanding housing poverty]. Tokyo: Yamabuki Shoten.

Iwama, Akiko. 2003. *"Shakai Kaisō Kenkyū to Shakai Kankei Shihon: Hōmuresu Jiritsu Shiensaku ni okeru Shakai Kankei Shihon no Jūyōsei"* [Social class research and social capital: The importance of social capital in homeless self-sufficiency policy]. *Wako Daigaku Ningen Kankei Gagubu Kiyou* [Annals of the Wako University Social Relations Studies Department] 7 (1): 19–37.

Iwata, Masami. 2000. *Homuresu/Gendai Shakai/Fukushi Kokka: "Ikite Iku Basho" wo Megutte* [The homeless/contemporary society/the welfare state: In search of a "place to live"]. Tokyo: Akashi Shoten.

Jacobs, A. J. 2005. "Has Central Tokyo Experienced Uneven Development? An Examination of Tokyo's 23 Ku Relative to America's Largest Urban Centers." *Journal of Urban Affairs* 27 (5): 521–55.

Jōhoku Welfare Center. 1999. *Jigyō Gaiyō* [Annual report]. Tokyo: Jōhoku Welfare Center.

———. 2013. *Jigyō Annai* [Annual guide]. Tokyo: Jōhoku Welfare Center.

Johnsen, Sarah, and Suzanne Fitzpatrick. 2010. "Revanchist Sanitisation or Coercive Care? The Use of Enforcement to Combat Begging, Street Drinking, and Rough Sleeping in England." *Urban Studies* 47 (8): 1703–23.

Joniak, Elizabeth. 2005. "Exclusionary Practices and the Delegitimization of Client Voice: How Staff Create, Sustain, and Escalate Conflict in a Drop-In Center for Street Kids." *American Behavioral Scientist* 48 (8): 961–88.

Keil, Roger. 1998. *Los Angeles: Globalization, Urbanization, and Social Struggles*. New York: John Wiley and Sons.

Kenworthy, Lane. 2014. *Social Democratic America*. New York: Oxford University Press.

Kitagawa, Yukihiko. 2005. "*Jiritsu Shien Sentā Riyō-keikensha Rojō Kikitori Chōsa Chūkan Hōkoku*" [An interim report on the street survey of former self-reliance support center users]. *Shelter-less* 25:153–70.

———. 2011. "*Tokubetsu-ku no Hogo Shisetsu nado Riyōsha Chōsa kara*" [From the survey of users of Tokyo's "special ward" hogo facilities]. *Hōmeless to Shakai* 4:77–81.

Koegel, Paul, M. Audrey Burnam, and James Baumohl. 1996. "The Causes of Homelessness." In *Homelessness in America*, edited by James Baumohl, 24–33. Phoenix, AZ: Oryx Press.

Kōgi no Hōmuresu no Kashika to Shiensaku ni kan suru Chōsa Kentō Iinkai (The Investigating Group for a Study of Making Visible and Supporting a Broadly Defined Homelessness). 2011. *Kōgi no Hōmuresu no Kashika to Shiensaku ni kan suru Chōsa* [A study of making visible and supporting a broadly defined homelessness]. Tokyo: Kōgi no Hōmuresu no Kashika to Shiensaku ni kan suru Chōsa Kentō Iinkai.

Kusenbach, Margarethe. 2003. "Street Phenomenology: The Go-Along as Ethnographic Research Tool." *Ethnography* 4 (3): 449–79.

Lee, Barrett A., Kimberly A. Tyler, and James D. Wright. 2010. "The New Homelessness Revisited." *Annual Review of Sociology* 36:501–21.

Liebow, Elliot. 1993. *Tell Them Who I Am: The Lives of Homeless Women*. New York: Free Press.

Lipsky, Michael. 1980. *Street-Level Bureaucracy: Dilemmas of the Individual in Public Services*. New York: Russell Sage Foundation.

Los Angeles Homeless Services Authority. 2006. "The 2005 Greater Los Angeles Homeless Count." http://www.lahsa.org/homelessness_data/reports.asp.

———. 2008. "The 2007 Greater Los Angeles Homeless Count." http://www.lahsa.org/homelessness_data/reports.asp.

———. 2010. "The 2009 Greater Los Angeles Homeless Count." http://www.lahsa.org/homelessness_data/reports.asp.

———. 2012. "The 2011 Greater Los Angeles Homeless Count." http://www.lahsa.org/homelessness_data/reports.asp.

———. 2013. "The 2013 Greater Los Angeles Homeless Count." http://www.lahsa.org/homelesscount_results.asp.

Lyon-Callo, Vincent. 2004. *Inequality, Poverty, and Neoliberal Governance: Activist Ethnography in the Homeless Sheltering Industry*. Orchard Park, NY: Broadview Press.

Luce, Stephanie. 2004. *Fighting for a Living Wage*. Ithaca: Cornell University Press.

Machimura, Takashi. 1994. *Sekai Toshi Tōkyō No Kōzō Tenkan* [Restructuring Tokyo as a world city]. Tokyo: Tokyo University Press.

———. 1998. "Symbolic Use of Globalization in Urban Politics in Tokyo." *International Journal of Urban and Regional Research* 22 (2): 183–94.

MacKnee, Chuck M., and Jennifer Mervyn. 2002. "Critical Incidents That Facilitate Homeless People's Transition off the Streets." *Journal of Social Distress and the Homeless* 11 (4): 293–306.

Maloutas, Thomas. 2007. "Segregation, Social Polarization, and Immigration in Athens during the 1990s: Theoretical Expectations and Contextual Difference." *International Journal of Urban and Regional Research* 31 (4): 733–58.

Marcuse, Peter and Ronald Van Kempen, eds. 1999. *Globalizing Cities: A New Spatial Order?* Malden, MA: Wiley-Blackwell.

Margolis, Abby. 2008. "Subversive Accommodations: Doing Homeless in Tokyo's Ueno Park." In *Cast Out: Vagrancy and Homelessness in Global and Historical Perspective*, edited by A. L. Beier and Paul Ocobock, 351–72. Athens: Ohio University Press.

Marpsat, Maryse, and Jean Marie Fiordian. 1998. "The Homeless in Paris: A Representative Sample Survey of Users of Services for the Homeless." In *Coping with Homelessness: Issues to Be Tackled and Best Practices in Europe*, edited by Dragana Avmarov, 221–51. Brookfield, VT: Ashgate.

Marr, Matthew D. 1997. "Maintaining Autonomy: The Plight of the American Skid Row and Japanese *Yoseba*." *Journal of Social Distress and the Homeless* 6 (3): 229–50.

———. 2005a. "Mitigating Apprehension about Section 8: The Positive Role of Housing Specialists in Placement." *Housing Policy Debate* 16 (1): 88–111.

———. 2005b. "Relationships between Self-Sufficiency System Users and Staff as Social Capital: A View from Former Self-Sufficiency System Users in Tokyo" [in Japanese]. *Shelter-less* 26:51–81.

———. 2012. "Pathways out of Homelessness in Los Angeles and Tokyo: Multilevel Contexts of Limited Mobility amid Advanced Urban Marginality." *International Journal of Urban and Regional Research* 36 (5): 980–1006.

Maruyama, Satomi. 2004. "Hidden Women in Shelters and on the Street: "Hidden Homelessness" in Japan." A paper presented at the Adequate and Affordable Housing for All: Research, Policy, Practice conference, Toronto, June 24–17.

———. 2013. *Josei Hōmuresu to shite Ikiru: Hinkon to Haijo no Shakaigaku* [To live as a homeless woman: The sociology of poverty and exclusion]. Tokyo: Seikaishishosha.

Marwell, Nicole P. 2007. *Bargaining for Brooklyn: Community Organizations in the Entrepreneurial City*. Chicago: University of Chicago Press.

Massey, Doreen. 1997. "A Global Sense of Place." In *Reading Human Geography: The Poetics and Politics of Inquiry*, edited by Trevor Barnes and Derek Gregory, 315–23. New York: John Wiley and Sons.

May, Jon, and Paul Cloke. 2013. "Modes of Attentiveness: Reading for Difference in Geographies of Homelessness." *Antipode* (early online view). http://onlinelibrary.wiley.com.ezproxy.fiu.edu/doi/10.1111/anti.12043/full.

McNaughton, Carol. 2008. *Transitions through Homelessness: Lives on the Edge*. New York: Palgrave Macmillan.

McPherson, Miller, Smith-Lovin, Lynn, and James M. Cook. 2001. "Birds of a Feather: Homophily in Social Networks." *Annual Review of Sociology* 27:415–44.

McQuarrie, Michael, and Nicole P. Marwell. 2009. "The Missing Organizational Dimension in Urban Sociology." *City & Community* 8 (3): 247–68.

Milkman, Ruth. 2006. *L.A. Story: Immigrant Workers and the Future of the U.S. Labor Movement*. New York: Russell Sage Foundation.

Ministry of Health, Labor, and Welfare. 2003. *Hōmuresu no Jittai ni kan suru Zenkoku Chōsa* [A national study of the conditions of the homeless]. Tokyo.

———. 2007a. *Hiyatoi Haken Rodōsha no Jittai ni Kansuru Chōsa* [A study about the conditions of dispatch day laborers]. Tokyo.

———. 2007b. *Hōmuresu no Jittai ni kan suru Zenkoku Chōsa* [A national study of the conditions of the homeless]. Tokyo.

———. 2011. *Hōmuresu no Jittai ni kan suru Zenkoku Chōsa* [A national study of the conditions of the homeless]. Tokyo.

———. 2014. *Hōmuresu no Jittai ni kan suru Zenkoku Chōsa* [A national study of the conditions of the homeless]. Tokyo.

Mitchell, Don. 2003. *The Right to the City: Social Justice and the Fight for Public Space*. New York: Guilford Press.

Miura, Mari. 2012. *Welfare through Work: Conservative Ideas, Partisan Dynamics, and Social Protection in Japan*. Ithaca: Cornell University Press.

Mizuuchi, Toshio, and Hong Gyu Jeon. 2010. "The New Mode of Urban Renewal for the Former Outcaste Minority People and Areas in Japan." *City, Culture, and Society*, supplement 1 of the journal *Cities* 27:S25-S34.

Morikawa, Suimei. 2013. *Hyōryū Rōjin Hōmuresu Shakai* [Society of aged mobile homeless]. Tokyo: Asahi Shinbun Shuppan.

Murphy, Stacey. 2009. "'Compassionate' Strategies of Managing Homelessness: Post-Revanchist Geographies in San Francisco." *Antipode* 41 (2): 305–25.

National Alliance to End Homelessness. 2013. *The State of Homelessness in America 2013*. Washington, DC: NAEH.

Ong, Paul, and Evelyn Blumenberg. 1996. "Income and Racial Inequality in Los Angeles." In *The City: Los Angeles and Urban Theory at the End of the Twentieth Century*, edited by Allen Scott and Edward Soja, 311–36. Berkeley: University of California Press.

Ong, Paul, and Abel Valenzuela Jr. 1996. "The Labor Market: Immigrant Effects and Racial Disparities." In *Ethnic Los Angeles*, edited by Roger Waldinger and Mehdi Bozorgmer, 165–91. New York: Russell Sage Foundation.

Ortiz, Vilma. 1996. "The Mexican-Origin Population: Permanent Working Class or Emerging Middle Class?" In *Ethnic Los Angeles*, edited by Roger Waldinger and Mehdi Bozorgmehr, 247–78. New York: Russell Sage Foundation.

Padgett, Deborah K., Victoria Stanhope, Ben F. Henwood, and Ana Stefancic. 2011. "Substance Use Outcomes among Homeless Clients with Serious Mental Illness: Comparing Housing First with Treatment First Programs." *Community Mental Health Journal* 47:227–32.

Pattillo, Mary. 2013. "Housing: Commodity versus Right." *Annual Review of Sociology* 39:509–531.

Peck, Jamie, and Adam Tickell. 2002. "Neoliberalizing Space." *Antipode* 34 (3): 380–404.

Piliavin, Irving, Bradley R. Etner Wright, Robert D. Mare, and Alex H. Westerfelt. 1996. "Exits from and Returns to Homelessness." *Social Service Review* 70 (1): 32–57.

Piliavin, Irving, Michael Sosin, Alex H. Westerfelt, and Ross L. Matsueda. 1993. "The Duration of Homeless Careers: An Exploratory Study." *Social Service Review* 67 (4): 577–97.

Piven, Frances Fox, and Richard A. Cloward. 1993. *Regulating the Poor: The Functions of Public Welfare, Updated Edition*. New York: Vintage.

Ravenhill, Megan. 2008. *The Culture of Homelessness*. Burlington, VT: Ashgate.

Reese, Ellen. 2002. "Resisting the Workfare State: Mobilizing General Relief Recipients in Los Angeles." *Race, Gender & Class* 9 (1): 72–95.

———. 2005. *Backlash against Welfare Mothers: Past and Present*. Berkeley: University of California Press.

Reese, Ellen, Geoffrey DeVerteuil, and Leanne Thach. 2010. "'Weak Center' Gentrification and the Contradictions of Containment: Deconcentrating Poverty in Downtown Los Angeles." *International Journal of Urban and Regional Research* 34 (2): 310–27.

Rindfuss, Ronald R., Minja Kim Choe, Larry Bumpass, and Noriko O. Tsuya. 2004. "Social Networks and Family Change in Japan." *American Sociological Review* 69 (9): 838–61.

Rivera, Carla. 2005. "Near Downtown Lies a Civic Problem." *Los Angeles Times*, August 25. http://pqasb.pqarchiver.com/latimes/access/886031791.html?dids=8860 31791:886031791&FMT=ABS&FMTS=ABS:FT&type=current&date=Aug+24% 2C+2005&author=Carla+Rivera&pub=Los+Angeles+Times&edition=&startpa ge=B.2&desc=Q%26A+%2F+SKID+ROW.

Robinson, Jennifer. 2010. "Cities in a World of Cities: The Comparative Gesture." *International Journal of Urban and Regional Research* 35 (1): 1–23.

Rossi, Peter. 1989. *Down and Out in America: The Origins of Homelessness*. Chicago: University of Chicago Press.

Rowe, Michael. 1999. *Crossing the Border: Encounters between Homeless People and Outreach Workers*. Berkeley: University of California Press.

Saito, Asato. 2003. "Global City Formation in a Capitalist Developmental State: Tokyo and the Waterfront Subcentre Project." *Urban Studies* 40 (2): 283–308.

Saito, Asato, and Andy Thornley. 2003. "Shifts in Tokyo's World City Status and in the Urban Planning Response." *Urban Studies* 40 (4): 665–85.

Santos, Maria C. L. 1996. "Paper or Plastic: A Comparative Study of Materials Used by the Homeless in Sao Paulo, Brazil and Los Angeles, USA." *Traditional Dwellings and Settlements* 99:35–64.

Sassen, Saskia. 2001. *The Global City: New York, London, Tokyo, Second Edition*. Princeton, NJ: Princeton University Press.

Schein, Edgar H. 1992. *Organizational Culture and Leadership*. 2nd ed. San Francisco: Jossey-Bass.

Schoppa, Len. J. 1995. "The Number of Homeless People in Los Angeles City and County, July 1993 to June 1994." Los Angeles: Shelter Partnership.

———. 2006. *Race for the Exits: The Unraveling of Japan's System of Social Protection*. Ithaca: Cornell University Press.

Shelter Partnership, Inc. 1995. *The Number of Homeless People in Los Angeles City and County, July 1993 to June 1994*. Los Angeles: Shelter Partnership, Inc.

Shinoda, Toru. 2009. "Which Side Are You On? Hakenmura and the Working Poor as a Tipping Point in Japanese Labor Politics." *Asia-Pacific Journal*. http://www.japanfocus.org/-Toru-Shinoda/3113.

Shlay Ann B., and Peter Rossi. 1992. "Social Science Research and Contemporary Studies of Homelessness." *Annual Review of Sociology* 18:129–60.

Small, Mario Luis. 2009a. "How Many Cases Do I Need? On Science and the Logic of Case Selection in Field-Based Research." *Ethnography* 10 (1): 5–38.

———. 2009b. *Unanticipated Gains: Origins of Network Inequality in Everyday Life.* New York: Oxford University Press.

Small, Mario Luis, David J. Harding, and Michèle Lamont. 2010. "Reconsidering Culture and Poverty." *Annals of the American Academy of Political and Social Science* 629:6–27.

Small, Mario Luis, Erin Jacobs, and Rebekah Peoples Massengill. 2008. "Why Organizational Ties Matter for Neighborhood Effects: A Study of Resource Access through Childcare Centers." *Social Forces* 87 (1): 387–414.

Smith, Curtis, Ernesto Castañeda, and Josia Heyman. 2012. "The Homeless and Occupy El Paso: Creating Community among the 99%." *Social Movement Studies* 11 (3–4): 356–66.

Smith, Sandra Susan. 2005. "Don't Put My Name on It: Social Capital Activation and Job-Finding Assistance among the Black Urban Poor." *American Journal of Sociology* 111 (1): 1–57.

———. 2007. *Lone Pursuit: Distrust and Defensive Individualism among the Black Poor.* New York: Russell Sage Foundation.

Snow, David A., and Leon Anderson. 1993. *Down on Their Luck: A Study of Homeless Street People.* Los Angeles: University of California Press.

Snow, David A., Leon Anderson, and Paul Koegel. 1994. "Distorting Tendencies in Research on the Homeless." *American Behavioral Scientist* 37 (4): 461–75.

Snow, David A., Susan G. Baker, Leon Anderson, and Michael Martin. 1986. "The Myth of Pervasive Mental Illness among the Homeless." *Social Problems* 33:407–23.

Soja, Edward. 1996. "Los Angeles 1965–1992: From Crisis-Generated Restructuring to Restructuring-Generated Crisis." In *The City: Los Angeles and Urban Theory at the End of the Twentieth Century,* edited by Allen Scott and Edward Soja, 426–62. Berkeley: University of California Press.

Sorensen, André, Junichiro Okata, and Sayaka Fujii. 2010. "Urban Renaissance as Intensification: Building Regulation and the Rescaling of Place Governance in Tokyo's High-Rise *Manshon* Boom." *Urban Studies* 47 (3): 556–83.

Sosin, Michael, Irving Piliavin, and Herb Westerfelt. 1990. "Toward a Longitudinal Analysis of Homelessness." *Journal of Social Issues* 46 (4): 157–74.

Southern California Association of Governments. 2000. *The State of the Region 2000: The Region at the Dawn of the 21st Century.* Los Angeles: Southern California Association of Governments.

———. 2005. *The State of the Region 2007.* Los Angeles: Southern California Association of Governments.

———. 2007. *The State of the Region 2007.* Los Angeles: Southern California Association of Governments.

Stuart, Forrest. 2011. "Race, Space, and the Regulation of Surplus Labor: Policing African Americans in Los Angeles' Skid Row." *Souls: A Critical Journal of Black Politics, Culture, and Society* 13 (2): 197–212.

Sugimoto, Yoshio. 2010. *An Introduction to Japanese Society.* 3rd ed. London: Cambridge University Press.

Suzuki, Bunji. 2012. *Hōmuresu Shōgaisha: Karera wo Rojō ni Oiyaru Mono* [Disabled homeless: What pushes them to the streets]. Tokyo: Nippon Hyōron Sha.

Swidler, Ann. 1986. "Culture in Action: Symbols and Strategies." *American Sociological Review* 51:273–86.

Tamaki, Matsuo. 2002. "*Tōkyō-to Hōuresu Jiritsu Shien Jigyō no Nani ga Mondai Ka*" [What is wrong with Tokyo's self-reliance support efforts?]. *Shelter-less* 15:19–31.

Telles, Edward Eric, and Vilma Ortiz. 2009. *Generations of Exclusion: Mexican Americans, Assimilation, and Race.* New York: Russell Sage Foundation.

Terao, Tōru, and Okuta Tomoshi. 2010. "*Hinkon Bijinesu-ron wo Koete: Posuto-hōmuresu Shien-hō Taisei wo Tenbō Suru*" [Beyond the theory of poverty business: Hope for after the Homeless Support Act system]. *Hōmuresu to Shakai* [Homelessness and Society] 2:8–15.

Tokubetsu-ku Jinji Kōsei Jimu Kumiai Kōseibu (Special Ward Personnel and Welfare Administration Union Welfare Division). 2010. *Jigyō Gaiyō* [Activities report]. Tokyo: Tokubetsu-ku Jinji Kōsei Jimu Kumiai Kōseibu.

Tokyo Metropolitan Government (TMG). 2004. *Hōmuresu no Jiritsu Shien nado ni Kan Suru Tōkyōto Jisshi Keikaku* [The Tokyo Metropolitan Government's report related to homeless self-sufficiency]. Tokyo: TMG.

———. 2007. *Tōkyō Hōmuresu Hakusho 2* [The second white paper on Tokyo's homeless]. Tokyo: TMG.

Tomoro, Kensaku. 2013. "*Kinnen ni okeru Todōfuken-betsu Hinkonritsu no Sui'i ni Tsuite—Wākingu Pua wo Chūshin ni*" [Recent changes in local poverty rates—a focus on the working poor]. *Yamagata Daigaku Kiyō/Shakaigaku* (Yamagata University Bulletin/Sociology) 43 (2): 35–92.

Toro, Paul A., Carolyn J. Tompsett, Sylvie Lombardo, Pierre Philippot, Hilde Nachtergael, Benoit Galand, Natasha Schlienz, Nadine Stammel, Yanélia Yabar, Marc Blume, Linda MacKay, and Kate Harvey. 2007. "Homelessness in Europe and the United States: A Comparison of Prevalence and Public Opinion." *Journal of Social Issues* 63 (3): 505–24.

Tsemberis, Sam, and Sara Asmussen. 1999. "From Streets to Homes: Pathways to Housing's Consumer Preference Supported Housing Model." *Alcoholism Treatment Quarterly* 17:113–31.

Tsemberis, Sam, and Ronda F. Eisenberg. 2000. "Pathways to Housing: Supported Housing for Street-Dwelling Homeless Individuals with Psychiatric Disabilities." *Psychiatric Services* 51 (4): 487–93.

Tsemberis, Sam, Leyla Gulcur, and Maria Nakae. 2004. "Housing First, Consumer Choice, and Harm Reduction with Homeless Individuals with a Dual Diagnosis." *American Journal of Public Health* 94 (4): 651–57.

Tsukada, Hiroyasu. 1991. *2001 nen no Tōkyō* [Tokyo in 2001]. Tokyo: Iwanami Shoten.

Tsukamoto, Takashi. 2012. "Why Is Japan Neoliberalizing? Rescaling of the Japanese Developmental State and Ideology of State-Capital Mixing." *Journal of Urban Affairs* 34 (4): 395–418.

Tsumaki, Shingo, and Keishirō Tsutsumi. 2011. "*Kazoku Kihan to Hōmuresu: Fujo ka Shikkoku ka*" [Family norms and homelessness: Aid or constraint]. In *Hōmuresu Stadiizu: Haijō to Hōsetsu* [Homeless studies: Exclusion and inclusion], edited by Hideo Aoki, 169–201. Tokyo: Minerva Shobō.

United States Department of Agriculture. 2012. "Reaching Those in Need: State Supplemental Nutrition Assistance Program Participation Rates in 2010." Washington, DC: USDA. http://www.fns.usda.gov/ora/menu/Published/snap/FILES/Participation/Reaching2010.pdf.

United States Department of Housing and Urban Development. 2007. "HUD Reports Drop in Number of Chronically Homeless Persons Living on Nation's Streets: Decrease Largely Attributed to Increase in Supportive Housing." Press statement, November 7. Washington, DC: HUD.

———. 2010a. "Costs Associated with First-Time Homelessness for Families and Individuals." Washington, DC: HUD.

———. 2010b. "The 2009 Annual Homeless Assessment Report to Congress." Washington, DC: HUD.

———. 2011. "The 2010 Annual Homeless Assessment Report to Congress." Washington, DC: HUD.

———. 2013a. *The 2012 Point-in-Time Estimates of Homelessness.* Washington, DC: HUD.

———. 2013b. "The 2013 Annual Homeless Assessment Report to Congress." Washington, DC: HUD.

United States Interagency Council on Homelessness. 2010. *Opening Doors: Federal Strategic Plan to Prevent and End Homelessness.* Washington, DC. USICH.

———. 2012. *Opening Doors: Federal Strategic Plan to Prevent and End Homelessness, Update 2012.* Washington, DC. USICH.

Vaughan, Diane. 2004. "Theorizing Disaster: Analogy, Historical Ethnography, and the *Challenger* Accident." *Ethnography* 5 (3): 315–47.

Vitale, Alex S. 2009. *City of Disorder: How the Quality of Life Campaign Transformed New York Politics.* New York: New York University Press.

———. 2010. "The Safer Cities Initiative and the Removal of the Homeless—Reducing Crime or Promoting Gentrification on Los Angeles' Skid Row?" *Criminology & Public Policy* 9 (4): 867–73.

von Mahs, Jurgen. 2005. "The Sociospatial Exclusion of Single Homeless People in Berlin and Los Angeles." *American Behavioral Scientist* 48 (8): 928–60.

Wacquant, Loïc. 2009. *Punishing the Poor: The Neoliberal Government of Social Insecurity.* Durham, NC: Duke University Press.

———. 2008. *Urban Outcasts: A Comparative Study of Advanced Marginality.* Malden, MA; Polity Press.

Wagner, David. 1993. *Checkerboard Square: Culture and Resistance in a Homeless Community.* Boulder, CO: Westview Press.

Waley, Paul. 2000. "Tokyo: Patterns of Familiarity and Partitions of Difference." In *Globalizing Cities: A New Spatial Order,* edited by Peter Marcuse and Ronald van Kempen, 127–57. Malden, MA: Blackwell.

———. 2007. "Tokyo-as-World-City: Reassessing the Role of Capital and the State in Urban Restructuring." *Urban Studies* 44 (8): 1465–90.

Wasserman, Jason Adam, and Jeffrey Michael Clair. 2010. *At Home on the Street: People, Poverty, and a Hidden Culture of Homelessness.* Boulder, CO: Lynne Rienner.

———. 2011. "Housing Patterns of Homeless People: The Ecology of the Street in the Era of Urban Renewal." *Journal of Contemporary Ethnography* 40 (1): 71–101.

Watanabe, Kaoru. 2010. *Jiritsu no Jubaku: Hōmuresu Shien no Shakaigaku* [Under the spell of "self-reliance": A sociology of homeless support]. Tokyo: Shinsensha.

Western, Bruce. 2006. *Punishment and Inequality in America.* New York: Russell Sage Foundation.

Wilson, William Julius. 1996. *When Work Disappears: The World of the New Urban Poor.* New York: Alfred A. Knopf.

Wiseman, Jacqueline. 1970. *Stations of the Lost: The Treatment of Skid Row Alcoholics.* Chicago: University of Chicago Press.

Wissink, Bart, and Arjan Hazelzet. 2012. "Social Networks in 'Neighborhood Tokyo.'" *Urban Studies* 49 (7): 1527–48.

Wolch, Jennifer. 1996. "From Global to Local: The Rise of Homelessness in Los Angeles during the 1980s." In *The City: Los Angeles and Urban Theory at the End of the Twentieth Century,* edited by Allen J. Scott, and Edward W. Soja, 390–425. Los Angeles: University of California Press.

Wolch, Jennifer, and Michael Dear. 1993. *Malign Neglect: Homelessness in an American City*. San Francisco: Jossey-Bass.

Wolch, Jennifer, and Geoffrey DeVerteuil. 2001. "New Landscapes of Urban Poverty Management." In *Timespace*, edited by Jon May and Nigel Thrift, 149–68. London: Routledge.

Wong, Yin-Ling Irene, Dennis P. Culhane, and Randal S. Kuhn. 1997. "Predictors of Exit and Reentry among Family Shelter Users in New York City." *Social Service Review* 71:441–62.

Wong, Yin-Ling Irene, and Irving Piliavin (1997). "A Dynamic Analysis of Homeless-Domicile Transitions." *Social Problems* 44 (3): 408–23.

Yamada, Sechi. 2005. "*Taisaku ga Hito wo Korosu Toki: Hōmuresu Chīki Seikatsu Ikō Shien Jigyō no Ura de*" [When a policy kills people: Behind the homeless movement to community support program]. *Shelter-less* 26:228–33.

Yamada, Sōshirō. 2009. *Hōmuresu Shien ni okeru Shūrō to Fukushi* [Welfare and employment in homeless support]. Tokyo: Akashi Shoten.

Yuasa, Makoto. 2008. *Han Hinkon: "Suberidai Shakai" kara no Dasshitsu* [Anti-poverty: Escape from "slippery society"]. Tokyo: Iwanami Shoten.

Index

Note: Page numbers in italics indicate figures; those with a *t* indicate tables.